My Animals
(and other family)

A Rural Childhood 1937-1956

Phyllida Barstow

MERLIN UNWIN BOOKS

Published by:
Merlin Unwin Books Ltd
Palmers House
7 Corve Street
Ludlow
Shropshire SY8 1DB
U.K.

www.merlinunwin.co.uk

The author asserts her moral right to be identified with this work.

Designed and set in Bembo by Merlin Unwin
Printed in Great Britain by MPG Biddles

ISBN 978 1 906122 13 3

To my grandchildren:
Molly, Beth and Robert Hindhaugh
and Edward Hart-Davis;
and in memory of my parents
John and Diana Barstow,
and my brother Gerry.

CONTENTS

Foreword

This is a rite of passage memoir, as well as an account of childhood in a vanished world. Phyllida Barstow weaves a refreshingly candid account of her developing personality into the fabric of the kind of eccentric, rural, educated upbringing that we seem too nervously conformist to give our children nowadays. The personalities are vibrant, from parents through sibling to sheepdogs and a succession of beloved ponies; and the arduous life on a Welsh farm is interleaved with civilising spells in seductive France, and the extraordinary rituals of the London season, especially for a girl whose heart lay more in dog baskets than handbags.

It is a book carried along by the author's own energy and appetite for life, and written with the clarity and elegance of someone who knows what they are doing.

Joanna Trollope
June 2009

CHAPTER ONE

Chapel House

THE SECOND WORLD WAR broke out just before I was two years old, and my first plunge into the dark soup of early consciousness in search of a flashback of memory finds me lying in a rumpled nest of clothes and rugs on the back seat of a car on a hot afternoon, thirsty and sticky, looking up into the anxious eyes of our nanny, Celia, shoe-horned into the luggage compartment among the suitcases and longing, like me, for the journey to end.

She was beautiful, gentle and beloved, and though there was no getting away from her strong personal aroma I knew exactly how she was feeling, tired of being cooped up and jolted about, but also like me, uneasily aware of tension emanating from the front seats, where my mother and brother were arguing over the map. She knew as well as I did that we'd better keep quiet because any complaint was liable to provoke an explosion. When I had begun to whine some time back I had been told in no uncertain terms to shut up and go to sleep, but how could I when their voices were getting ever louder and snappier?

'That can't be right,' Mummy exclaimed.

'It is! I'm sure it is,' insisted Gerry, on the brink of tears.

'But we've tried that way already.'

'We didn't go far enough. There's another turning,'

'There isn't.'

'Then we're lost,' said Gerry gloomily, and the word hung in the air with a dreadful finality. I wanted to cry, but knew it would be a mistake to attract attention. So long as Celia and I kept quiet, we wouldn't be – what? Blamed? Shouted at? There was nothing either of us could do to improve the situation. The safest option was to keep a low profile.

For the past eternity, it seemed, the car had been moving in short spurts then halting, reversing, making about-turns and sudden changes of direction, but now it had been stationary for several minutes although the engine went on girning away, puffing out evil fumes. Sprawled on the back seat, I could see sky and trees and a signpost leaning drunkenly and I was dimly aware that it would be a calamity if the engine stopped. There was something wrong with the battery. Only that morning it had taken several men to push the car downhill before Mummy let in the clutch with a jolt and, calling 'We're off!' had driven jerkily away from the hotel where we'd spent the night. Now the sun was beating on the roof, the heat in the back was building up and along with the thermometer, tempers were rising.

As soon as the long-expected, long-dreaded war broke out, the even tenor of our nursery routine in London – meals, walks in the park, play with parents, bath, bed – had become unsettled, as nannies and nursery-maids came and went. Gerry and I never knew who would be looking after us next. Mummy volunteered for the First Aid Nursing Yeomanry (FANY) and became an ambulance driver. Daddy put his legal career on hold and, being already a territorial captain in the Honourable Artillery Company, was soon appointed major in the 12th Regiment (HAC) Royal Horse Artillery, guarding vulnerable points in London.

By late summer of 1940, when my mother was expecting a third baby, she applied for a discharge from the FANY so that she, and we, could follow the drum, perching in a series of chilly and uncomfortable boarding houses as Daddy's regiment was posted first to Hertfordshire and then to the East Coast, the car becoming more battered and our possessions more scattered with every move.

We were living at Skegness in what we called the Mungle Bungalow when news reached my mother of the British Expeditionary Force's retreat from Dunkirk. Fear of an immediate German invasion prompted the authorities either to remove roadside finger-posts or turn them the wrong way round in the hope of confusing the advancing enemy, and this

2

well-meant initiative made a nightmare of our long slow cross-country journey from East Anglia to Chapel House, my grandparents' house in Wales. Daddy and his regiment had vanished in conditions of secrecy without even saying goodbye, and Gerry, only two years older than me, was pitch-forked into the role of man of the family.

Along with the heat and the smell, I remember feeling hopeless and helpless as tension mounted in the front of the car, and the cowardly way I squeezed my eyes tight shut when Mummy asked, 'How's Phylla?' and Gerry peered over the back of his seat to report, 'Asleep,' adding with a tinge of envy, 'Lucky thing.' No doubt he wished he could shed his responsibilities as easily.

I lay doggo, hoping to escape further notice, feeling a strong bond of sympathy for Celia, though our immediate needs were different. I was longing for a drink, while she was bursting to be milked, but we were both scared of triggering one of Mummy's sudden explosions. Patience was never among my mother's many virtues, and at this moment she had enough fears and frustrations to justify an outburst of wrath.

With my father, along with most men of fighting age, in uniform, swept up in the war machine that was stuttering fitfully into action, her own future must have looked bleak and uncertain, and although she was good at giving a positive spin to circumstances – looking on the bright side, as she would have said – it can't have helped to know that Daddy's new life showed every sign being much more dramatic and enjoyable than hers.

This was not only unfair; it also upset the dynamics of their marriage, pushing each of them into an unfamiliar role. Hers was the quick, bold, enterprising spirit whose love of adventure verged on recklessness and whose threshold of boredom was correspondingly low, while my father, calm, steady, tolerant, good-humoured and nine years her senior had always acted as a brake on her impetuosity and gently teased her out of her wilder enthusiasms.

Now it was up to her to behave sensibly and responsibly – virtues which she instinctively despised. Fun, along with food and petrol, was in short supply. The threat of a German invasion hung over the country like a black cloud and the whole family was tormented by anxiety about my father's younger brother, Oliver, who had not been in touch since the retreat from Dunkirk.

At this pivotal and terrifying moment of English history, staying in the depths of the country to look after small children was an unappealing prospect, and now she couldn't even find the right road.

'All right, we'll try your way,' she said in an exasperated tone that boded ill for Gerry if he was wrong. The growl of the engine grew louder as she revved, the car jerked forward a few yards, and then to my dismay, it faltered, coughed a couple of times, and died.

'Thank you, God, for a lovely day,' said Mummy bitterly into the silence, and at that point my flash of recall cuts off as abruptly as an eyelid closing.

Did it happen? The memory is sharp and vivid, but even a cursory check casts doubts on certain points. For a start, could a three-year-old remember in such detail? Isn't it more likely that I have run several different journeys together and come up with a composite scenario? Certainly we did drive for three days across the breadth of the country during the blackout, with Gerry asking passers-by for directions because the signposts had been removed, but what about the goat? Would the hotels we stayed in have put her up too? Would there even have been room for her along with the suitcases and the rest of our clobber in BYK 2, our little Standard 9 ?

Whatever the truth, she is firmly there in my memory as a comforting presence when the rest of the world seemed chaotic and frightening, and even nowadays the slightest whiff of that half delicious, half disgusting goaty smell brings my wartime childhood instantly to mind.

Celia was a handsome British Saanen, white all over with a sensitive aristocratic face and ears that pricked alertly like a sheep rather than hanging spaniel-fashion. Her fine silky summer coat was soft and warm to the fingers, her tail flicked jauntily upward, and her neat small rubbery hoofs were almost prehensile in their ability to scramble and cling. Though svelte of figure, she had a prodigious appetite and she liked the best of everything – the youngest, most succulent leaves and shoots, the unopened buds of flowers, the newly-baked cake on the kitchen table.

Contemptuous of thorns, she made short work of roses and, balancing on her hind legs in a heraldic pose, she could reach up to strip the lower branches of most garden shrubs, which did not endear her to gardeners. She was meant to spend her days tethered to an iron peg firmly hammered into the ground, with a revolving ring and a long light chain attached to her broad leather collar, but Mummy worried that she would tangle the chain and garotte herself. She therefore spent much time and energy constructing secure areas where Celia could roam free, but from which she always managed to escape.

'Diana! Your goat's in the garden!' was a frequent cry from the house-proud owner of wherever we happened to be staying, for Celia was a Houdini *par excellence*, and naturally enough preferred the delights of the *potager* to the rough grass and brambles of her official diet.

Gluttony was her besetting sin, and nearly cut short her career when, in her giddy youth, a rare over-estimation of her digestive powers inspired her to binge on rhododendron leaves. The result was severe – potentially fatal – colic. Like donkeys, goats are seldom ill, but when they do succumb they have very little fighting spirit and are inclined to give up without a struggle.

My mother nursed her with gruel and hot water bottles for two days and nights and then, exhausted, accepted an offer from Celia Johnson, bright star of stage and screen and wife of my parents' friend Peter Fleming, who happened to be staying, to spend the next night in the goat shed, and since it was on Celia's watch that the patient turned the corner, she was named in her honour.

She led easily and was an excellent traveller, jumping into small spaces in the back of cars as readily as a dog. When we travelled by train, she made herself comfortable in the guard's van. I can visualise myself leading her down the platform, past the snorting, grimy, sulphurous engine, past rows of dingy maroon carriage doors, with Mummy directing and Gerry helping a porter with the luggage, until after what seemed an endless trudge we reached the goods' van with its ramp resting on the platform and a tangle of bicycles in the corner.

There we would construct a pen from boxes and suitcases, and Celia would settle down equally to chew her cud as the train thundered and rattled towards London, Glasgow, Ayr, Cambridge or wherever we were bound.

As a mobile milk supply she was usually a welcome guest in friends' houses, though landladies were apt to go into mild hysterics when she pattered into the kitchen and leapt lightly on to the table to be milked. This was her party trick, and you could see from her sly complacent glances that she enjoyed an audience. She had a fine bold squarish udder, pink and slightly freckled, and teats like ice-cream cones from which milk cascaded into the shiny bucket in a frothing stream, making a high-pitched *ping-ping* which deepened to a soothing *swish-swish* as it covered the bottom.

Mummy's clever monkey paws, (as I used to call her small strong hands), were good at milking, and took only a few minutes to fill the bucket with more than enough for nursery needs. She would reward Celia with a scratch behind the ears and a cabbage leaf, quickly pour the foaming brew through a wire sieve to strain out bits of dirt, and pour the warm, rich, nutty milk into a Breton jug decorated with figures of country dancers in traditional knee-breeches and stiffened head-dresses prancing round its middle.

Goat's milk is now considered a rather specialised taste, and even then I remember some grown-ups objecting to putting it in their tea, which puzzled us because we thought it the normal thing to drink. Celia must have produced more than we needed because the kitchen or nursery ceiling always seemed to be festooned with dripping muslin bags full of sour milk. The idea was to strain off the whey and make soft cheese from the resulting solids, but more often the evil-smelling dangling shrouds became a booby trap for any grown-up who forgot to duck, and splatted on the floor, leaving an ineradicable smell of sick.

When this happened to my grandfather as he paid a rare visit to the nursery, even his legendary tolerance snapped. With most uncharacteristic sternness, he forbade any more cheese-making upstairs, and thereafter all further experiments were conducted in the cellar.

We spent most of the war years in Wales. Childhood memory is capricious and selective, and I remember very little about moving to Cambridgeshire for a few months when Daddy's regiment was stationed near the village of Hinxton, except that I was sent to the village school where, on the very first day, children gathered round in the playground to tease me – one could hardly call it bullying – by calling me 'Philadelphia.' Where they got the word from, I can't imagine, but I can still see their jeering faces and taunting mouths, which turned to shocked astonishment when I fled out through the gate and ran all the way home. Being a kind responsible brother, Gerry came with me, found a grownup and explained what had happened, then returned to school himself, but to my eternal gratitude, I was never sent there again.

Nor has our next sudden translocation to Ayr, on the east Coast of Scotland, left much impression. It must have been during the summer, because Gerry got badly stung by a jellyfish, and I put my bare foot on a broken bottle while wading in a pond, and remember my surprise at the blood and fuss made of a wound which had hurt so little that I hadn't even noticed it while in the water.

Then the regiment embarked for North Africa, and we made our slow way back to the Wye Valley.

Chapel House – Chapho in family-speak – had been just a small plain-fronted Welsh cottage on the valley slope above the river Wye when my great grandparents, who owned the big, black-and-white fishing lodge called Abernant, bought it as a wedding present for their daughter and son-in-law Enid and George Barstow. Some thirty years later, when I was born, the little house next to the chapel had been largely rebuilt, with two new wings which more than doubled its original size, and had become a substantial, rather handsome family home.

A garden on several levels had been carved out of the steep fields all round the house. Orchard, rose garden, lily pond garden, tennis court and shrubbery stretched away to the right, and rock garden, paddock and green-houses to the left. For some reason there were two kitchen gardens, their paths lined with espaliered apple trees, one either side of the house, each with its own fully equipped tool shed, and even in wartime two gardeners and a boy to tend them.

Mr Hadley, the head gardener, was tall, thin, twitchy and sour-faced. He had been shell-shocked in the trenches, poor man, and detested children, and we hated him right back. 'I wish Mr Hadley was Deaf, Dumb, Blind and Wounded!' we used to chant from a safe distance.

However Watkins, his second-in-command, was our friend, a

limping, wizened, good-tempered Welshman whose face for some reason always reminded me of a dandelion bud just before it opens – something about the shape of his cheeks, I suppose. Watkins bustled between the upper and lower vegetable gardens with his big wooden barrow's wheel crunching on the chipping paths. He let us cadge tomatoes from the green-house and delicious raw peas, and he could often be found with his lame leg propped on a log-box, reading the *Brecon & Radnor* as he munched his elevenses and swigged from a bottle of cold tea. (At least I imagine it was cold tea. It was certainly brownish; but in retrospect it seems odd that he chose to drink it in the tool-shed when his neat cottage and bun-like wife were only yards away on the other side of the orchard.)

Separated from the house by the valley road, then little more than a quiet lane, and a single grass meadow which frequently flooded, the broad gleaming surface of the River Wye could be seen from the dining room window, and both there and on the loggia at the end of the house, powerful binoculars were kept handy for checking the state of the water and assessing fishing prospects.

Into this children's paradise, Gerry and I settled happily, and there our sister Olivia was born in January, 1941. Grandfather, who worked all week in London and came down by train on Friday evenings to be picked up by Granny at Three Cocks station, heroically allowed his library to be turned into a nursery in which we played and did our lessons and also ate. It was immediately above the kitchen, which greatly facilitated the exchange of hostilities between a succession of nannies and cooks, who could screech abuse at one another out of the windows without being heard in the dining-room.

Nursery food was uniformly bland and disgusting. I remember my gorge rising uncontrollably when Gerry said pensively, 'Just think ! Some little animal once depended on this,' as he pushed the sheep's brain about his plate, and our refusal to eat the bitter scorched skin on milk puddings led to tremendous scolding and lectures about the starving millions in China.

Dining room food – as we discovered when we were allowed to eat downstairs – was little better. I don't think this was entirely due to wartime shortages, nor because it was difficult to get staff; it was more because neither Grandfather nor Granny was in the least interested in what they ate; in fact Granny amazed us once by saying she could never remember being hungry in her whole life. She considered it bad manners to discuss food, particularly at meals. You simply ate what was put on your plate and that was that.

Though she would meticulously plan the day's menu every morning when the current cook came up to her bedroom to collect her breakfast tray, she never commented on – let alone criticised – the result, which was usually overdone, under-seasoned, and lukewarm after its journey by double-decked trolley from the kitchen, across the hall, and into the serving-room's warming cupboard, where it became desiccated beyond redemption.

'The carver is either a knave or a fool,' Grandfather would say ruefully when he found he had left little or nothing for his own helping, but he would never have dreamed of sending out to the kitchen for more. He was as frugal by nature as Granny was extravagant – 'Have you nothing more expensive?' my mother once heard her ask a jeweller – but both of them were prepared to sacrifice their own comfort if it helped the war effort. Just as Uncle Trevor had given his four lovely hunters to the Army to serve their country as cavalry chargers in the First World War, Grandfather sold his large luxurious Packard to the Army for £20 in the Second.

This was actually more of a sacrifice for Granny than himself, since he never learned to drive, which was probably just as well because he was short-sighted and kack-handed. I once saw him measuring with knicker-elastic the space needed to hang a picture, though at lawn tennis, as he always called it, when well into his seventies he could still wear out any grandchild by lobbing the ball from one side of the court to the other with slow, remorseless accuracy.

Granny, on the other hand, was a bold and dashing driver. She had never taken a test, and had a fine contempt for traffic laws. Much later I remember the Humber Hawk which replaced the Packard swooping from one side of the river road to the other as if on a dance-floor as the strains of the Blue Danube Waltz crackled from the radio, and her map-reading was rudimentary. 'The roads go like spaghetti in my head,' she explained.

Dull though most Chapel House food was, few cooks can really spoil roast chicken, and this was our regular Sunday treat. 'White or brown?' Grandfather would enquire as he distributed the meat — a question largely redundant nowadays since there is little difference in colour between leg and breast of chicken — but before mass-production, the farmyard roosters we ate had long brown muscular legs like footballers. We used to clamour to be allocated the wish-bone which, when picked clean, would be returned to the warming cupboard to dry and later two children would hook their little fingers into either side of it and ceremoniously pull until it snapped . The pieces were then compared and if yours was the longer you closed your eyes and wished.

Though we all inhabited the same house, children and grown-ups led parallel lives, and very little of the drama and turmoil of war penetrated nursery consciousness. Even when Uncle Oliver, who had survived the fighting at Dunkirk, was killed in Greece, our parents' and grandparents' distress was carefully concealed from us.

Peter Fleming had asked Oliver to join him, together with a few other adventurous spirits backed up by a handful of Grenadier guardsmen, on a mission of sabotage as the Germans advanced on Athens, capturing trains, blowing up bridges and in other ways harassing the enemy, which they did with a good deal of success and enjoyment, until they were eventually forced to flee, along with the Legation staff, which included Oliver's sister Nancy and brother-in-law Harold Caccia, with their young son and daughter.

Packing and leaving in a hurry, they sailed from the Piraeus for Crete, moving by night and hiding on islands by day. Most of the party were picnicking ashore on the small island of Polyaigos when German planes spotted their caique in the harbour and repeatedly dive-bombed it, killing Oliver, who was on guard aboard, while Nancy and her children watched in horror from the shelter of a cave.

Losing their youngest son was a terrible blow to my grandparents, and for weeks the grown-ups must have talked of little else, but so insulated were we children that no word that I can remember reached the ears of the nursery party. As far as we were concerned, the tragedy simply meant that our cousins, David and Clarissa Caccia, appeared one day like magic and were absorbed into the household.

They were exciting technicolor newcomers in the quiet Welsh valley, sun-tanned to a deep apricot, against which their large pale blue eyes stood out startlingly. Their fair hair was bleached almost white by the Aegean sun, and they had a fund of thrilling stories about a world of which we knew nothing.

Though much the same age – David younger than Gerry but older than me, Clarissa younger – they were far better than us at running and jumping, and instead of a nanny they were attended by a tall sailor called David Yellowlees. Most exotic of all in my eyes, they had a smattering of demotic Greek. Soon they had me and Gerry counting to ten: *ina, thea, tria, tesera…* and singing anti-Government ditties learnt in faction-torn Greece:

> *Zito, zito, cucoides!*
> *Zito, zito M and V!*
> *Dirty water, compo tea/*
> *Zito, zito, cucoides!*
> *ELAS at the windows*
> *Andartes on the wall,*
> *They've pinched our ammunition,*
> *We're done for good and all!*

Our thoughtless chanting must have been horribly painful for Grand-father and Granny, but they never – as far as I remember – tried to stop us, nor raised more than the mildest protest as we put on the wind-up gramophone another favourite record with the refrain:

> *Oh, what a surprise for the Duce, the Duce,*
> *He can't put it over the Greeks.*
> *Oh, what a surprise for the Duce, the Duce,*
> *He's had such a kick in the breeks!*

The last line seemed to us so uproariously funny that we would roll on the floor in hysterical laughter; and the moment it stopped would lift the arm back to play it over again, the triangular fibre needle grinding round relentlessly, until at long last it skidded across the grooves and ruined the track for good.

11

With five children in the house, the nursery party split into the Big Ones – Gerry, David, and me – who did lessons every morning with the two governesses. Miss Cover for me and Gerry, Miss Oldershaw, aka 'Oshie', for David, and were occasionally allowed to lunch in the dining-room, and the Little Ones – Clarissa and Olivia. I remember very clearly the moment when I learned to read. Everything suddenly fell into place and I thought, So that's how it works! Why didn't anyone say so before?

The Little Ones, meanwhile, remained in the charge of the current Nanny and the naughty, flighty, irrepressible nursery-maid, Florence. She was thin, freckled and star-struck, adored going to the flicks, as she called the cinema, sang, *I'm Forever Blowing Bubbles...* and *It's Foolish but it's Fun* and, with comb, water and kirbigrips, tried unavailingly to put waves in our straight, floppy hair.

Florence was one of a large family and, aged fourteen, already had a boyfriend. He would call at the kitchen door on her day off and carry her away on his motorbike while we watched enviously from the nursery window. She paid no heed to the frequent scoldings she got from Cook and the governesses, but one evening when we were having our bath, her fecklessness went too far. Hearing the scrunch of wheels on gravel in the front drive, she scrambled on to the high tiled windowsill to see who had arrived, and the movement caught my grandfather's eye as he got out of the car.

He looked up and waved in a friendly way, whereupon Florence ducked out of sight so hastily that she toppled backwards into the bath on top of us, cracking her skull on the rim.

'She'd a lump on her head the size of a turkey egg,' Cook reported to Nanny with ghoulish relish. Whether she was subsequently sacked or gave notice I don't know, but as far as we were concerned that was the end of her. As we grew older and took to riding bicycles and ponies, life seemed to be one long round of minor injuries. David was the most adventurous and accident-prone. He couldn't see a tree without wanting to climb it, or a stream without falling into it, and his elbows and knees were always patched with grubby Elastoplast.

'The falling was all right, it was the landing that hurt,' he would say stoically when someone sympathised with his latest crash. He was a one-off – a true original – and from an early age an outstanding mimic and raconteur in the Peter Ustinov tradition, doing all the accents and noises with tremendous brio. He also had the useful knack of making the grown-ups laugh, thereby deflecting criticism or punishment. With fascinated dread, my mother once watched him, at the age of five, plodding round Chapel House in his gumboots with a stone in his hand, squaring up to each window in turn and drawing back his arm as if about to hurl his missile, then lowering it and moving on to the next tempting target.

'Why were you doing that?' she asked when she managed to collar him, and he said he wanted to know what it would sound like.

I found him wholly captivating, and the my first-ever reversal in love came when we were splashing through puddles on the valley road, with Nanny Price pushing Olivia's pram fifty yards behind, on an afternoon when it was too wet to play in the garden. I asked him to marry me and to my consternation and distress he refused, explaining that later on I would meet someone I liked better than him and (this was the bit that really hurt) he would find someone he liked more than me. I remember the horrible hollow feeling of jealousy in the pit of my stomach, but I didn't believe him and continued my secret hopes.

Like most girls at that time, I yearned to be a boy. Not only were Gerry and David older than me, but they seemed to have all the fun, and one would have had to be blind not to notice that they were Granny's favourites. It rankled that when Grandfather brought home two golden sovereigns, they were presented to the boys, mounted on cards inscribed: *Granny's wish is quickly told, Be like St George, be good as gold*, while Clarissa, Olivia and I got nothing.

Even in the matter of clothes, the boys got preferential treatment. We were not a dressy family and most of the time both sexes wore identical blue Aertex shirts and grey shorts with plimsolls in summer. But come wintertime the boys were kitted out in splendid shiny black boots with little yellow tags at the back, while I had to wear boring lace-ups. On one occasion, I kicked up such a fuss in the shoe-shop in Builth that, much to the disapproval of the proprietor, Mr Eadie, Mummy bought me boots, too, and I wore them proudly though I found them stiff, heavy, uncomfortable, and inclined to rub my heels, just as Mr Eadie had predicted.

Below the house a broad terrace of flagstones – deadly slippery when wet – stretched the length of its facade. A flight of steps led down past two more grass terraces separated by a flowerbed, the whole forming the obstacle known to us as the Whee-air jump. 'Doing the Whee-air' was a rite of passage which we all undertook with varying degrees of dread. You had to screw your courage to the sticking-point and leap boldly out from the upper grass terrace, over the roses, and land with a tooth-rattling thump on the grass at the bottom, and any child who started the run and then 'refused' at the last moment suffered irretrievable loss of face, no matter how convincing his or her excuses.

Sipping their drinks in wooden garden armchairs on the sunny terrace, the grown-ups used to encourage us to hurl ourselves over the drop in a way that might surprise parents nowadays. I suppose they thought it was a good way for children to let off steam. Though I never really enjoyed the nervous anticipation of launching off or the shock of landing, I did love the resulting murmurs of approval and, except on the occasion when David rode his bicycle over the Whee-air, none of us ever suffered more than bumps and bruises.

These in themselves were a bonus if the damage was deemed worthy of a smear of the delicious-smelling cure-all we called 'Bermarderveen', whose faint scent emanated from the wall-mounted medicine cupboard outside Granny's bedroom. I guess it was arnica compounded with wintergreen and other healing herbs: a thick yellow grease which turned transparent as one rubbed it into the skin and brought instant relief.

Later I discovered that this magical embrocation was the famous 'Pomade Divine,' expensive and difficult to obtain in those days, and therefore used very sparingly. You needed to suffer more than a common or garden grazed knee before you were taken upstairs to sit on the oak chest outside the linen cupboard, and the stopper was pulled from the greasy little container, which was shaped like a flat-bottomed bulb.

Before it was applied, though, there was the grisly business of picking dirt and grit from the wound, during which moans and squeaks were given short shrift. 'Worse things have happened at sea,' was a recurring phrase, and even the most spectacular falls from the dour little solid-tyred Fairy Cycle on which we were taught before graduating to a proper bicycle were casually dismissed as 'a bit of a smeller.'

The grown-ups were always trying to toughen us up physically, no doubt feeling that if the country was invaded and we were forced to take to the hills, we ought to be prepared for hardship, but neither Gerry nor I was naturally hardy. As soon as we could read we preferred curling in an armchair with a book to building dens in the garden, and I think this was a disappointment to our mother, who had so passionately longed to be Tarzan of the Apes in her own childhood.

'Run like a village child, not a governess!' she would shout as we trotted about with our knees knocking together, and she made great efforts to improve our action with built-up insteps and, in the case of my sister Olivia, fearsome medieval-looking leg-irons which were supposed to straighten bandy legs.

During the governesses' reign, however, we saw little of either my mother or Aunt Nancy until six o'clock, when we would be brushed and scrubbed and buttoned into tidy clothes in order to spend a civilising hour in the drawing-room before bedtime.

Feeling constrained and chilly in white socks, ballet pumps, and either a white silk dress smocked in red (my favourite) or a much-hated organdie number that prickled under the arms, we would be lined up on the stairs, told to behave, and then propelled through the opened door into the long low room set about with sofas and armchairs, a grand piano, two big black-and-gold Chinese cupboards adorned with golden dragons and brass locks that Granny had brought back from Pekin in 1936, glass-topped tables full of precious oddities and, on the far mantelpiece, a row of figurines of Chinese musicians which were supposed to have come from a princess's tomb.

You had to move with care in the drawing-room, because there were so many things to trip or knock over. The grown-ups would have finished their tea from the double-decked trolley, but there might well be delicate sandwiches or a rather dry cake left over beside the slop bowl and silver tea-pot. Granny would be sitting on the sofa beside the fire, carefully adding milk and sugar to a saucer of weak tea for each of the Siamese cats, Proust and Pooh-Hi, who sprawled elegantly on blue silk cushions with gold fringes, their long chocolate-gloved paws stretched out before them.

Proust was the elder, and actually belonged to my father, but sharing his life with my mother's dogs, Chinky the stroppy wire-haired terrier and Brioni, aka 'Boney,' the Dalmatian, would not have suited him, and when Daddy married, Proust preferred to continue his luxurious existence at Chapel House throughout the war years. By the time I remember him, he must have been ten or eleven, dark for a Siamese, and with a placid careworn expression. Solid of figure and stately of pace, he was perfectly prepared to let children lie close beside him while they tried to imitate his deep rumbling purr. We thought that was why he was called Prrroust, and were later surprised to discover his name's true origin.

His companion, Pooh-Hi, was very different – lighter in colour, frame, and temperament, quick-moving and unlikely to let children near enough to stroke him. He would leap to the back of the sofa if you so much as stretched out a yearning hand, and glower at you with blazing blue eyes, daring you to come closer. All his love was reserved for Granny. A true one-woman cat, he dogged Granny's footsteps about the house and garden, and chatted to her in his plaintive Oriental yowl. He was even allowed to curl up at the foot of her bed.

He, too, was wary of Mummy's dogs. She had trained Chinky to shut a door by flinging his solid little body at it in the hope of dislodging a sugar lump balanced on the handle. It was not a very labour-saving trick, since you had to get up in order to position the sugar lump before ordering Chinky to perform, but he loved doing it and both Granny and the Siamese cats used to flinch at the resulting bang. At Chapel House, their expressions said, doors should be closed soundlessly.

Boney the Dalmatian was tall and handsome and supposed to be utterly brainless, but when we lived in London his wits were sharp enough to recognise the butcher's boy's whistling as he hurried down the street with his big wicker basket, delivering meat. The boy would ring each bell and place the order on the windowsill, but before the householder came to the door, Boney would make a lightning raid and be away round the corner with the chops or sausages in his jaws. He had an even more uncultured predilection for lifting his leg on any upright, sentient or non-sentient, that he passed – once, to Mummy's consternation, on the line of waitresses holding trays just inside Lyons Corner Shop. Horrified, but nearly helpless with laughter, she described the way each black-stocking-inged leg lashed out in fury as Boney anointed it, while she hurried on pretending he was nothing to do with her.

Like many Dalmatians, he was hard of hearing and difficult to train. It was impossible to know whether his disobedience resulted from deafness or sheer natural bloody-mindedness, but in either case it was the cause of his premature death, knocked down in the road by a car.

Back in the drawing-room at Chapel House, shining and slicked, we would be kissed and briefly admired before Mummy and Aunt Nancy found some excuse to leave on affairs of their own, telling us to be good and to play quietly with the Big Toys, which were kept in the Chinese cupboards. These were pretty basic. Various board games and large-format books, a babyish wooden roundabout, and a box of large wooden blocks and planks of various sizes, from which a child of architectural bent could build the houses of rather brutalist design shown on the lid.

We preferred to stack them higher and higher in tottering towers, for the fun of hearing them crash when a vital support was removed – at least the boys did. I was drawn like a magnet to the beautiful pea-green gipsy caravan, with shafts and a swingle-tree, and a removable roof. It had dear little furniture inside and was pulled by a thick-set wooden horse we called Bonny, and I was horribly chagrined when one day it disappeared, given to a neighbour's child who was dying of leukaemia.

Gerry had a good treble voice, and would sometimes sing while Granny accompanied him at the grand piano, her stubby be-ringed fingers totally assured on the complicated black-looking chords of Victorian favourites like *The Lordly Ones* and *The Last Rose of Summer*.

Then the wall-mounted grand-daughter clock would chime the half-hour and it would be time to read. This was much the best bit of our drawing-room time. Granny would sit on the sofa with her back supported by a drum-shaped Chinese bolster and her legs covered by a fringed shawl, because the little Bratt Colman fireplace gave only minimal heat, and we would sit or lie on the hearth rug while she worked steadily through *The Wind in the Willows*, both the *Jungle Books* and the *Just So Stories*, Charlotte M Yonge's *Dove in the Eagle's Nest* and *The Little Duke* and many more I don't remember, reading clearly with each word beautifully pronounced, never skipping, never hurrying, and continuing until she reached a suitable break-off point even when half-heard sighs and scuffling behind the door indicated that the nannies had come to fetch us to bed.

As petrol became scarcer, my mother's thoughts turned to pony-power. She bought a two-wheeled, round bodied 'tub' cart in a ruinous condition, had it done up and smartly painted black and yellow, and picked up from somewhere a set of harness to fit an animal between 12 and 13 hands high. There was no shortage of beautiful, spirited, Welsh ponies with attractively dished faces and legs like deer available for between £10 and £20 in Hereford market; the trouble was that most of them were straight off the hill and wild as hawks.

After a flighty black mare appropriately named Blackbird had kicked over the traces and smashed the front panel of the tub, and her successor, Nutmeg, had bolted on the main road when her driver took a handker-chief from her pocket, Mummy gave up the dream of bowling around the Wye Valley road behind a swift-stepping well-mannered driving-pony, and settled instead for a shiny, chunky little black five-year-old named Micky. He had very neat short ears, which barely poked above his bushy mane, a chiselled face and large kind eyes. Best of all, it was claimed by the vendor that any child could ride him.

Well, maybe – provided he or she was superglued to the saddle, but merely sitting on is not the same as being in control, and Micky was very hard to stop. At an early age he had taken part in local 'flapping races,' where the contestants are handicapped by distance rather than weight, which had fired his competitive spirit to such a degree that a jointed snaffle was no more use in his mouth than a wisp of hay.

In rapid succession Mummy tried out all the bits in my uncle Trevor's tackroom – pelham, Kimblewick, gag and so on – but the only one to make any impression on Micky's iron mouth was a straight-barred Liver-pool with long cheeks and a tightish curb. In this Gerry could control him most of the time, but in common with most boys he disliked feeling he couldn't stop when he wanted, and it was several years before he and Micky really saw eye to eye.

He was also reluctant to be caught in the field, though for some reason he would – if sufficiently bribed – always come to me. The trick was to avoid looking him in the eye as you approached. Humans, with forward vision, are predators who stare at their chosen prey. A horse, whose best defence is flight, has widely-spaced side-set eyes so that he can watch all round for attackers and long experience has taught him that anyone who stares fixedly at him is up to no good.

When close to one another, with no need to neigh or whinny, horses communicate by very small movements of the lips, and I found if I looked at Micky's muzzle rather than his eyes, and sort of drifted obliquely towards him rather than marching up purposefully – while concentrating on the kind of simple thoughts that occupy horses' brains: *Food. Good. Safe*, and so on, to counter his own negative reflections which probably focused on *Danger, Pain* and *Exertion* – he would approach cautiously and, with his weight still braced backwards ready for instant flight, stretch out his nose towards my handful of oats.

I would spin these out as far as I could, while he gradually became more confident, and slowly pivot until we were both facing the same way and I could slip the leadrope over his neck. Once haltered, he was quiet and obliging, and though I knew perfectly well that it was the oats he loved, not me, it gave me a great buzz to be the only child who could be sure of catching him.

No-one feeds ponies oats nowadays. It is recognised as a sure way to send them scatty, like pumping children full of fizzy drinks. But before the invention of pony-cubes and balanced equine nutrition, we used to stuff them with as many as we could scrounge from the cart horses' and hunters' rations. Oats would cascade from my pockets when I undressed, much to the annoyance of the housemaids, and we never made the connection between this unsuitably high-octane diet and the ponies' erratic behaviour.

Nor were we ever formally taught to ride. Mummy's method was to put a child on a pony and lead it about, first on foot, then from a horse. When it seemed to be getting tired of being constrained, she would dispense with the leading-rein and – hey presto! – the child could ride. We never wore any kind of head protection – nobody did in those days unless they were showing or hunting. A penny would be placed between each knee and the saddle, and if you still had it there at the end of the ride, you were allowed to keep it. As a result, we rode like monkeys up sticks, gripping hard with our knees and hardly using our seat or lower legs at all. Bad habits acquired as a child have resisted all my efforts to eradicate them, and even today I feel most at ease on horses that closely resemble Micky.

He would, no doubt, have been a very different character without the oats, but as it was, in his rather hepped-up condition, he was great fun for a lightish grown-up like Mummy to ride on the hill – lively, tireless, sure-footed, and extremely sharp. Even on the steepest slope he always had a leg or two to spare.

He was the classic type of old-fashioned Welsh pony, in the mould of early champions like Starlight of Grove, much cobbier than today's show ponies, but since judges tended to be gentlemen of riper years, Micky was a favourite at local shows, and though he considered jumping a mug's game and preferred to keep his nice round feet firmly on the ground, he was brilliant at gymkhanas, particularly bending races, snaking round the end pole so slippily that his rider risked being shot over his shoulder.

About the time we acquired Micky, I had had the luck to inherit our cousins' pony Mincepie at the end of a glittering career in the Cotswolds. One after the other, she had carried Libby, Robbie, Jenny and John Lawrence to glory in Pony Club and hunting field, and when they all finally outgrew her she was far too much part of the family to sell. She was small, dark, long-tailed and fiery, and wore a pad saddle secured (more or less) by a crupper, though she was expert at blowing out her belly when you did up the girth, so unless checked later it had a horrid habit of sliding round and depositing you on the ground. She was well over twenty when she transferred to our branch of the family, but still a great goer who, despite stiffening joints, would cat-jump small obstacles with tremendous brio, though whether she and her rider landed together was largely a matter of luck.

The foothills of Mynydd Eppynt rose steeply behind Chapel House. A rough winding track skirted the fields belonging to Abernant Farm, and where it forked you had the choice of continuing uphill over a couple of shaley shoulders to the farm called Alltmawr, or turning left across a stream and up through a still steeper wooded slope to its neighbour, Pentwyn.

Not that there was much to see when we got there. If they happened to be outside in the farmyard, plucking chickens, chopping wood or tending stock in their faded cotton dresses and sacking aprons, heavy stockings and cracked leather boots, Mrs Williams Alltmawr and Mrs Price Pentwyn would respond politely to our greeting and duck back indoors as soon as they decently could, while the farmer himself stared at us with rheumy pale-blue eyes as if we were beings from another world. There was a high incidence of goitre in the area, caused by lack of iodine, and with most able-bodied young men and women away at the war, those that remained were often simple-minded (or, as it was tactfully called, 'delicate') hapless victims of centuries of in-breeding.

Landscape and farming practices had scarcely changed since the days of George Borrow. In an era of agricultural depression and scarce manpower, Welsh hill-farming meant subsistence living of a kind that is almost unimaginable today – perhaps the nearest equivalent would be Romania at the time of Ceaucescu, but without the sunshine. Despite beautiful views on every side, the climate of mid-Wales could only be described as depressing, as all-year-round Atlantic weather systems brought heavy rain and dumped much of it in the Wye Valley.

'We do reckon,' an old carpenter once said gently to Mummy, 'that we do have nine months winter and three months middling weather.'

How right he was. Year after year, a wet summer ruined the hay, and constant rain rotted wooden posts and rusted wire until the fences would hardly keep a cow in, let alone those incorrigible escapers Welsh mountain sheep. Tractors were few and far between in those days before the little grey Fergie 20 revolutionised farm work, and most of the power on a typical hill farm was still provided by a single carthorse with, perhaps, a Welsh cob to work in double harness when needed, or take the family to market.

To Alltmawr or Pentwyn and back was about as far as children cared to walk – in fact I always loathed forcing my legs uphill and could never decide which was worst: the long gradual slope to Alltmawr or the short steep struggle to Pentwyn – but nannies and governesses were united in their view that no afternoon was complete without a walk. I suppose they reckoned it would cut down on mischief in the evening.

Ponies, however, extended our range considerably and gave us a whole new governess-free territory to explore. In a matter of twenty minutes or so, Gerry and I could ride up to the hill gate – previously the ultimate boundary – and discover beyond it an unbroken expanse of undulating open country stretching as far as eye could see, its ancient turf quilted by wind and snow into firm, springy cushions, and its great tracts of bracken or heather intersected by alluring green tracks. These were former drove roads, part of the great network of mountain trails whose soft surface was kind to the hoofs of cattle making the long trek to market, years ago; and little by little we learned where they led until we could ride with fair confidence over the hill to Builth – say – or Erwood in the other direction, or even to watch the sheepdog trials at Cwmowen, which really did seem the back of beyond, and avoid the main road along the river.

A few years later this became important to me when Mincepie went to the great Hunting-Field in the Sky and Mummy bought me a charming gentle blue-roan Exmoor with a fluttery ginger muzzle called Sally, a perfect child's pony in every respect except for her ineradicable fear of lorries. Taking Sally to the blacksmith in Builth was an anxious business, because even if you rode over the hill, the last mile to the forge took you through the back streets right into the centre of town, where you were almost bound to meet one of her bugbears.

As soon as she saw it, her head would go up, her muscles would tense, and her eyes would start to roll while I signalled urgent appeals to the driver to switch off his engine. If the monster fell silent, Sally would – with much legging and urging – eventually agree to pass it, but if it didn't, she would either rush into the nearest garden, alleyway or shop, or whip round and bolt back the way she had come. Even with Micky between her and the lorry, she could not overcome her terror, and I was always thankful to get her inside the high corrugated-iron walls surrounding the forge where the lorries could not trouble her.

Oh, the hours we used to spend waiting for our ponies to be shod! Whole mornings would go by as we perched uncomfortably among the broken implements and heaps of worn-out shoes, trying not to mind that Charlie Evans the blacksmith seemed to be attending to everyone else's needs before ours, though to be fair it was probably more important for him to finish mending some vital bit of farm machinery than making shoes for children's ponies.

Men in trilby hats and flat caps would drift in and out of the forge, chatting and laughing, and Charlie, his high-arched eyebrows and turned-up nose giving him a look of perpetual surprise, would blow up his fire and put down his hammer, and join in the gossip, while we fidgeted silently, not daring to go shopping in Builth in case we got pushed even farther down the queue of customers.

When at last he did get around to dealing with our ponies, he made the shoes from scratch, like a proper craftsman. No ready-made cold-shoeing for him. He would cut, heat, hammer, and bend the fullered bars of iron on his anvil, the rapid hammerstrokes bouncing and ringing, then carefully shape them to the pared hoof, not the other way round, while I would silently prayed that the pony (chilled and bored from the long wait), would not disgrace me by snatching her hoof away and knocking over the tripod. Charlie was teetotal and a pillar of the Methodist Church, and would never have sworn in front of children, but if a pony was obstreperous he would stand back with his hands on his hips, and blow out his lips in disgust, and say he wouldn't be able to finish if she didn't behave better.

It was a fearful threat, but luckily never carried out. At long last the job would be done, the four neat hoofs finished with a slick of tarry-smelling oil, and I would fish from my jodhs pocket the 'five bob a leg' he charged for a full set, and go out to face the lorries again.

Riding on the hill was not without its hazards, but they were natural ones. It was very easy to lose your way amid those continuous false horizons and tussocky ponds which all looked very much alike. There were bogs, and rabbit-holes into which a galloping pony might put a hoof, and sometimes a bossy little Welsh stallion would leave his bunch of mares and foals and trot over, with wild mane flying and plumed tail held high, to fancy Sally and squeal angrily at Micky.

We would hurry on our way, knowing he would not pursue us very far; and we soon learnt that if a mist came down to blot out the landmarks, the ponies were as good as compasses and could be relied on to find their way home.

Children on their own are usually pretty cautious, and in fact on both the occasions when we got into serious difficulty on the hill Mummy was with us – indeed, most of the trouble was directly attributable to her.

I remember it was an unusually fine warm April afternoon when we rode up to the lake called Pant-y-llyn, with my mother on a hunter called Lucky Lark, borrowed from our great-uncle Trevor, who lived at Abernant. In the middle of the lake were a number of marshy islands, white with noisily-nesting gulls, and Mummy was inspired to strip to her underclothes and half-wade, half-swim out to the nearest, in quest of their delicious pink-yolked eggs.

Holding her horse and our ponies on the bank, Gerry and I watched in growing alarm as she began to swim from one island to the next, her head a mere blob among the dancing ripples. From time to time we'd see a pale flash as her arm reached into a nest, abstracted an egg, then tested it in the water. If it was fresh, it would sink. If it floated, it was certainly addled or contained a chick near hatching. Selecting suitable eggs took a long time, and we became increasingly anxious as she went ever farther from the shore.

We were both rather short-sighted, and what with the dazzle of sun on the water it was difficult to keep her in view; but eventually we had to recognise that the head was no longer visible. Mummy had vanished. We looked at each other in dismay, wondering what to do. We couldn't let go of the horses and there was nothing to tie them to. Nor could either of us swim that far.

The sun went in, a chilly wind blew, the ponies fidgeted and tugged at the reins, and we stood there in frozen indecision.

Then Gerry said, 'There she is!'

I saw it, too. A confused splashing on the edge of one of the islands, a faint halloo, and to our huge relief we saw Mummy haul herself out of the water and collapse among the rushes. She lay there, pummelling her legs, trying to get up and falling down again.

After what seemed an age she stood up and waved to us. We caught the one word, '…Back,' and saw her lower herself into the water. With hearts in our mouths, we watched her swim slowly and splashily towards us, and Gerry thrust all the reins into my hands and waded deep into the water to help pull her out. His clothes were soaked when they both staggered up the bank, and Mummy's arms and legs were mottled green and red in patches, like condemned meat fed to lions at the zoo, and she shivered convulsively. We tried to dry her off with heather, but it was too scratchy, and gorse was plainly not an option, but after a bit she managed to pull on her clothes and began to look more herself.

'I got cramp. Too silly! But look...' And she showed us the clutch of little greeny-khaki eggs she had brought back, knotted into a big spotted handkerchief.

'Don't tell Granny. She's got enough to worry about,' she said as we rode home; but of course by degrees the story came out. After constant re-telling it became enshrined in family lore as a rather jolly adventure, but I remember the whole episode was very frightening.

Muffled echoes of the war reached the nursery from time to time. I don't think there was any deliberate policy of keeping children in the dark; merely the general assumption that we wouldn't be able to understand why people in uniform kept coming and going, or where Daddy was fighting, so there was no point in trying to explain. The words 'Sidi Barani,' 'Monty,' and 'Alamein' gradually penetrated our consciousness, however, and one Sunday there was extra praying in church, and we were told Daddy had helped win an important victory and had been made a Colonel.

With St Mauritius' Church actually inside the perimeter of the garden, there was no escaping its fortnightly services, ('Singing communia – hell of a row,' remarked Olivia, aged 3, when asked where Granny was) but along with the inevitable boredom of sitting still and quiet, there were compensations. Not only were the boys allowed to ring the bell and take round the little red felt collection bags, but we were all encouraged to invade the tiny vestry and count the proceeds, heaping coins – there were never notes – into little stacks and checking and re-checking one another's totals before the Rector filled in the Church Attendance ledger.

We sat on the narrow polished benches of the high-sided 'loose-box' at the back of the church, hidden from the rest of the congregation, and free to play cards or jacks or read whatever we had managed to smuggle into the pew. From time to time one of us would stand on the seat to see how things were going, or a burst of giggling would bring a parent or nanny to haul out the offender and make him or her sit in an ordinary pew under supervision.

There was much that puzzled me about Church, but questions were not encouraged. Why, for instance, was Jesus always in such jolly spirits – 'Merrily, merrily I say unto you' – when his subject matter was plainly serious in nature? Why should an unfortunate lamb be killed so that its blood would wash away your sins? It sounded very much like putting the blame on someone else, and everyone knew that blood stained : you couldn't wash with it. Why should anyone but a cannibal want to eat His flesh and drink His blood? I thought – and still do – the whole idea bizarre and revolting, and was thankful that children were not obliged to go up to the altar rail. Those sinister little discs looked all too like dried skin, and if I'd had to eat one I would have been sick on the spot.

But I enjoyed the hymns, however silly the words, especially when I was allowed to turn the pages for Granny at the wheezing, temperamental harmonium. She and Miss Jones Alltmawr played the voluntary and hymns at alternate services, their faces rapt and feet pedalling furiously. So anxious was I not to miss the quick nod indicating the turn that I often muffed it and flicked over the page several bars too early. It was nervous work.

Grandfather read the Old Testament lesson, taking off the spectacles which seemed a part of his face in order to focus on the small black print. His enormous memory encompassed whole books of *Paradise Lost*, and all Shakespeare's Sonnets, but he also had a taste for doggerel, and was apt to indulge it to commemorate family events – hence that heroic ballad *How Grandma Lost Her Knickers When She Went To See The King*, (set to the tune of *The Wearing of the Green*) and *My Wife's a Cushion-Plumper, A Picker-Up and Thumper*, and he composed verses of a vaguely Biblical nature to amuse us thus: *Joshua the son of Nun/And Caleb the son of Gefunneh/Were the only two/Who ever got through/To the Land of Milk and Honey.*

Being a Yorkshireman, he made a point of retaining the short 'a', so:

Goliath of Gath
Stood in the path
When poor little David came by.

26

He took out his sling
And gave it a fling
And hit the old fool in the eye.

One Sunday he abandoned Scripture, and his verse had a triumphant ring:

All you people, do you know?
Daddy's won the DSO.
First he crossed the ocean wave,
Then he was extremely brave,
And with all his shells and guns
Pounded those disgusting Huns!

The citation put it rather differently, but the substance was the same. As the Allies battled their way up the spine of Italy towards the narrow pinchpoint of Monte Cassino, where the Germans had taken over the monastery and sited their guns to command the approaches, Daddy had crouched for days in a dangerous forward position, directing the fire of the Royal Horse Artillery guns where its could do most damage. After a prolonged struggle, the monastery was flattened and the German guns silenced, and Daddy's bravery recognised with the award of the Distinguished Service Order.

Not long afterwards, when the identical twins Adam and David Block won identical awards, Mummy's congratulations were in the same vein:

All you people, run and flock,
Here we have the brothers Block
In battle they have won their fame,
And added glory to their name.
When to Buck Palace they both go
To fetch their well-won DSO,
The King will have a bit of trouble,
Think that he is seeing double.
Say, as he scratches royal pate,
'Do I do this in duplicate?'
'Nay, Sire,' they'll say, 'Survive the shock,
For here we have the brothers Block,

Alike in size and shape and girth,
Two of the finest chaps on earth!'

Despite her energy and ready wit, Mummy believed in keeping children on a tight rein. She liked them to be a) busy, and b) useful, and the last lines of *Once in Royal David's City* – 'When like stars, thy children crowned/All in white shall wait around,' used to provoke a derisive snort.

'Not if I'm there, they won't!' she would mutter.

We were kept in our place quite strictly, and disrespectful remarks were slapped down with a crushing, 'Don't be pert'. We were not allowed to question her decisions, and explanations were kept to a minimum.

Aunt Nancy could be just as fierce.

'You know, Mummy,' David once began helpfully, 'women like you and Granny with short thick necks should always...'

'Stop right there,' ordered his mother. 'I see no future in that sentence.' And so we never heard what women with short thick necks should always do.

Real naughtiness – scribbling on walls with lipstick, telling lies, peeing in the sandpit – brought a spanking with the back of Mummy's Mason Pearson hairbrush, which stung even through the overworked pair of Austrian lederhosen passed around between us. Worse than the discomfort – one could hardly call it pain – was the gruesome anticipation as one waited in one's bedroom for the footsteps of the avenging angel, hearing sobs and howls from other rooms as justice was dispensed.

Actually retribution was often far from just. Gerry was spanked along with the rest of us for the sandpit episode, although he was completely blameless and, indeed, had warned us not to do it. But having decided that some crime merited a spanking, I think Mummy just gritted her teeth and punished guilty and innocent alike, rather as Dr Keate, the Flogging Headmaster of Eton, beat the entire confirmation class he found gathered outside his door under the misapprehension that they were defaulters.

Punishment – or escaping it – was largely a matter of luck. One summer evening after a long drive the Caccias and I raced down to the river, leaving Gerry to help Mummy unpack the car. There, tied to its mooring alongside a croy projecting into the smooth dark water of the

Boat Pool, was Uncle Trevor's fishing-boat, newly painted a beautiful green.

We climbed into it and pretended we were shipwrecked sailors for a time. Then we got out the oars and pretended to row, and presently David untied the tow-rope and said, 'Let's go across to the other side and explore.'

It seemed a marvellous idea. He pushed off and gave me one oar while he took the other, and Clarissa sat in the middle, but rowing was much more difficult than we expected. We couldn't make the boat go straight.

'Come back!' shouted Gerry, who had been sent to fetch us for supper, but already the boat was out of control, sweeping downstream at a frightening speed, David and I were struggling to turn it, and Clarissa was screaming.

'We're going to drown! These are our last moments!'

Brutally I whacked her on the head with my oar and she flattened herself in the bottom of the boat. We had left the relative calm of the Boat Pool and were going sideways down a wide strong run known as the Woodstream, unable to point the bows across the current. Not far ahead we could see broken water with rocks sticking out.

We flailed away with the oars, desperately trying to get beyond the full force of the current, sometimes catching a crab and sprawling backwards, sometimes dipping so deep that the oar wouldn't move at all. David stood up and tried to pole like a gondolier, but the water was too deep and he nearly went overboard. We were pretty well exhausted and in despair when the boat suddenly slid into smooth water, grounding on gravel just a few yards from the Radnorshire bank.

On the Breconshire side, Gerry had run downstream to keep level with us. He yelled through cupped hands, 'Pull – it – back – up,' and though we couldn't actually hear the words, gestures got his point across. Somehow or other we were going to have to cross again, and if we started from the place where we had grounded, and the same thing happened, we would certainly be swept into those jagged rocks.

With all three of us heaving at the mooring rope, we managed to wade and drag the boat upstream until we were opposite the croy where we had embarked on this foolish voyage, and with hearts in mouths we began the return trip.

I don't remember this as being nearly so frightening or difficult. Perhaps the swirl of the current was more favourable, because although I was now so tired I could hardly row with my oar, it seemed only a few minutes before Gerry, up to his waist in water, had seized the gunwale and was hauling us into the bank.

'You idiots,' he said. 'Look how you've scraped the paint. Uncle Trevor will be furious.'

Chastened and soaked, we staggered up to Chapel House, hoping to get inside unnoticed, but our mothers were enjoying a drink in the loggia and spotted us at once. 'What's happened? ' they shrieked in unison, and there was nothing for it but to confess. Then the lottery element of punishment kicked in.

Gerry and I were scolded, spanked, and sent to bed without supper. David and Clarissa were scolded, spanked and sent to apologise to Uncle Trevor. He was a daunting figure and set in his ways – the quintessential cavalry colonel, tall, thin, upright, moustached, a Master of Foxhounds and lifelong bachelor who was never at ease with children at the best of times, and when he understood that his boat had been taken without permission – and damaged – he was indeed furious.

'He swore – horribly!' reported Clarissa, saucer-eyed and shaken.

But when Gerry and I were sent to Abernant after breakfast next morning to apologise, Uncle Trevor had completely recovered his temper. He offered us toast and marmalade and hardly mentioned the boat at all. It just went to show the truth of one of Mummy's favourite sayings: 'Life's not fair, and nobody ever said it was going to be.'

It never occurred to me that she might dislike spanking us as much as we disliked being on the receiving end. There was a great gulf between grown-ups and children at that time, and we found it difficult to believe that our elders had feelings.

We were seldom warned and certainly not invited to contribute our opinion on future plans, however closely they concerned us. One evening when we were fetched from the drawing-room, instead of being put to bed, Gerry and I were surprised to be bundled into a car and driven for several hours to a hospital in Cardiff. I remember holding my breath as long as I could when the little pink mask, like an inverted cup, was placed over my mouth and nose, and the noxious smell of ether when at last I was forced to inhale.

I woke up with a cracking sore throat, having had my adenoids removed, but details of Gerry's operation were concealed from me, though clearly it hadn't been the same as mine because his throat was fine. For two days I lay in bed, eating ice-cream, and then – whoosh, swoop – without a word of warning we were whisked back to Chapel House.

I don't suppose we moved much more often than other families with fighting fathers, but it seemed to me that no sooner were we settled in one place than something would happen to uproot us again. More adventurous children would probably have enjoyed the excitement of new surroundings, but I was a conservative child who disliked change. Particularly I hated packing and unpacking, sudden orders to look for things I didn't know where to find, the grime, cold, haste and tension of forcing possessions into boxes and overflowing suitcases and cramming these into overloaded cars, the endless waiting for grown-ups to be ready, so often followed by dashes back to the house to fetch things that had been left behind. I was, besides, miserably car-sick.

So when one day Mummy announced that we were going away to live in Hertfordshire, I immediately began to argue.

'We can't! What about the ponies?'

'We'll take them with us.' She tried to cheer me up. 'We're all going. The Caccias as well.'

I wailed, 'I don't want to leave Chapel House.'

'Don't be silly. We'll come back for holidays, but we need to be near London so Daddy doesn't waste all his leave travelling.'

Deep down I think I had always known that our life at Chapel House was too good to last, but I sensed she was in a mood for concessions. 'Can I keep rabbits at the new house? Angora rabbits?' I had seen the white powder-puff babies at the North Breconshire Show and fallen deeply in love with them.

She hesitated for a long agonising moment, no doubt weighing up the considerable nuisance of adding captive rodents to her roll of dependants against the benefit of getting me on-side, and eventually nodded. 'All right. But you'll have to groom them and muck them out yourself.'

'Oh, I will, I will!'

The following week she got in touch with the rabbit breeder, and before we packed up to leave Chapel House for life at Much Hadham, Herts, two beautiful pure white does with red eyes and pink insides to their ears joined the household. They were full sisters, and I called them Snow White and Rose Red.

CHAPTER TWO

Much Hadham

RABBITS DOMINATED my thoughts for the next three years. They were charming pets and the more I had of them, the more I loved them. At one stage pretty well the entire lower lawn at Gaytons, the long rambling house fronting on Much Hadham's main street which Mummy and Aunt Nancy had rented, was covered by rather wonky wood and chicken-wire runs in which my young stock, who had been weaned and were advertised for sale, spent their youth. They did a better job on the grass than the push-mower, but little for the look of the garden.

My foundation does, Snowy and Rosy, had been well handled as babies and were very tame. You could let them run free in the walled garden and catch them again with ease, and unlike most animals, they actually seemed to like being cuddled. There is nothing so soft and luxurious for a child to bury her nose in as the thick silky fur of an Angora rabbit, and this amazing fluffy fleece kept growing, even when they were shorn twice a year.

The shearing was quite a performance, requiring time, patience and nerve – all heroically supplied by Mummy, armed with dressmaking scissors, while I held the rabbit as still as possible on the kitchen table. Angoras have rather loose, curiously yellow skin, which makes them unsuitable for culinary purposes – or so the Breed Society advice booklet informed us, and even in the hungriest days of the war none of us would have dreamed of popping them in the pot. However, the loose wrinkles were all too easy for the amateur barber to nick with her shears, thereby ruining the snowy fur from which I derived most of my pocket-money.

In those days you could get ten shillings an ounce for white Angora wool, though it always astonished me what an enormous mound of the airy fluff had to be heaped into the scales to achieve that tiny weight. The company which bought all we could supply probably weighed it at their end, too, but they paid up faithfully, never less than the sum I billed them for.

Not having proper clippers, Mummy's attentions left the shorn rabbits' coats covered in ridges and they looked very odd for a few weeks until the fur began to grow again. Rosy, however, never endured this indignity because by some fluke we had chosen from the breeder's large litter a show champion.

To my eye, she was almost indistinguishable from her sister, but when I took them to a Breed Society show in the nearby town of Bishop's Stortford, Rosy came home with six first prizes and a cup, while poor Snow White won precisely nothing. One of the judges told us that shearing would spoil her looks, so to the end of her life she remained as nature intended, a gigantic powderpuff who had only to appear on a show bench for honours to be showered on her.

The drawback was that this made her a high-maintenance female, who needed daily grooming and ultra-clean living conditions. Feeling through her coat for mats was something I could do in my sleep; as soon as your fingers encountered the smallest seed or blade of grass that could form the basis of a clump, you had to tease it out very gently, gradually easing it away from the skin until at last it was loose enough to pull free without tweaking. Snowy, in contrast, was the ultimate in easy-care – two strokes of the brush and she was perfectly soignée.

For about a year, the two sisters lived a peaceful celibate existence in a big hutch just outside the stables, but things changed dramatically with the coming of Snowball. I can't remember if I nagged Mummy into buying him, or if she got him off her own bat, being now quite as keen on the rabbits as I was. Anyway, we let him into the outer compartment of the does' hutch, and almost immediately had to take him out smartish as they erupted from their sleeping-quarters in fury at the invasion, scratching and kicking until their precious fur began to fly

A tactical rethink suggested introducing them on neutral territory, one at a time, and this was more successful. I felt sorry for Rosy, left alone in the big hutch while her sister cavorted with the young buck, jumping over one another, boxing and nuzzling playfully, but when we felt sure they weren't going to damage one another we left them alone for a few days, and later repeated the exercise with Rosy. The result was two cracking litters, and soon an urgent need for extra housing.

The temptation to peek inside the sleeping-quarters at the newborn rabbits was overwhelming but had to be resisted, because if the doe caught you at it, she was liable to eat her naked helpless offspring. In any case, the deep nest of fluff in which she cradled them hid all but a tiny movement of the top layer to confirm that the babies were there. It always seemed an age – but must have been about ten days – before they opened their vivid pink eyes and ventured out into the open section of the hutch. Then there was the excitement of counting them, handling them to make them tame, and determining their gender – not easy, and one always hoped for a preponderance of females, for which there was more demand.

Snowball was a prolific progenitor, smaller and faster-moving than the laid-back does. He was also quite aggressive, kicking and scratching when transferred from one pen to another, so my arms and legs were usually decorated with long parallel lines of half-healed scabs.

I wasn't altogether sorry when he was killed by a visiting terrier which broke into one of the wonky pens, but by the time that happened we were almost snowed under with rabbits, despite selling as many as we could bear to part with. It was like that poem by W.B. Yeats about seagulls in a storm:

First there were two of us, then there were three of us, then there was one bird more,
Four of us wild white seagulls, treading the ocean floor,
And the wind rose and the sea rose and the angry billow's roar,
With four of us, eight of us, ten of us, twelve of us seagulls on the shore.

He goes on about: 'A wild white welter of winnowing wings...' which in our case was more like a wild white carpet of fluffety fur, but when Mummy eventually called a halt to the breeding programme because I was going away to weekly-board, we had twenty-seven rabbits to feed, muck out, and house according to age and sex, and the sense of overcrowding had become acute.

Great armfuls of greenstuff had to be gathered for this horde, from the lane that led to the allotments in summer, where you could be sure of finding cow parsley and hogweed, dandelions and hazel wands, all of which were rabbit favourites. In winter we scrounged leftovers from several different greengrocers – cabbage and sprouts, carrots and parsnips. It was before the days of pelleted feedstuffs, but I remember we also gave them oats and flaked maize, on which they did very well, but providing for them all and keeping the cages clean took a lot of time.

Just once I remember Mummy finding the water-bottles empty, and giving me a tremendous talking-to. 'If you take away an animal's freedom and put it in a cage so it can't fend for itself, you are the only person it has to depend on, and unless you care for it properly it will die and it will be all your fault!'

What with the sales of young stock and angora wool, rabbit-breeding was quite a lucrative little business, but although the money was nice, better still was the sense of shared endeavour with the person I most wanted to please. Like most middle children, I schemed and dreamed of having my mother all to myself, and since none of the others was much interested in rabbits, I could always secure her attention with news of the latest litter or behavioural problem. It marked a great change in our relationship. In this area, at least, we were colleagues – even conspirators – building pens, planning matings, chosing which rabbits to show and which to sell, and debating anxiously which of our friends could be trusted to look after them properly. On one embarrassing occasion, I charged a form-mate's mother ten shillings for a young doe, only for her to shriek with disgust when she spotted fleas in its ears.

The move to Much Hadham brought the war much closer. The village was only about thirty miles from London, so misdirected bombs and doodlebugs sometimes ended up nearby, and all the rules and regulations which various Ministries kept spewing forth were applied much more strictly there than in Wales.

Rationing, for example. At Chapel House the big vegetable garden and adjacent farm provided plenty to supplement official quantities of eggs, butter, bacon and so on, but at Much Hadham our ration-books with their funny little grids and different coloured pages suddenly assumed great importance.

Actually there was only one page, an orange one towards the back, in which we children took an interest, and that was because it contained the 'points' we needed to buy sweets. Mummy would tear out these pages and send us off to the Post Office to choose our week's ration, a long-drawn-out process fraught with argument. Should one splurge the whole week's allowance on two Mars bars, which was all you would get for your week's points, or four tubes of Rowntree's Clear Gums, or simply masses of Smarties? Or go for a mixed bag which might include striped humbugs from a tall glass jar, lemon sherbets which fizzed excitingly in the middle, and boring boiled sweets? Was a Venus bar (white in the middle) slightly more delicious than a Mars? Chocolate was so heavy on points that a plain bar of it wasn't worth considering, and it contained so little cocoa that it tasted very nasty.

Mr Groom the postmaster would wait patiently while we changed our minds forward and back, and eventually weigh out our choices in little white paper bags, twisted at the corners, and we would dawdle home with bulging cheeks.

The rest of the household's ration books were kept centrally, and I remember long debates between Mummy and Nan, the Scotch cook, when supplies ran low, because by then there were a lot of us to feed. Besides Aunt Nancy with two children and Mummy with three, there was Nan with her legitimate son, plus a baby she had unwisely borne to her husband's best friend, the dashing moustached Hector Macfarlane, and wanted to get adopted before her husband came on leave. Then there was Nan's unmarried sister, who acted as a sort of unofficial kitchenmaid, and was later replaced by Lily, a big-boned, simple-minded girl who had been rejected for war work because of an uncontrollable twitch that affected her left arm. This defect made her less than ideal as a parlourmaid, and as the breakages mounted exponentially, Aunt Nancy decreed that keeping her was too expensive and she must go.

Soon we were joined by Mummy's French sister-in-law Marianne, with her two baby sons, and Aunt Nancy's friend Ann, a fragile-looking divorcee with large soulful eyes and a yearning expression. She, too, was accompanied by her sons Peregrine and Hugo, but before long her gentle charm attracted a rich, wisecracking bachelor friend of the Caccias, who fascinated us children by eating – or pretending to eat – spiders, and they left us to get married.

Finally – and most importantly – there was Grandfather, who took the train to work in London every day, and for whose benefit Nancy had taken the house in the first place. She hoped it would be more peaceful for him than living in London during the Blitz, but sharing a house with this shifting mass of women and children must have been anything but tranquil, even though all of them weren't there all the time. People came and went; as work and war dictated. There were camp beds in odd corners and unexpected faces at meals.

One advantage of having so many children on the strength was the special vitamin-rich foods devised by the MOF to stop us getting rickets. Very small blue-labelled tins contained a blackcurrant puree so strong and sweet that it brought out beads of sweat on your forehead. Rosehip syrup had a gloopy delicacy that seemed half-taste, half-smell, and the creamy gruel known as Midlothian Oat Food made a pudding fit for the gods.

We all shared two or three to a room, and privacy was not something you could count on. It was, for instance, often difficult to find a lavatory unoccupied, and when I felt desperate to indulge an addiction I never dared admit to Mummy, I had to hang about for ages at the top of the stairs where I could keep an eye on the shelf known as 'Exchange and Mart' because everyone dumped things on it, and the built-in cupboard above it. This was where bottles of vinegar were kept, along with tins and boxes of emergency stores.

I would listen carefully until I knew the coast was clear, then make a dash to climb onto Exchange and Mart and jerk open the cupboard door. Kneeling uncomfortably, I would uncap the vinegar bottle and take an enormous swig, which turned the world black for a moment, and then gave me a tremendous high as the blood seemed to rush through my veins and my head spun vertigiously. I don't know if Mummy or Nan ever wondered why the vinegar kept disappearing, but from time to time a new bottle would be added, and since I was never accused of stealing from the store cupboard, I suppose they never noticed the loss.

Although housekeeping in such circumstances must have been quite a challenge, even preoccupied as I was with rabbits and ponies and school, I sensed that Mummy was happier than she had been at Chapel House.

Certainly she was much less strict with us. Anyone who has watched a bitch with an unruly litter punish a puppy for unacceptable behaviour by growling and shaking it and pinning it down until it rolls over in jellified subservience will have been tempted to say, 'Oh, the poor little thing! How can she be so cruel?' But they will also have noticed that the puppy doesn't repeat the offence. In the same way, Mummy – who had a great respect for the maternal skills of animals – may have instilled the basics of civility into her brood with a certain ferocity, but once it was well established where the boundaries were, she could afford a degree of latitude.

Another reason may have been that, despite the daily struggle to keep us all fed and clean and happy, (and constant worry about what was happening to Daddy), at least at Much Hadham she was in command of the household. However much she loved and admired her parents-in-law, it must have been a strain to live in their house and make her children conform to their standards for so long, especially since during Granny and Grandfather's Victorian upbringing children were supposed to be seen but not heard. Grandfather had been only half joking when he threatened to disinherit the lot of us if he heard another shout of, 'Finished! Come and wipe me!'

Nominally, of course, it was a shared command at Gaytons. Renting the house had been Aunt Nancy's initiative, but she was out all day, working as a Progress Chaser in a factory near Finchley that made bomb sights. There her diplomatic skills ensured she got the best from the tired girls on the production line, and also helped her frustrate attempts by communist agitators to go slow, undermining the war effort, but it meant that Mummy had to look after five children rather than three, as well as running the household.

She was stoical about this burden of work and worry, and only once do I remember seeing the brave mask slip. It was a summer morning in 1944 when I burst into her bedroom to wish her a Happy Birthday, and thrust into her hands a badly drawn card with the brutal message, *Now You Are Thirty!*

For a moment she stared at it, still half asleep, and then her face seemed to crumple. 'Thank you, darling. It – it's lovely,' she said shakily and, to my consternation, burst into tears.

Puzzled and dismayed, I backed out of the room, dimly aware that the card was not a success. Poor Mummy! The war – the bloody war – had swallowed five precious years of her youth. Her twenties, and all the fun that should have gone with them, were vanished for ever and *now she was thirty.* Just for that moment, it was more than she could bear.

Gerry, David and I had outgrown governesses, and were sent to The Barn School, at the other end of the village. On the way we had to pass the village school, where the boys inside the railed playground would shout insults at us and we at them, while surreptitiously increasing our pace in order to get out of earshot as quickly as possible.

Most of the little toffs in the neighbourhood went to The Barn, which consisted of a single-storey Gothic-looking building with knapped flint walls, where the smallest children struggled to make shopping-bags out of raffia and milk-bottle tops, and alongside it a long low wooden hut with a bare plank floor, where the rest of us worked at proper desks. It was divided into two classrooms by a flowery curtain on a rail, through which you could all too easily be distracted by whatever was going on the other side.

Not that short, dark, dynamic Mrs Clukas or wispy-haired, steely-eyed Miss Cookson (who owned the school) allowed our thoughts to wander for long. Even David's diversionary tactics cut little ice with them, beyond, 'Yes, dear. Very amusing, but now perhaps you'll finish your work…' and when a particularly naughty little boy called David Moller was rumoured to have actually sworn at 'Cookie' and kicked her on the shins, a frisson of horror ran through the school. No-one was surprised when he vanished, never to be seen again.

Boys aged seven were only at The Barn on sufferance in any case, and the moment they passed their eighth birthdays were booted out into the harsh male world of boarding-school. Gerry went away to Horris Hill, near Newbury, and David to Summerfields, Oxford, their trunks stuffed with stiff new clothes and tuck-boxes, while the left-behind girls drew closer, and work with Cluky and Cookie became more geared to female tastes.

Mrs Bentley, our Drama teacher, used to put on surprisingly ambitious plays, bold chunks carved out of Shakespeare which she tailored to fit our acting capacity. I remember particularly the drinking scene and teasing of Malvolio from *Twelfth Night*, in which I was cast as Feste, the Fool, and sang, *O Mistress Mine*, in a breathy, feeble pipe which could have been audible only to the first row of the audience.

A more successful effort was *Pyramus and Thisbe*, the play-within-a-play in *A Midsummer Night's Dream*, where we in the cast were deeply puzzled at the way our audience was reduced to hysterical giggles by our wrestles with Shakespeare's jokes, which we hardly understood. However, the production that shattered my ambitions for an acting career and severely dented my self-esteem was a musical version of *The Sleeping Beauty*.

All the girls, naturally, wanted the part of the Beauty and after a series of highly competitive auditions, it was alloted to me. '*Briar Rose Bud was a pretty child, a pretty child, a pretty child,*' ran the opening line, and alone in the bathroom I practised expressions of swooning prettiness in front of the mirror. Full of wicked pride, I turned up at the first rehearsal with lines already word-perfect, only to be brusquely informed that I had been supplanted. Jocked off. A curly-haired, blue-eyed blonde of chocolate-box loveliness called Victoria was to play Briar Rose Bud, and I was relegated to the role of the 'Ugly Fay'.

Talk of adding insult to injury. In vain Mummy argued that any fool could play the Sleeping Beauty, and the Witch was a far more interesting character. I refused to be comforted, and my acting career withered before it had even bloomed.

More animals were joining the household, though none were as specifically mine as the Angora rabbits. Olivia's special pet was a magnificent fudge-coloured cat with white paws, called Mittens. He would sprawl on her bed like a pasha, eyes slitted, reaching out a velvety pad at times to touch her face. He killed baby wild rabbits and brought them into the porch to devour them, but was clearly perplexed by the Angoras because they didn't give a damn when he went into stalking mode. When they were loose on the lawn you'd see him moving stealthily towards them, and lying prone with lashing tail, prepared to pounce, only for his prey to hop right up to him and shove him casually in the ribs. The buck, Snowball, went so far as to deliver a flurry of boxing blows at poor Mittens, which must have been a dreadful humiliation.

More of a threat to my rabbits were the miniature Sealyham terriers, Beret and Betsy, which Mummy was given by an admirer. As a gift, it turned out a bit of a poisoned chalice, since Betsy had eczema and Beret suffered from fits. These were frightening, because he would howl and yelp and dash round and round the kitchen table, under chairs, under the bed, trying desperately to find somewhere dark. The best thing seemed to be to throw a blanket right over him, and by degrees the twitching and trembling would die down and he would go into a sort of cataleptic trance.

Bright light, even sunlight, could trigger a fit, and so could white bread, which in the absence of proper dog biscuit Mummy used as a 'filler' to eke out his tins of Chappie. He was short-tempered, too, and apt to snap at children. All in all, Beret was rather a nightmare, but Betsy – gentler and more obedient – so appealed to Granny (whose adored Pooh-Hi had recently died) that Mummy thankfully handed her over to a life of calm luxury at Chapel House.

Petrol was scarce – the ration had to be hoarded for essential journeys – but now Dustyfoot, the redoubtable piebald Shetland, entered our lives. She was smaller than either Micky or Sally, with a short thick neck, short thick legs, and a disproportionately large head, all of which made her very uncomfortable to ride, but in the little tub trap she went splendidly, hammering along like a metronome, taking us to picnics and tea-parties, with the weight of the cart counterbalanced nicely against her heavy head.

David was an athletic boy, and much the best at staying on top of Dustyfoot, though my hunting journal notes that when hounds met at the Much Hadham ford, Dusty rolled with him in the water, and he only just got off in time. He was also decanted in the plough several times that day, and arrived home with spring wheat apparently growing out of his shoulders.

It was simply no good getting into a fight with Dusty, because she always won. With secret glee I remember watching her deposit David, Mummy, and Aunt Nancy on the ground in quick succession when they tried to make her jump over a very small log. David (who half expected it) bounced off without damage. Mummy took his place, lengthened the stirrups, gave Dusty a few hearty wallops, and was sent flying over her head; Aunt Nancy induced her to canter right up to the offending log as if she really meant to go over it, and then at the last stride Dusty ducked out from under her and she nose-dived over the obstacle alone.

With three ponies, the problem was finding grazing. Though Gaytons had a neat little stable yard with two looseboxes, a haystore and tackroom, there was no paddock, and the large field behind the garden at which Mummy looked so longingly remained obstinately arable throughout our tenancy. Farmers were working hard to increase food production, so every acre that could grow corn did so. The needs of children's ponies had a very low priority if, indeed they figured in the local agricultural picture at all.

Much Hadham was a horsy village, strongly supportive of the Puckeridge Hunt, but nobody who was lucky enough to own a paddock wanted three extra ponies in it. However Mummy did discover a sheep-farmer at a nearby village, Green Tye, who agreed without much enthusiasm to let her some grazing along with his ewes. Mr Turner was a taciturn old man, soured by the loss of his right hand. His hook made him a figure of dread to us children when we bicycled the three miles to his farm in winter, with buckets of boiled potatoes mashed with porridge oats swinging from the handlebars. This mash, which the ponies loved, smelt so appetising that we often scooped out a handful to eat as we pedalled, even though the spuds were unpeeled frostbitten ones from a clamp, not fit for sale, which Mummy had been given for nothing. There was good hacking around Green Tye, but it took so long to get there and back that we were all glad when the Hadham butcher agreed to let our ponies join half a dozen other grass-liveries in his big field near the ford.

Here Sally, who had been covered the previous summer by a beautiful burnished chestnut Anglo-Arab stallion called Dropscotch, but was thought not to be in foal, surprised everyone by producing a lively colt with long wobbly legs and a fluffy tail. Mummy found her in a corner of the field one April morning, gallantly protecting her offspring from the interest of the other horses and most of the Barn schoolchildren, since the butcher's field was close to our playground, and hastily summoned me and a strong sensible friend called Joanne out of school to help get her back to Gaytons, a distance of nearly two miles.

It was a slow anxious business for me to lead her along the back road behind the main street, whinnying and reluctant to go forward, with her head turning constantly to make sure her foal was still following, while Joanne and Mummy bundled him along between them. When we turned in through the double gates into the sunny Gaytons yard, the little colt dropped down and lay flat on the cobbles, utterly flaked out.

For the rest of that Spring and Summer, Jock Scot (as we named him) accompanied his mother wherever we rode, and became splendidly blasé about traffic, wandering nonchalantly into the path of lorries rumbling through the village, confident that they would stop, unlike poor Sally who still went into a quivering jelly at the sight of anything bigger than an Austin 10.

Suddenly the war was over, we were told, and we had won, but everything went on much as before. Daddy was still abroad. Rationing was tighter than ever, and the grown-ups talked wistfully about getting things on the Black Market, particularly petrol and nylon stockings, though I don't think either Mummy or Aunt Nancy knew how to contact the shady purveyors of such coveted goods.

After VE Day was declared, there were low-key celebrations in the village. A fancy-dress parade with a prize for the best decorated bicycle, children's races, a tug-of-war, and a competition in which the biggest boys and one dauntless girl tried to sandbag one another with pillows while seated on a greasy pole over a stream. Of course she won, to the accompaniment of much muttering. 'Couldn't hit a girl, now, could I?' grumbled a bad loser.

The local Home Guard and anyone else with a uniform marched to church with banners and brass bands for a service of thanksgiving, but although the Scouts and Guides were invited to accompany them, the Brownies were not, to my infinite chagrin, since I had polished my little brass badge within an inch of its life in the hope of joining the parade. Instead, we sat at the back of the church in our everyday clothes, and

I think this was the first time I realised how scruffy our family looked compared to others.

Just in front of us sat our school friends Dione and Kirsty, wearing – as they did every Sunday – identical blue velvet berets over their neat blonde plaits, well-cut tweed jackets with velvet collars, swinging kilted skirts pinned at the side, with little leather straps at the waist, long beige socks with tasselled garters peeping out of the turnover tops, and polished brown shoes, again with a tasselled flap. The whole outfit was smart, practical, carefully put together – and then I looked down the row at my siblings and cousins, by comparison a tatterdemalion crew with cardigans over our usual blue Aertex shirts, the boys in grey flannel trousers and the girls in skirts that were either too long or too short, having been passed on by cousins to whoever was nearest in size, ankle socks, far from clean, ditto our scuffed shoes. The contrast was striking: not the result of penury, as one might have supposed, but of Mummy's basic lack of interest in clothes, and underlying contempt for fashion.

She herself was so beautiful that she could get away with wearing superannuated garments that Aunt Nancy, for example, wouldn't be seen dead in, and she regarded with amused contempt other women who agonised over the scarcity of clothing 'points,' and tried to keep their wardrobe up to date. She had a few well made good quality clothes bought in London before the war – a sealskin coat, for instance, and coats-and-skirts by Nissen – and wore them to the point of disintegration, confident that her own looks could carry them off.

Much the same was her attitude to beauty care. At night she washed her face with soap and water, and allowed it a dollop of whatever greasy substance came to hand – vaseline, olive oil, Nivea creme, lanolin – then secured two 'snails' of hair with kirbigrips just above her ears, and that was that. In the morning more soap and water, a touch of lipstick rubbed into the cheeks in lieu of rouge, and a dusting of loose powder before the snails were brushed out in curls and the rest of her hair swept back from her strong widow's-peak, and she was ready for the day. No woman felt properly dressed then without bright red lips, and Mummy was expert an 'putting on her mouth' in any situation – even when driving – without the help of a mirror.

'What *I* could have done with your face!' Nancy once exclaimed with a mixture of exasperation and regret. She herself was handsome rather than beautiful, with large, flashing, deep-set eyes and strong dramatic features which could have been Italian or Greek, whereas Mummy's beauty was emphatically English. Through force of circumstance, they had worked well in harness during the war and overcome all sorts of difficulties, but they didn't really have much in common and – apart from a shared love of painting – their cultural tastes were very different.

Take music, for instance. Though Mummy had a good enough voice and enjoyed singing, she was indifferent to classical music and found Nancy's enthusiasm for opera, with its ridiculous plots and endless repetitions, quite inexplicable. Why did they drag everything out so long? Why couldn't they just get on with the story? All right, Mimi – or Gilda, or Aida, or Violetta – was dying, everyone had grasped that, but why must she make such a tremendous fuss?

Nancy was sophisticated, well informed, widely travelled. She had a large social circle and a sharp tongue – 'A baby? I thought she'd have a litter,' she once remarked of an friend who had forfeited her regard by marrying an admirer of her own – so to her life at Much Hadham must have seemed pretty parochial once the war was over, and it would have been strange if the sisters-in-law had not begun to get on one another's nerves. As the British cultural scene began to revive, and Uncle Harold's career in the Diplomatic Service moved ever upward, she and her children returned to live in London, and we Barstows expanded gratefully into the extra space.

From then on, we only saw David and Clarissa during the long summer holidays which we all went on spending in Wales, sometimes camping, sometimes at Chapel House or a rented cottage, but whenever we all got together the old, easy, quasi-sibling relationship reasserted itself as if it had never been disrupted.

The ponies always came to Wales, too. Not in a lorry, but travelling in great style and comfort by rail from Hadham station to Builth Road in a special wagon adapted to the needs of horses, with a ridged floor to prevent slipping, a manger, water-bucket holder and, beyond a sliding panel, a groom's compartment in which Gerry once made the journey to see what it was like .('Rather fun,' he reported. 'Lots of time to read.)

It was a cross-country route, starting in the hands of the LNER (London and North Eastern Railway) then transferring to the care of the GWR (Great Western Railway.) There were two scheduled stops for watering, scrupulously observed, the loosebox always arrived at the right time, and the whole operation cost remarkably little.

The ponies travelled loose, with head-collars in the groom's compartment in case they were needed, they ate their hay-nets quite placidly and never seemed to sweat up, despite all the bumping and banging as the box was shunted in and out of sidings, and attached to different trains, though the time they reached Builth Road they were very keen to stretch their legs on the way home.

If the Much Hadham VE Day celebrations had been muted, those marking VJ Day in August, 1945, when atom bombs dropped on Hiroshima and Nagasaki precipitated the Japanese surrender and brought the war to a real conclusion, were something I shall never forget, though bunting and fireworks had little to do with their impact.

We were camping at the time in the Alltmawr field above the Chapel House orchard, with three sleeping-tents – for boys, girls, and Mummy – a store tent, and a kitchen tent all neatly pitched with their backs to the prevailing wind in the best Baden-Powell style, a camp-fire ringed with big smooth stones, and a latrine tent with two wooden bars over a shallow trench pitched at a discreet distance. Carrying up all the camping gear had taken the best part of two days, the ponies' loads continually slipping as they plodded up the winding track and I, a lazy, inefficient child who was going through a bolshy phase, had felt outshone by Clarissa, who was always extremely helpful and quick in the uptake, seeing what needed to be done before she was told to do it, whereas if not given definite orders, I would try to sneak off and read.

Lying in my sleeping-bag on the hard, hard ground on our first morning under canvas, I heard rain drumming on the roof of the tent, and idly traced my name on the side which, in those days of primitive water-proofing, we had been specifically told not to do. Sure enough, by the time Mummy came to roust us out of bed, water was trickling through in a steady stream, and with the writing a dead giveaway, it was no good pretending that Olivia or Clarissa was responsible.

So the morning began badly, and got worse. I managed to burn the porridge over the camp fire, making it taste truly disgusting, and when sent to fetch milk from the Abernant dairy, I tripped over and spilt half of it. We were meant to rest on our camp-beds in the afternoon, because of the celebration supper and fireworks that evening, but as soon as Mummy had gone down to Chapel House to confer about the travel arrangements, David and I slipped away to explore the wooded gorge just below our encampment, at the bottom of which was an old mill.

The upper reaches of the millstream were shallow, but as the gorge became steeper and shaped more like a funnel, the water tumbled over rocks in a series of mini-waterfalls, and the slope of the wood ever more precipitous. At the narrowest point was the mill-race, where the channelled water would have swept through with enough force to turn the great wooden wheel.

That was long gone, but still the water flowed deep and strong between the sheer sides it had carved out of the rock. As we scrambled along the crumbly overgrown bank some fifty feet above it, I began to lag behind, unable to keep up with David who was swinging from one handhold to another as nimbly as a monkey.

'Come on!' he urged, glancing back. A moment later he rounded a shoulder of hill and disappeared.

'Wait!' I called, reaching out for a projecting root, but as I put my weight on it, the rotten wood gave way and to my horror I began to slide downhill towards the precipice that overhung the mill. Desperately I snatched at ferns, stones, branches, but nothing arrested my slide. Down, down I went, bringing with me a small avalanche of powdery earth and leaves which preceded me over the drop just as I came to a stop with my legs actually overhanging the lip of the precipice.

Far below – how far? Twenty foot? Thirty foot? Quite enough to break my neck – I could see the swooshing water and shiny rocks with their fringe of weed, and the jagged walls of the ruined mill. Far above were the scrubby trees which offered the only possible handholds for me to climb back to safety.

I don't know how long I sat frozen with fear like a treed cat, but it seemed an eternity and the memory still haunts my dreams. David had gone on, thinking I was following. How long would it be before he noticed I wasn't there? I was too frightened even to shout, and in any case my voice wouldn't have carried far against the noise of the water.

Then the corner of my eye caught a movement, and a moment later I heard his voice above and to the left. 'Don't move. Don't look down.'

He kept talking as slowly, cautiously, he inched downhill, traversing the steep slope at an angle, testing every clump of bracken or tuft of grass as he came. At last he was close enough to reach out and flip the sleeve of his shirt into my hand,. 'Hang on to that,' he said. 'Wriggle back a bit.'

'I can't.'

'Yes, you can.'

'I'm going to die,' I wailed.

'No, you're not. Come on! I'll pull you up. Get hold of the bracken roots. They're the toughest.'

I still sweat at the thought of crawling back up that slope, slipping from time to time, clutching brambles, bracken, anything that promised the least support, but at last we made it to the top and collapsed on the blessedly flat turf.

'What are you doing here?' asked Mummy, spotting us there as she walked back to the camp. 'You're meant to be resting.' She looked at me more closely. 'How did you get so dirty?'

'We were looking for a better place to get water,' said David, an inspired excuse because the campsite's principal drawback was the lack of a handy source.

'Did you find somewhere?'

We looked at one another, and David said, 'Not really...'

'Oh, bad luck! Never mind. At least you tried.'

We basked in her approval, transformed from naughty, disobedient children to enterprising resourceful campers, and no more was said about missing our rest.

That evening we went to Builth, where celebrations were taking place on the Groe – the public park on the Breconshire bank of the Wye. Long tables draped in sheets were flanked by narrow wooden benches, and spread with festive fare: sandwiches with the crusts cut off, some with fish paste, others with jam, potted meat, or sandwich spread which looked like sick but was my favourite because of the vinegar. There were jugs of orangeade and lemonade, cups of tea, iced buns, a sparsely fruited cake, and paper cups full of brightly coloured jelly.

There was probably something in the way of strong drink to get the grown-ups going, and when everyone had finished and the tables were cleared, members of a local male voice choir made their way up to a stage and started the singing, which went on for a long time. We stuck it out through a dozen choruses, solos, duets, getting very chilly but determined to see the fireworks, though when at last they were set off on the far bank of the Wye, they were disappointing, as fireworks usually are – bang, fizz, twinkle and out.

It must have been after ten by the time we got back to Chapel House, and stumbled shivering and yawning out of the fug of the car into cold, starlit night. Mummy led the way with her big torch, and we straggled behind her, following the wavering beam up the winding lane to the flat top of the Alltmawr field. Everyone was cold and tired, longing to dive into a sleeping-bag and crash out, but a sudden exclamation from Mummy dashed that hope.

'The tents! They've gone!'

They hadn't, but there wasn't a single one standing. As Mummy swept the beam back and forth, we picked out bit by bit the ruins of our camp – billows of collapsed canvas, poles, and tangled guy-ropes. Bedding dragged into the fire. The suitcases in which we kept our clothes burst open, their contents scattered. The store-tent completely demolished, tins and bottles smashed, and long streamers of loo-paper draped over every-thing. It was a scene of total destruction.

Mummy was the first to speak. 'How *could* they?'

'They must have known we'd be out,' said Gerry in a low, shaken voice. 'So they waited till the coast was clear.'

It was horrible to think of someone lurking about, waiting to despoil our nice little campsite.

David walked towards the remains of the fire, tripped over something large and warm, and let out a yell . 'Who's that?'

At once there was a loud, indignant snort which made us all jump, and then the darkness seemed to erupt with huge black bodies as half a dozen bullocks lumbered to their feet and charged off down the hill, loo-paper still trailing from their horns. We burst into hysterical laughter, clinging together as our fright dissolved in a frenzy of relief and hilarity.

'Well, obviously we can't sleep here tonight,' said Mummy at last. 'We can do the clearing up tomorrow,' and without a backward glance we left the scene of devastation and ran down to seek shelter at Chapel House. It seemed a fitting end to the VJ celebrations.

It was not until the late autumn of 1945 that Daddy was at last demobbed, and by then I had a new and very special pony – a real Rolls-Royce of a pony whose purchase had stretched the family budget almost to breaking-point. 'I can't wait to see the £70 pony!' he had written, tongue in cheek, from the valley of the Gurk in Austria, where 12 RHA had been put in charge of the horses and grooms of a regiment of Cossacks, descendants of White Russians who had left their homeland when the Communists assassinated the Tsar during the First World War, and had fought for the Germans in the Second. It was a problem to find accommodation for 2,000 horses, and Daddy described how, being unable to picket so many, he ordered them to be turned loose into an enormous rope enclosure. Carrying halters, the Cossack grooms would go confidently into the milling throng, and call out their own horses, just as a huntsman draws his pack before a day's hunting.

That summer every British officer had as much riding as he wanted. The regiment organised gymkhanas and mounted games, and a good time was had by all. Only years later did Daddy describe to me the grim aftermath of this happy interlude, and time had done nothing to lessen his anger.

In a disgraceful piece of political chicanery, the British government agreed to the vengeful Stalin's demand that they should hand over their Cossack prisoners for forced 'repatriation,' even though none of them had ever been to Russia.

The prisoners were under no illusions about their fate. Some hanged themselves. A very few – with the connivance of British guards – managed to hide in the PoW camp long enough to escape the round-up. For the rest, officers and men were forced onto separate trains and sent to certain death at the hands of the Communists. The episode remains a black stain on British honour.

Back to 'the £70 pony.' Considering that, throughout the war, a single £5 note sent by registered post from Daddy's bank covered all Mummy's weekly expenditure, to pay £70 for a child's pony, sight unseen, seems reckless extravagance, but Taffy came strongly recommended by a trusted friend, and like so many reckless extravagances, she proved to be worth every penny. Her previous owner had been a boy who, when he reached his teens, suddenly shot up to six foot. 'He looks ridiculous,' said his mother mournfully. 'His feet nearly touch the ground, but while we've got Taffy, he won't ride anything else.'

She must have been about nine when we bought her, a bright bay with a bold, confident, can-do look about her, and she came with a much-creased certificate signed by a vet and declaring her height to be 13.2 hands, although she looked bigger – more like a small horse than a pony. Time and again in the next years, ring-stewards would challenge her right to compete in 13.2 classes, but crafty Taffy would spread out her legs and dip her back, and scrape under the stick. She was nice-looking, not particularly beautiful, but unlike our other ponies she was absolutely straightforward, no nasty tricks, no hang-ups about traffic or anything else, and she jumped like a dream.

Until then, jumping had hardly figured in our riding activities, and I had no idea what fun it could be.

Oh, Taffy, my Taffy, there's none to compare!
Oh, Taffy, my Taffy, you float through the air!

I sang in an ecstasy of love and admiration. 'Float' was perhaps coming it rather high, for Taffy was too cavalier in her attitude to flimsy coloured poles to be much of a show-jumper, and in the ring she usually collected faults in double figures, but the glorious thing was that she would have a go at anything. With neither hesitation or deviation, she would canter determinedly up to the obstacle and launch herself over it. You hardly felt her take off or land, but hey, presto! there you were on the other side. Needless to say, she was the perfect hunter: keen but biddable, and even when I fell off (which happened quite often) she would stand like a rock to let me remount.

Thanks to Taffy, I quickly became over-confident, but a chance invitation to ride Cadwal, a handsome young Welsh Section A stallion, at a local show soon exposed my limitations.

Mrs Peebles, his owner, wanted to sell him as a child's pony, and gave such a glowing account of his looks and virtues that I would happily have hopped up on him for the first time in the show-ring, but luckily Mummy insisted on a trial ride. She and I drove Dustyfoot in the governess cart over to the farm a couple of miles away, where Mrs Peebles was waiting with Cadwal ready saddled. He was iron-grey in colour, with one wall eye, no more than 12 hands, like Micky, but full of power and presence, from his sharply-pricked ears to his long kinky tail.

He snorted suspiciously at the handful of oats I offered, scattering them to the wind, and Mrs P said quickly, 'Don't go spoiling him, he's not used to it. Come on, now. Up you get. We'll go round the field together till you get the feel of him.'

She held his head while I mounted, for which I was grateful because the moment I settled on his tense, resistant back I had the doomy sense that we weren't going to see eye to eye.

All went well as Mrs Peebles on her steady cob led me down the lane, and into a ploughed field surrounded by high blackthorn hedges with a narrow rutted track round the perimeter.

'All right?'

I felt thoroughly insecure, but it seemed rather wet to say so.

'Good. Follow me, then. We'll trot down to the bottom, and have a canter up the far hedge.'

Off she went, her cob's hoofs throwing up clods of mud, and I followed right on her tail, unable to hold Cadwal at a proper distance. He tucked his head in to his chest and stiffened his crest while I bounced uncomfortably, digging the knuckles of one hand into his withers and yanking against it with the other, but two could play at that game and Cadwal was an expert. If it hadn't been for the cob's fat hindquarters blocking the track, he would probably have bolted then and there.

We rounded the end of the field at a butcher-boy trot, with Cadwal resolutely refusing to break into a canter.

'Use your legs!' shouted Mrs Peebles, lolloping along on the cob.

'I can't!'

'Don't be so feeble!'

In desperation to stop the relentless bouncing, I whirled the end of the reins and slapped Cadwal on the shoulder. The result was immediate. Down went his head. Up went his heels, and I flew face-down into sticky black plough. It was soft enough and no harm would have been done if only both feet had come out of the stirrups. Unfortunately, one of them stuck fast, and Cadwal continued on his way with me bumping along the ground at his side, and roaring at Mrs Peebles to stop.

My jacket and shirt rode up as I was dragged for what seemed like miles but was probably just a hundred yards or so, unable to free my foot, with Cadwal, now thoroughly alarmed and just as anxious to be rid of me, kicking out sideways. Luckily he was unshod and in no position to do much damage, and when at last my shoe came off and Mummy rushed to my aid, although I looked a mess of mud and blood I had suffered nothing more serious than scraped ribs and a severe dent in my pride.

Mummy, too, had had a nasty fright watching from the gateway as her elder daughter was dragged through the plough. 'Stupid woman,' she said as steady, sturdy Dustyfoot jogged gently homeward. 'That pony's only half broken. She'll be lucky to sell him like that.'

Daddy came to England briefly in the spring of 1945, and Mummy rushed to spend two nights with him in London, but there wasn't time to visit Much Hadham, and when he was finally demobbed in the late autumn, it was so long since we had seen him or he us that the actual moment of reunion was tinged with awkwardness. In three years we had changed a lot, and so had he. The slim, serious, music-and-literature loving young solicitor who had gone to war returned two and a half stone heavier, his complexion was florid and hair that had been receding in 1939 was now almost gone. Most striking of all was his air of authority, a kind of jovial imperturbability that nothing could seriously disturb. He had seen the war through from beginning to end, coming out of it not only unscathed but with honour. Nothing would ever be so bad again – and the whole horrible business was now over for good.

We were staying at Chapel House at the time, and so were the Caccias, but once he had sorted out which were his children and which his nephew and niece, we quickly slipped into an easy relationship, and Gerry was at last relieved of the burden of being the Man of the Family.

The biggest change was in Mummy. Ever since 1942, she must have been under intense and wholly unacknowledged strain, organising, working, handling finances, taking family decisions, and secretly worrying that she might be widowed right up to the last day of the war, and now that long dreary ordeal was ended and she had her husband to lean on and laugh with again she seemed years younger – happy, jokey, even frivolous – as they both flung themselves into making up for the time they had missed.

There were no more spankings that I remember, and fewer sudden outbursts of anger. '*Aequam memento rebus in arduis servare mentem,*' Daddy would say when she looked like going off the deep end about something, and although at the time I had no idea what it meant, it had a miraculously calming effect.

He didn't often talk about the war, and the only bits we managed to weasel out of him made it sound like one long adventure in the company of brave kindred spirits, dangerous at times but essentially very good fun. He was always humming and singing, and his big booming laugh echoed from one end of the house to another. On long car journeys we could sometimes persuade him to teach us regimental songs ranging from the innocuous (*The HAC have Dirt Behind their Ears* and *Marching up the Valley of the Arno*) to the definitely-unsuitable-for-children: (*Messalina, she was the Dirtiest Roman of Them All*) which would make Mummy say, 'Johnny!' in such pretended horror that we never heard the song right through.

He was so determined to put the war firmly behind him that it took a long time for me to realise how hotly his anger still burned against the nation that had robbed him of his brother, his first years of marriage and his children's childhood; and his underlying contempt both for the French and for our American 'cousins' who had been so painfully slow to join the struggle against Hitler.

Although Taffy had stolen most of my heart, I was still deeply into rabbits. Degrees of kindred and affinity had to be closely considered when contemplating matings, for though the *Rabbit Breeder's Handbook*, my Bible, permitted relationships between kissing cousins, full-blown incest – whether pharaonic or father-daughter – was strictly taboo, though sometimes difficult to avoid.

Immersed in the Angoras' complicated love lives, I completely failed to notice that Mummy, too, had changed shape, and any reference to her pregnancy must have gone right over my head. I was therefore astonished and far from pleased when, after Mummy had taken a brisk and uncharacteristic run up to the allotments one December evening, Olivia and I were told that we must go to her bedroom after breakfast the next morning to meet our new baby sister, Miranda.

Aren't we enough for her? was my immediate jealous thought – a fairly universal one among older children – but although the baby was quiet and good and hardly impinged on my convenience in any way, she unfortunately brought with her an absolute harridan of a monthly nurse, who took a sadistic delight in telling us our 'noses would be out of joint now,' and similar nasty digs designed to emphasise our loss of status. She bossed us around and made dictatorial rules about meals and bedtime which were not, strictly speaking, anything to do with her, but our own minder at the time, a gentle, artistic soul named Irene, who had been engaged as a sort of gardener-cum-mother's help, was incapable of checking her tyranny.

Furious and resentful, I responded in the classic way by becoming rude and naughty, teasing and tormenting Olivia and also Josie, the daughter of Cope, who had been Daddy's army batman, and his wife, who had now become our cook. Josie was a pretty, plump child with long dark ringlets, easily moved to tears by my bullying, and it may have been partly anxiety lest the Copes should decide to leave that prompted Mummy to arrange for me to weekly-board some fifteen miles away near Ware with Mrs Baird, and do lessons with her granddaughter Johanna and three other girls, two of whom, oddly, had the same-sounding name, though Moona was Irish and Muna a rolypoly little Egyptian.

I remember a long, dim, melancholy house covered in creeper, with a wide gravel sweep overhung by sodden bare branches (it must have been winter.) Mrs Baird seemed immeasurably old, her voice faint and querulous, and the only animal in the household was definitely not child-friendly: a yappy white terrier with pink skin showing through his sparse, wiry coat. No wonder, because he was washed daily, poor brute, and scratched continually – eczema, probably – and if Pixie Sykes, our governess, hadn't taken him with us on our ultra-boring 'botanical walks' through the flat, cold, featureless Essex countryside, he would hardly have stirred all day from his favoured position under the legs of his mistress's armchair.

Pixie was not the elfin figure her name suggests, but a short, sturdy, lantern-jawed little woman with iron-grey curls, ruthlessly netted at night. She dressed in twin-sets, pleated skirts and sensible brogues. She was not an ambitious or talented teacher, limiting her curriculum to English literature, botany, music, and the most basic of maths. Nor did we work long hours, just between half past nine and twelve and an hour in the afternoon, followed by one of those dire walks.

This left us plenty of time to amuse ourselves as we pleased, providing we didn't make too much noise and disturb Mrs Baird, so we read and ragged and gossiped, and played a game we called 'Slave Girl', loosely based on a story I had read about harem life in Abyssinia, in which the heroine was captured and tied to a bed so that the robber baron could have his wicked way with her.

We knew instinctively that the grown-ups would not approve of this game, and Johanna often warned me and Moona to watch out lest Pixie should catch us at it. She was a renowned passage-creeper at night, but during the day she spent so much of her time ministering to Mrs Baird that we thought we were safe enough – and so we were until the day when she did, indeed, walk in on us in Moona's bedroom, and there was hell to pay.

Moona had me well trussed up on the bed, wearing nothing but my white cotton bloomers, and was standing over me whip in hand in the character of the brigand chief when Pixie suddenly opened the door and stood staring at us. There was quite a long silence, and then a torrent of accusation and reproach burst over our uncomprehending heads. She called us dirty and immoral, deceitful and shameful, and wouldn't listen to a word of our stumbling explanations.

'We're acting a story,' I wailed, but it did nothing to stem the flow. Finally, with the dreadful threat that she was *going to tell Mrs Baird*, she stormed out of the room, leaving me and Moona perplexed and shaken.

Sex was never discussed in front of children in those days, and despite my years of rabbit-breeding, we were woefully, hopelessly ignorant about human desires and practices, and had never heard of sado-masochistic bondage. Even the mechanics of procreation were a closed book. If I had ever considered the matter (which I hadn't) I might have guessed that our parents had gone about it in the same way as the Angoras.

I was never a cuddly child, being sallow of complexion, thin and gawky in build, all elbows and knees. Indeed I looked on cuddling as an invasion of my personal space, and actively disliked being mauled around, especially if what had begun as fondling degenerated into surreptitious massage in a futile attempt to improve my bandy legs or some other less than satisfactory part of my anatomy. So although we'd had an inkling on some subconscious level that the frisson we got from games of 'Slave Girl' was not the kind of pleasure Pixie had in mind when she told us to go and enjoy ourselves, we would have been amazed to be told it was pre-pubescent sex-play, and couldn't see why she was making such a tremendous fuss.

For three days we waited anxiously for Mrs Baird's reaction. When at last Moona and I were summoned to see her in the long dim cluttered drawing-room, we advanced into the gloom with shaking knees, and stood in silence for what seemed a long time before she spoke.

'Pixie tells me you girls have been very naughty,' quavered the faint querulous voice from its nest of rugs.

Had we? Why?

'Well?' more sharply. 'Speak up! What have you to say?'

'Sorry,' we said, choosing the safest option though we had no idea what we were apologising for.

'She thinks I ought to send you away. To expel you.'

Now that we could understand. At the time, *His First Term* by John Finnemore, and its sequel, *Teddy Lester, Captain of Cricket* were quite my favourite books, and I still regard the moment when The Lubber gets expelled as one of the high spots of schoolboy fiction. But the wicked Lubber had, among his many misdemeanours, set a mantrap that nearly took the leg off a choleric baronet, and richly deserved expulsion. Surely our naughtiness was not in the same league?

'But I have decided to give you another chance,' quavered Mrs Baird. 'I will let you stay, providing you promise never to do it again. Well? Do you promise?'

Still baffled, we promised, leaving the room no wiser than we'd come into it, and that was the last time I ever saw Mrs Baird. Within the week, there was a night full of door-bangings and car-revving and scurrying feet, and when we came down to breakfast next morning Pixie told us, between sniffs and dabs at her eyes, that her employer had died in the night.

So we were sent home after all, though not expelled, and Muna came to stay with us at Gaytons until her father could be summoned from Egypt. When he finally arrived – short, stout, oily and mustachio'd – Shawa Bey made an opportunistic pass at Mummy, and was indignantly repulsed despite his lavish presents of scent and nylon stockings. Daddy roared with laughter when he heard about this, and Muna and her father departed for home, never to be heard of again.

CHAPTER THREE

Old Dalby

THE QUESTION OF where to continue my education caused a good deal of parental soul-searching. Having burned her boats with The Barn School, Mummy could hardly ask them to take me on again, and anyway there was at the time speculation that Miss Cookson planned to sell up and retire. At nine, I was still too young for the senior part of a girls' boarding school, but rather too old to infiltrate into any junior section.

Besides, it was the wrong time of year, since schools preferred pupils to start in the autumn term.

Before any decision was taken, in 1947 we were gripped by the coldest winter weather anyone could remember, its discomforts exacerbated by postwar shortages of every description – food, electricity, transport, fuel. There were powercuts and much cursing of the Labour government: as the Minister responsible for power, Mr Emmanuel Shinwell came in for particular excoriation in our household. My parents had been shocked and astonished when Winston Churchill had been thrown out of office in the General Election after the war, and in their eyes Mr Attlee's government could do nothing right.

For us children, the extreme cold was fun. The Rectory pond froze for weeks – plenty long enough for us all to learn to skate – and we tied a toboggan behind Dustyfoot and made her drag us round the back road behind Hadham's main street. There was no means of braking the sledge except by digging your feet into the snow, and as it grew more icy we became adept at baling out quickly when it threatened to run on to

Dusty's heels because she had no inhibitions about kicking. My circulation has always been poor and I suffered torments of itching from chilblains on fingers and toes, though I was far too squeamish to adopt what Mummy claimed was an infallible remedy and pee on them.

All the grown-ups were run down both physically and mentally by the long strain of the war, and for them the bitter winter which led inexorably to illnesses seemed the last straw. One after another we children went down with whooping cough and, since it was a struggle to dry sheets and towels fast enough to keep our beds fresh, the whole house smelt of sick.

Another supposedly infallible remedy current that winter was that breathing the air near a gasworks cured whooping cough so Mummy, who had considerable faith in old wives' tales, took us to the nearest – outside Bishops Stortford, I think – and made us walk all the way round the perimeter fence guarding the huge cylinder on a cold February afternoon, exhorting us to breathe deeply. Far from curing us, the exercise made us cough all the harder, and for weeks the wretched illness dragged on with no improvement.

Emptying buckets and carrying laundry up and downstairs, Daddy must have longed to be back in the Army and one day, suddenly deciding he had had enough of sickbeds and shortages, he announced to our amazement that he was taking us to Switzerland for the remains of the school term. Hang the expense – we were all going to St Moritz. When? In three days' time.

It was a long complicated journey which involved car, train, taxi to Waterloo, boat train, storm-tossed cross-Channel ferry, two French trains, the second a splendid wagon-lit with couchettes, and finally a sparkling clean, wooden-seated, typically Swiss little electric chuffer that hauled us up to the snowy slopes. True to form I was sick on nearly every stage, but this in no way detracted from the glamour and strangeness of it all. The war had ensured that none of us children had ever been abroad, and Mummy had last crossed the Channel in 1938. Like English travellers at the end of the Napoleonic wars, we were hungry to expand our horizons, and ready to marvel at everything we saw.

To my sleepy eyes as we emerged at night from the ferry's bunks after a rough crossing, the French train with its engine belching sparks looked monstrous, far bigger than the ones we were used to, its wheels and pistons dangerously near our legs because there was no platform. While Daddy dealt with the tickets, Mummy hustled us aboard. Having spent much of her childhood in Normandy, she spoke fluent French and I remember my pleasure in realising that books we'd ploughed through at the Barn School about tiresome Madame Souris and her très jolie maison formed part of a language that people here understood. Obviously there wasn't much call for remarks about Mme Souris on a French train, but it might come in useful some time.

The next great surprise was the food: rich, lavish, and delicious. As the train rattled through Northern France, we sat in its dining car in a state of gluttonous delight, gorging on fish mousse that melted in the mouth, thick steaks charred on the outside and almost raw within, and puddings swirled and swathed in cream. It was a revelation. Accustomed as we were simply to refuelling ourselves with whatever could be cooked with dull wartime rations, neither Gerry nor I had ever imagined that eating could be such a pleasure.

How could it be that the French, who had been under the Nazi jackboot for most of the war, had access to food so infinitely superior to that eaten by the poor saps across the Channel? We knew nothing of the tacit agreement whereby the occupied French continued their lives in considerable comfort despite the jackboot so long as they agreed not to rock the boat, which was why the activities of the Resistance were regarded with grave disapproval by *les honnêtes gens* who had no wish to jeopardise the delicate unspoken accord between themselves and the occupying power. Our parents, however, were well aware of it.

The sleeper into which we were ushered by a porter when we changed trains at Lyons had neat little double-bunk couchettes with clean smooth sheets and ingenious basins hidden under the dressing-table. I was allocated the top bunk and drifted in and out of sleep amid the shouting and whistles, muttered exchanges with ticket collector and frontier police, heavy clanking over points, and sudden flashes of orange light as we passed through stations. We awoke to blue sky, dazzling white snow, and jagged peaks so high you could hardly bend your neck back far enough to see their tops.

'The Alps,' said Daddy, sliding open the window to let a piercing breath of mountain air slice through the couchette's overnight fug. 'Come and have breakfast. There are only two more stations before we get the electric train.'

We stayed at the Posthaus, a family-run pension at Celerina, then a small quiet village a few miles from St Moritz itself, near the end of the Cresta run. In the brilliant sunlight reflecting off snowfields, everything had an unreal, toy-like perfection. Wooden chalets had brightly painted barge-boards, horse-drawn sleighs had tinkling bells. There was no motor traffic on the smooth, packed-snow tracks and, with nothing to make it dirty, everything looked unnaturally clean. A greater contrast with dingy, grimy Britain at the fag-end of winter could hardly be imagined. Our spirits soared and the whoops disappeared within days.

Our host at the Posthaus was called Hansel, and Trudi was his tubby, ever-smiling wife. We were the only family staying with them at the time and as well as giving us the pick of their comfortable rooms, each with its view-facing balcony, they bent over backwards to make our holiday fun. He was sturdy and thickset with the blunt, craggy features that you see on a carved wooden bottle-top, and wore green lodencloth breeches and a stand-collared jacket, while she was a marvellous cook, and always wore a checked pinafore over her dark dress. Both had a few words of English and, judging by the visitors' book in which they pressed us to write, had entertained swarms of English tourists before the war, during which neutral Switzerland had not exactly covered itself with glory. It was clear that they both looked forward keenly to the revival of this lucrative business and hoped the Barstow family represented its first green shoots.

Through the swing door from Trudi's kitchen came tray after trolley after tray of wonderful food. As morning sun flooded the light, bright dining-room with its wooden tables spread with white cloths gaily embroidered in cross-stitch, crisp rolls with luscious snails of pale unsalted butter would appear, and black cherry jam lumpy with globs of squishy fruit that exploded in your mouth – a far cry from the carrot-and-wood-chip gunge we were accustomed to spread on our bread and marge. There were croissants that crumpled into melting flakes when you bit into them, and proper coffee for the grown-ups. For us, there was something even better: thick, rich hot chocolate, like a whole bar melted in the cup, and this was *for breakfast*. We could hardly believe our luck.

'Eat. Is good,' said smiling Trudy, watching us guzzle. '*Viel gut.*'

It sounded like 'feel good,' and even more delightful was the discovery that the words, '*Bitte, Schockolade,*' produced not bitter chocolate, which I disliked, or even a bit of chocolate, but a noble slab of the sweet-to-sickliness nut-laden milk variety nestling alongside the salami and cheese-stuffed rolls and hard-boiled eggs of Trudy's packed lunches, which we would eat on the sunny wooden balcony of the cafe at the top of the nursery slopes after a morning at ski school.

The first morning Hansel took us to his cousin's sports-shop, a virtual forest of tall coloured skis, luges of every description, and padded jackets with matching trousers, at which Mummy cast covetous glances, though she confined herself to buying us padded waterproof gauntlets and bright woollen headbands with flaps to protect our ears. The shop was so small and so full of kit that it was almost impossible to move, the whole place redolent of hot wax.

One at a time, the cousin fitted us for boots and skis, closely supervised and advised by Hansel. The skis themselves were long and narrow, your height plus your upstretched arm, and awkward to carry as they cut into your collarbone and shoulder. They were not easy for beginners to manoeuvre. They had grooved bottoms and metal edges, and after every day's skiing you had to rub them with wax – different colours for different types of snow – and put them to dry overnight in the warm basement at the pension.

Boots at that time were just ankle-high, with a deep groove at the back into which was positioned the loop of the spring-binding bolted to the ski. To put on the skis, you had to kick your toe hard between two metal clips, then bend forward and press down the lever that tightened the loop of the binding and held your boot firmly in position. At least, that was the theory. In practice, I found it almost impossible to exert enough pressure on the lever to tension it tightly enough, with the result that my skis were always coming off unexpectedly.

'*Achtung! Ski verloren!*' I learned to shout as the liberated and potentially lethal board flew like an arrow down the slopes, but luckily these were sparsely populated in 1947 and lost skis seldom caused any damage, though dot-and-carrying down the hillside to retrieve them was a great nuisance.

There was a good deal of debate about whether to fork out a fortune for an English-speaking guide from the Ski Club of Great Britain or to opt for the local ski-school, where the instructors' English would be fractured but they would at least be locals. In the end we plumped for a small class with two instructors, stolid Swiss-German Dieter in the morning, and dashing, dark Swiss-Italian Ludo after lunch.

Dieter was endlessly patient as we fell and fell again before getting the hang – more or less – of snow-plough, stem-turns, and side-slipping, which last manoeuvre I found particularly difficult.

His mournful foghorn bellows of, '*Berg ski vor!*' followed me about the slopes as I continually leaned into the slope instead of out over the drop. '*Vite on the louwer ski, Fräulein!*'

At six, Olivia was too young for ski-school, but she got closer to the country than either Gerry or me, since her Swiss nannie/au pair, the wild-haired, high-spirited Lisa Schneller, not only took her to spend a few days with her own parents in a nearby village but, when they rejoined us at the Pension, used to take her up on the drag-lift between her own skis, and then swoop down the nursery slopes together, with Olivia shrieking with delight.

We would all meet up to eat our packed lunches, and sunbathe in deckchairs, faces upturned to the blazing sun without so much as a smear of protective cream until our ear-tips blistered and Daddy turned a dangerous shade of magenta.

Though Mummy had skied as a teenager and was reasonably competent if inelegant, skis well apart as she zigzagged in slow parallel turns, he was a complete beginner, recklessly brave and seldom in control, a fifteen-stone unguided missile before whose path whole ski-school classes scattered like blown leaves. You could pinpoint his position by successive explosions of snow, deep craters at the side of the piste, and resounding shouts of laughter.

In the afternoons we skied en famille, led by the dashing Ludo down long easy runs – Chanterella, Corviglia – that generally ended in St

Moritz itself, where we joined the chattering, sunburnt crowds thronging the tables at Hanselmann's, or the old-style Chesa Viglia, to gorge on eclairs and mille-feuilles oozing whipped cream before skiing down to Celerina along the shiny hard-packed piste beside the Cresta Run.

Like all the best holidays, time went too fast. I knew nothing of Dr Faustus but would have echoed his plea, *'O lente lente currite, noctis equi,'* as the final week galloped towards our last day. The ski-school held tests on Saturday morning, followed by races in the afternoon, and Dieter wanted me and Gerry to take the easiest test, and win the infinitely covetable badge with a bronze Swiss cross on a tiny shield.

Gerry performed creditably and got an approving nod from the examiner, and a pat on the back from Dieter. Wobbly-kneed with excitement, I made a complete hash of every manoeuvre, fell headlong when I tried to turn, and practically did the splits in the sideslip, digging in my edges and bringing down flurries of snow. The examiner looked dour.

'Now the Schüss,' he said curtly. 'Without turning, go directly to the ski-stick.'

Off he swished, and planted a ski-stick a fair way down the slope just where it began to level out by the drag-lift.

'Go!' urged Dieter, giving me an encouraging grin.

Grimly determined not to fall again, I fixed my eyes on the stick and pushed off as hard as I could, crouching low, feeling the wind sting my cheeks and dry up all the spit in my mouth. I was hypnotised by that stick – it drew me like a magnetic force ever nearer, ever faster. On the hillside behind me, Dieter was shouting something as I hurtled towards the one slim straight pole on an otherwise empty slope until my skis went either side of it. The handle struck me in the face. The spike at the bottom flipped over and buried itself in my leg.

It made a small hole in my gaberdine ski-pants, a bigger one in my woolly tights, and a large ragged rent in the skin of my inner thigh.

'Naturally you are insured, Madame?' the examiner asked Mummy, who had pushed her way through the forest of legs topped by red-brown faces surrounding me as I lay writhing and gasping.

Luckily we were. Within minutes I was strapped head-down on a blood wagon – a considerable thrill – and whisked away to the wood-smelling hospital where the wound was cleaned and examined.

The doctor was fat and bespectacled, with a cynical French mouth. 'It requires stitches, ' he announced laconically, reaching for a needle.

Up till then I had behaved fairly stoically, partly because although it looked a mess and was bleeding profusely, the wound didn't hurt much and I was enjoying being the centre of attention. It seemed, in a way, to mitigate the disgrace of the ski-test. But the thought of that needle sewing my skin unnerved me completely.

'No, no, no!' I howled, kicking and struggling. 'I'll heal. I don't want stitches.'

'Control yourself, mademoiselle. It will not take long.'

But I roared and wriggled and made it impossible for him to approach.

'*Que voulez-vous, madame?*' he asked Mummy. 'Without stitches there will be a scar. It will not look pretty. What if she should become an *instructeur de gymnastiques?*'

The thought of her clumsy uncoordinated daughter choosing so unlikely a career made Mummy laugh, and much to my relief and the doctor's disapproval, she asked him to forget about the stitches. A nurse applied a dressing and I was driven back to the pension in a horse-drawn sleigh, which nearly made up for missing the ski-races.

I lay on a chaise longue the rest of the day, being thoroughly spoiled. Trudi made special chocolate mousses for each of us, decorated with individual motifs drawn in whipped cream. I remember mine was a Christmas tree.

Daddy gave me an edelweiss brooch which I had yearned for and Mummy had said was ridiculously expensive, and a little carved chamois standing on a rock. Gerry told me all about the races and who had won what, and showed me his bronze ski-test badge.

Then he grinned and said, 'Oh, and they asked me to give you this,' and handed me a small box. My heart thumped incredulously as I opened it. Was it...? Could it be...? Surely not...?

But it was. There on a scrap of velvet lay a second badge – a consolation prize, I suppose – but who cared how it had been acquired? I certainly didn't though, as it turned out, the French doctor was quite right. It was lucky that I was never tempted by a career as a gym instructor, because the ugly scar on my thigh has been with me for life.

For a single term, in the spring of 1947, I lived at home and did lessons privately with Mrs Bentley, who was a wonderful teacher of all my favourite subjects– history, English literature, drama, geography, French – but as far as I remember we did nothing in the science line, and no maths at all.

At Chapel House in the Easter holidays, I reduced poor Grandfather almost to tears by my inability to understand how to do long division. He had worked in the Treasury for forty years and gone on to be chairman of the Prudential Assurance Company, so maths to him were as natural as breathing, but unfortunately he was a hopeless teacher and as I tried to follow his instructions I became more and more confused.

We were sitting at the small oval breakfast table in the dining-room, with April sunlight blazing in through the wide span of river-facing windows, and I began to sweat with anxiety as I tried again and again to divide one three-figure number by another. My brain seemed to seize up so I could hardly even add or subtract. Grandfather tried to be patient but I could tell he thought me deeply stupid as he copied out the sum yet again, made me watch as he worked it out, then set another for me to attempt.

I just couldn't do it.

Praying that someone would join us and put an end to this torture, I fell back on what is still my default setting when people try to teach me the rules of Mahjongg after dinner or how to de-bug my computer. Bright smile, intelligent look, several slow nods.

'Aaah! *I* see. So *that's* how it works. Yes. Erm, so you mean I just have to do *this*, and *that* – whoops, no, that can't be right...' And nine times out of ten the impatient instructor will solve the problem him or herself, which is fine and gets me off the hook for the moment, but leaves me none the wiser.

I don't know whether Grandfather voiced his worries to my parents, but soon after I was told I had outgrown Mrs Bentley's tuition, and other plans were afoot for me.

In the course of a jolly lunch at the Garrick Club, Daddy had mentioned the problem of my schooling to his old Oxford friend Denny, whose wife Barbara had been a 'Thirties Beauty who, like Zuleika Dobson, bowled over a generation of undergraduates. Daddy would pretend to sigh over a carefully-posed photographic portrait of Barbara in perfect profile, sidesaddle on her hunter, which she had sent to a select band of her admirers, but Mummy, who was not in the least vain herself, thought this bit of blatant self-promotion a bit *off* .

'And then she went and married dull old Denny!' Daddy would say with mock indignation, though he willingly agreed to stand godfather to their elder daughter.

Now he heard from Denny that their younger daughter Tessa, who was my contemporary, was sharing a governess with two other girls in Leicestershire, and having a wonderful time. They did lessons in the morning and rode in the afternoon, and every Monday in winter they hunted with the Quorn. Perhaps they might like to add a fourth to the class. Why didn't he put us all in touch?

Letters were written, a visit arranged, an instant rapport established. When Mummy and Daddy returned from Leicestershire on Sunday night, it was all arranged, and at the start of the summer term 1948, Mummy drove me north to meet my new schoolfellows in a large and beautiful house near Melton Mowbray. A week later Taffy – very smart in a new blue rug with red edging – travelled up by train to join me.

Polly and Hubert, who owned Old Dalby Hall, were the kind of people who give the English squirearchy a good name: friendly, generous, deeply and benevolently involved with local affairs, and devoted to outdoor sport, particularly those in which horses played a part. Since two of their four children had gone off to boarding-school, they had decided to make good use of the big house by importing companions to be educated with the younger two. Thus Cilla, who was nearly ten, would share her governess Miss Smith with Tessa, Joanna, and me; while Charles, a bonny, blue-eyed rosy-cheeked four-year-old, lived with his own small contemporaries and a staff of nannies and cooks in a nursery wing that operated as a completely self-contained unit behind the main building.

It is a rare ten-year-old who interests herself in toddlers, and I wish now that I'd paid more attention to the logistics of life at Old Dalby Hall. I never knew exactly where all the children in the nursery wing came from, but my impression was that more were constantly trying to join them. Could they have been the offspring of unmarried mothers, or families displaced by the war? Or even the children of working women who paid to have them looked after?

Polly was generous and open-hearted to a fault. Anyone down on his or her luck could be sure of her help, and that included animals. From the moment you pushed open the heavy oak door into the great hall, with its double-branched staircase at one end, long refectory table and mighty open fireplace at the other, you found animals in such abundance that our own menagerie at Much Hadham seemed sparsely populated in comparison. Most of them had some disability that made them worthy of special care.

There was Mickey, the black-and-white mongrel with a paw missing; Maggie, a one-eyed magpie, and cats who had lost ears or tails before being taken in and nursed back to health. There were terriers and labradors and hound puppies at walk, and a beautiful conservatory opening off the hall, a jungle of exotic greenery with a floor-to-ceiling cage of canaries, doves, and budgerigars.

In addition to our four ponies: Cilla's wilful black Cinders; Tessa's disillusioned grey Arctic, Taffy herself and Jo's slab-sided Icelandic dun with a black stripe down his back who was known as Rikki, or Reykjavik, there was a stableyard full of hunters and broodmares, run like clockwork by tall, thin, trilby-hatted Mr Sandford and his staff of three.

We fought a long-running war of attrition with Sandford, who quite rightly objected to our stealing the hunters' oats, and went so far as to put a lock on the feed-shed. We saw where he hung the key on the back of the farm office door, and one sunny afternoon Jo and I sneaked in and stole it while Sandford was at lunch. Whether one of the stable-boys saw us and alerted him, I don't know, but there we were, filling our pockets from the bin, when he loomed up in the doorway in vengeful fury.

He made us empty our pockets, then walloped us soundly, an action which no doubt relieved his feelings but nearly cost him his job when Polly got to hear of it. For several days the matter hung in the balance before Hubert came home and pointed out that sacking Sandford for a moment's loss of self-control would have been grossly unfair, and besides, head grooms of his calibre didn't grow on trees. So in the end, Jo and I were made to write him letters of apology, and the matter was somewhat uneasily smoothed over.

On one side of the house, smooth lawns swept down to a wide-spreading cedar under which, in the best English tradition, we used to have tea on summer afternoons. An old pony pulled the clanking triple-mower, shuffling along in leather boots that prevented his hoofs marking the turf. Beyond the lawn lay a haha, and if you were lying on the grass you could often see the cattle's long pink tongues licking upward at the lawn, which they evidently considered more delicious than the rough grass growing in the park. Hazy in the distance were the bulrushes surrounding the lake, and further off still a semi-circle of tall beech trees that blended into the thick, brambly woods where foxes were carefully preserved.

The other side of the house was flanked by the rose garden, where we pony-mad children played our favourite game of 'horsing.' This involved trotting and cantering on all fours – very hard on the wrists if you did it properly – and from this position jumping over the rose-beds, landing on your hands. We preferred to do it wearing only our knickers, for maximum freedom, and were surprised by Miss Smith's disapproval.

'You girls are getting too old for that kind of silliness,' she would say with a tremendous sniff.

Polly, however, thought pretending to be a horse perfectly natural. She was immensely tolerant, indeed some might have thought her eccentric, but from our point of view this touch of wackiness was irresistible in a grown-up. Slight and elegantly bony in her checked shirts and faded corduroy trousers, she looked her very best on her bay thoroughbred, Cottage Pride. I can see him now in my mind's eye cantering across the Park, with Polly gently swaying in rhythm to his long flowing stride, as much a part of her horse as a female centaur. Both her daughters, Sarah and Cilla, had her fair complexion and long serious face, but their striking deep blue eyes were just like Hubert's.

During the war, he had been badly wounded – losing a lung, I think –while rescuing his gunner from their blazing tank and was still convalescent, though well enough to run the farm, and would occasionally, in response to our nagging, take us joyriding in his four-seater Miles Messenger, which lived in an improvised hangar in the biggest flattest field on the estate.

The little plane was so light and frail it could easily be pushed about by two men (and four excited ten-year-olds) and though we couldn't all get in at once, Hubert was scrupulously fair about turns. It was the greatest thrill to bounce down one of the four long straight green runways mown through whatever crop happened to be growing, with the engine roaring ever louder until suddenly you saw the ground drop away beneath the plane, and you were tipped back steeply, heading for the clouds. I don't remember any kind of helmet or intercom, just a seat-belt, and Hubert used to lean across, shouting in his hoarse, breathless voice, pointing out what we were seeing below. My sense of direction has never been strong, and the fields, woods, buildings and roads which we knew well were altered beyond recognition from a bird's-eye viewpoint.

Swooping down on the field at last, we would bounce and bump to a halt before the hangar's concrete apron, and climb out of the plane with trembling legs and woozy heads, more exhausted and elated than if we'd galloped the same distance on our ponies, though delighted to have missed the morning's lessons.

Miss Smith, who tried endlessly and largely unavailingly to impose order on the laissez faire chaos of the household, would be less than delighted. She was the quintessential maiden lady – late forties, I guess, spare, round-shouldered, thin-haired and with a naturally red nose which she kept well powdered, but she had a bewildering array of talents. She was a good pianist and skilful needlewoman, very well educated with beautiful handwriting, she corresponded with Oxford dons and read learned periodicals and, when suitably buttered up and begged to do so, cooked magnificent birthday cakes, light as air and layered with lemon cream. She tried to show me how to make one, but I was too slapdash about weighing the correct quantities and my cake was a pale shadow of her towering masterpiece.

'Wash as you go,' she insisted. 'Muddle makes more muddle,' but where Polly was concerned, this advice fell on deaf ears. At times it seemed to me that she took a mischievous pleasure in shocking our governess, and there were occasions when – although I adored Polly – I found myself on Miss Smith's side. For instance I found it disturbing – what I called, 'Yerk!' – to see Cilla in bed with Mrs Purr, her white cat, ecstatically sucking her nipples, but Polly simply said that if they both enjoyed it, why not?

On the cookery front, Polly had been brought up with a houseful of servants, so, like Mummy, had learned by trial and error during the war. Like Mummy, too, her cuisine ranged from the inspired to the absolutely disgusting. Her Yorkshire puddings, for instance, were marvellous, crisp billows of golden batter which we ate as pudding, rather than with roast beef, slathering them in golden syrup and Guernsey cream, but basic hygiene had a low priority in her kitchen.

I remember once when visitors were coming to Sunday lunch and I was lackadaisically helping to lay the dining-room table, drifting in and out of the kitchen collecting plates and cutlery, seeing Maggie, the one-eyed magpie who liked to perch on the plate-rack, deposit a copious yellow-white dropping into the fresh pea soup which Polly had left on the draining-board.

'Look what Maggie's done!' I said, pointing.

She turned, frowned and, without missing a beat, seized a ladle and scooped most of the mess into the sink. Then she plonked a large spoonful of cream into the soup, swirled it round and put it back on top of the stove.

'You *can't* give them that!' said Miss Smith.

But she did. When it came to my turn to be helped, I shook my head and Polly's mischievous smile flickered down the table at me.

'Just a taste,' she urged. 'You'll like it.'

'Delicious,' confirmed the Vicar's wife. 'Fresh peas – such a treat.'

But neither Miss Smith or I could bring ourselves to swallow a mouthful. She was very much an indoor person, intensely private, and quite how she came to be living in an environment which was about as alien to her interests and inclination as one could imagine is a mystery I have never resolved. Nor did I ever know what her first name was. Did M stand for Mary, Margaret, Muriel? Although Polly and Hubert were unusually modern in encouraging children to call them by their Christian names, Miss Smith insisted on formality between herself and her employers and always addressed them as Major and Mrs. She had her own room at the top of the right-hand branch of the double staircase, next to the schoolroom, and there she led a self-contained, rather lonely existence, it being clearly understood that when she retired to her room she was off-duty and any child disturbed her at its peril.

In addition to teaching us everything from History to Needlework, Piano to Latin, she was expected to keep track of all our clothes and equipment within the house (though she drew the line at saddlery), and the concluding *Conduct* paragraph of my reports always seemed to end with a lament for returning my underclothes in such poor condition.

I have always been lucky in having a blotting-paper memory, which made me teacher's pet in every subject except the dreaded maths. Jo, too, was a quick learner, but Tessa and Cilla were painfully slow, and in the horrid manner of little girls I used to mock and taunt their stupidity, a practice which eventually proved my undoing.

Miss Smith loved poetry herself, the more dramatic the better, and encouraged us to learn it by heart. I still reel off *Lepanto*, or *The Pied Piper of Hamelin*, or even Alfred Noyes's *Highwayman* when walking uphill, because the flow of words takes my mind off the boredom and exertion, but for me Miss Smith's most enduring legacy was her doggerel verses on British monarchs. These, when combined with the well-known *Willie, Willie, Harry, Stee* aide-memoire, gave us a useful historical framework for every major upheaval between the Romans and Queen Victoria.

> *Julius Caesar first arrived*
> *From Gaul in BC 55*
> *Hengist and Horsa, covered in brine,*
> *Landed at Thanet, 449*
> *Alfred of the toasted bun,*
> *His reign began 871*
> *We may not know our dates too well,*
> *But one we all can fix.*
> *It is the Norman Conquest in*
> *The year 1066...*

And so it went on, crisp, succinct, easy to remember. Historically speaking, Miss Smith was by no means even-handed. Monarchs she approved of were allocated four or even six lines, whereas baddies got two at most. After Henry I, King Stephen was briskly dismissed.

His nephew Stephen seized the throne in 1135,
And all the land was in a brawl when Stephen was alive.

That whole chaotic period encapsulated in a couple of lines. After all, what else do you need to know Stephen? But Henry II was definitely a goodie.

Henry Two —One one five four,
Wed Aquitainian Eleanor
And thus his pennants braved the breeze
From Scotland to the Pyrenees.
The Church was proud. He tried to check it
Which led to all that fuss with Becket.

She regarded the Hanoverians as a dull lot and some got particularly short shrift. So:

George the Fourth in 1820
Reigned ten years, and that was plenty

Miss Smith noted crisply, but she went to town with her particular heroine:

Victoria had a long, long run
From '37 to 1901.
She died. It seemed so strange to sing
No more The Queen. 'God Save the King!'

Alas, there her verses ended abruptly, with the result that the dates of the last five sovereigns have never fully registered in my mind.

When morning lessons ended, we were free for the rest of the day, and on afternoons when it was too hot and flyey to ride, we used to gravitate to the lake.

The shallow water covered a layer of vile-smelling mud at least waist-deep, so it wasn't really a bathing practicality, but with enormous labour we constructed a rickety raft out of planks and empty petrol cans, and poled this about the reed-fringed margins trying to catch minnows in jam jars.

We discovered a whole colony of mud-dwelling clams, great sullen lumps weighing a couple of pounds each, which we located by probing the mud with a stick, at grave danger of falling in. As the others hung on to your legs, you thrust an arm deep into the ooze, squidging it through your fingers until they touched the hidden treasure, then eased it into an old trout-net to bring it to the surface.

Loading them into a wheelbarrow, we brought them back to the house in triumph. What should we do with them? we asked Polly.

She was busy that afternoon and suggested vaguely that people in the village might like to buy them, but this proved optimistic. Although Polly and Hubert were well-liked locally and tremendous benefactors as well as employers, not a single household was prepared to shell out hard cash for our smelly and unprepossessing wares. Nobody went so far as to set the dogs on us, but there was a good deal of door-slamming and half-heard remarks about dratted children.

Finally, tired and disillusioned, we wheeled the whole load back to the lake and threw them in. It was a disheartening venture into commerce.

Considering her many commitments, it was extraordinary how much time Polly used to spend playing with us.

'What shall we do today?' was a favourite question, immediately followed by: 'I know, let's have a gymkhana/treasure hunt/paperchase/ picnic by the lake.' Sometimes she wrote little plays in very loosely-rhyming couplets for us to act, or inspired us to dramatised versions of *How We Brought the Good News From Aix to Ghent*, and *Young Lochinvar* (I was delighted that she cast Taffy as the best steed in all the wide Border). Whatever she organised was bound to be fun – with one exception: her dreaded musical rides.

I suppose that with a quartet of pig-tailed ten-year-olds, all reason-ably well mounted, at your command, and an instinct for showmanship, a horsy mum's thoughts are liable to turn in that direction, but Polly's enthusiastic, 'I know! We'll rehearse the musical ride,' would evoke from me at least a suppressed groan and the knowledge that aeons of tedium and criticism lay ahead.

I had never learnt to school a pony properly, nor did Taffy enjoy working on a circle. For a while she would co-operate, but as she grew bored she would start to lean on the bit, stick out her nose in an ugly line and, in response to my increasingly frantic aids, simply hammer round at an ever-faster trot, refusing to break into a canter. Orders to 'Collect her,' and 'Use your legs' had not the slightest effect, and I always ended the session hot, tired and humiliated.

Besides, the old grass tennis-court where we rehearsed was not only the wrong shape but too small for the kind of ambitious mounted manoeu-vres Polly remembered from watching performances by the King's Troop. The corners came up too quickly on the short ends, and it was difficult to time diagonal cross-overs unless all the ponies reached the turning point at the same time. So we sweated away in the hot fly-buzzing afternoons with Polly, standing on a chair in the middle of the court, shouting herself hoarse as she changed or muddled the sequence of movements, and the ponies grew fractious and sullen, and I longed to be reading quietly in the shade.

By contrast the treasure-hunts were enormous fun. Polly would produce a list of perhaps a dozen highly specific objects for us to collect: a curl from Mrs Williams' poodle; the smallest horse-shoe in Mr Page's forge, an envelope with a tuppeny-ha'penny stamp and so on, and send us off on ponies or bicycles in teams of two to scour the neighbourhood, with a promise of a treat for whoever got back first. In this way she could secure herself an afternoon's freedom, and no matter how humdrum the treats turned out to be, we competed for them keenly.

Judging from photographs, it must have been the summer holiday after my first term at Old Dalby that a freakish accident altered my appear-ance for the worse. Though the nose I was born with had never looked likely to rival Cleopatra's, up till then it had been the standard type and size from Mummy's side of the family – what one might call the Elephant's Trunk model, rather long and slightly retroussé – sported by my brothers and sisters.

Visiting the Wye Valley that summer was John , our first cousin once removed, being the son of Granny's brother Geoffrey Lawrence, who had recently presided over the international court for the trial of Nazi war criminals at Nuremberg.

Since his uncle – and our great-uncle – Trevor Trevethin was at the time Chief Scout for Wales and never (as we have already noted) fully at ease with children, he had summoned John to help him entertain several troops of Scouts who were holding their annual camp in the Abernant meadow. Naturally enough, John soon gravitated towards Chapel House. Though hardly taller than me, he was in his teens, and as the former owner of Mincepie he was a glamorous figure in my eyes, so I keenly undertook to show him the garden and all our favourite haunts.

He was bouncing a golf ball off walls and paving-stones as we wandered here and there, and presently began throwing and catching it against the big wooden doors of the garage.

'Can I have a go?' I nagged.

'Catch!' He threw the ball to bounce off the door at an angle. I grabbed at it, missed, and it struck me sharply on the nose.

'Butter-fingers,' he laughed. 'Are you all right?'

My eyes were watering, but I attempted a devil-may-care grin. 'I'm fine,' I said and we wandered on to look at the tennis court.

As the week went on, though, my nose felt increasingly sore, as if a boil was brewing in its tip. We spent the Scouts' last evening eating charred sausages round the campfire, finishing with a rousing singsong, and it was when I squeezed through a wire fence on the way home, just touching the end of my nose against the top strand, that I felt a sickening pain.

Mummy rushed me to the doctor, and then down to Cardiff for an operation, but the damage was done. The golf ball had broken my nose and the bone was so badly infected that the surgeon had no option but to remove the end of it, leaving the kind of squashy blob one associates with prizefighters. Antibiotics were still at the cutting edge of medicine in those days, seldom used on children, but I was lucky to have a go-ahead surgeon who boldly blitzed the infected bone with penicillin, thereby saving the bone above the break.

'That's all we can do until she's stopped growing,' he told my parents. 'We'll have another go at it when she's eighteen.'

Although that seemed immeasurably far away, it was comforting to have a plan to repair the damage, so that I could say, when people asked curiously what had happened to my nose, that it was going to be properly mended when I was eighteen. During the intervening years I don't remember feeling much embarrassed by its odd appearance, and Daddy made me laugh by quoting the young man of Redcar, Who had a most terrible scar. *'My face I don't mind it, For I am behind it. It's folks out in front gets the jar!'*

Back at Old Dalby for the autumn term, we found great changes as the whole household geared up for the hunting season. Being a mere seven miles from Melton Mowbray, fons et origo of the smartest pack in the Shires, most meets in the Quorn's Monday country were within easy hacking distance for our ponies and, being keen to encourage the young entry as the sport got back into its stride in those early post-war years, from highest to lowest the hunting hierarchy gave us children every help and kindness.

Quorn, Sherby Crossroads, Taffy, the entry in my hunting journal for December 3rd, 1948 is headed. *Meet held in brilliant sunshine. Moved off to draw Ragdale Wood… very soon there was a view holloa from the other side. However, I saw the fox and tally ho backed him and we waited for ages. Then with no warning the fox broke cover and soon the whole pack was after him. A nice well-laid fence was the first jump and Taffy and Arctic took it abreast. Hounds checked after a wild 15 minutes and worked slowly towards Hoby, when Hubert holloaed him and we galloped on. Tessa and I were together going down a field when we suddenly plunged into a vast and muddy ditch. Tessa got out quickly and helped me for I was deeper in, though she lost a shoe and I didn't. We hopped over a small gate and hedge before the fox went to ground in Curits (sic) Gorse. It was one of the runs of the season.*

Famous coverts: Ragdale, Hoby, Curate's Gorse… the crème de la crème of British foxhunting, and all on our back doorstep. Glamorous ladies riding sidesaddle in full war-paint, veil, topper, and beautifully cut habit would call, 'I know a way round!' when they saw a fence too big for our ponies to jump. Major Aldridge the Hon. Secretary would solemnly collect the half-crowns which was all we were charged as a 'cap' and tell us we were the 'best people in the hunt to give them in.' It was kind Major Aldridge, too, who sometimes deliberately made a hole in a hedge so the ponies could hop through after him.

One way and another, I can see now that we were grossly over-indulged – for Polly and Hubert's sake, no doubt – and it is no wonder that a somewhat complaining note pervades my hunting-diary recording the days Taffy and I had with the Puckeridge Hunt during the Christmas holidays. The country was flat, the plough heavy, the wind bitterly cold, the only obstacles blind ditches and, far from being an amusing novelty, pushy little girls on hairy ponies were regarded by regular subscribers as, frankly, rather a nuisance. Come January and the start of the Spring term, I was only too glad to return to Old Dalby and the Quorn's charmed circle.

I was also vaguely conscious of stresses and strains within our own family that winter. With four children to school and rear, money was fairly tight, and the family budget wholly reliant on Daddy's salary as a partner in Trower, Still, and Keeling, the firm of London solicitors for whom he worked. Being a friendly, gregarious person – 'Colonel Barstow is so jovile,' a small friend of Olivia's once wrote in a thank-you letter – he had settled very happily into Much Hadham life. There was cricket in summer, with his former batman, Cope, the star of the team, and shooting parties in the winter. There were concerts, and amateur dramatics, and a year-round carousel of birthday, anniversary, dinner and cocktail parties.

Now he was back in harness with an easy daily commute to his handsome ground-floor office looking out on the green lawn of New Square, Lincoln's Inn, with interesting work and agreeable clients as well as colleagues, he was perfectly happy to stay put. We didn't own Gaytons, so the rent was effectively money down the drain, but one day in the dim and distant future he would inherit Chapel House, and that would be time enough to start thinking of moving back to Wales.

He had also discovered many kindred spirits both among Much Hadham's Old Guard who had lived there for years – Normans, Bedding-tons, De la Mares, Kemp Welches – as well as all the younger, less Hertfordshire-rooted families with commuting fathers and children of school age. Although the village was deep in the country, communications were good, and it was easy enough to pop up to London for the theatre or dinner at the Garrick Club. One way and another, he felt he had fallen on his feet.

Mummy's viewpoint was rather different. She was tired of cosy, gossipy, cheek-by-jowl village life.

A longstanding joke among villagers concerned the supposed rivalry between the owners of the four grandest houses:

In the villages you know and I know,
Someone is always the Squire,

(began the opening song of a fund-raising revue put on by the self-styled 'Hadham Follies' in 1949)

His house is much bigger,
His face and his figure
Proclaim that his status is higher.
But that isn't the case in Much Hadham.
It doesn't apply here at all
We have lots of large places
And eminent faces
At The Lordship, Moor Place, The Palace, The Hall.

The skit went on to poke fairly affectionate fun at quirks of the four pseudo-squires, but it was the final verse that really hit the spot:

Oh, fortunate folk of Much Hadham,
With four of a kind you're supplied.
Our vices divided, our faults coincided,
Our virtues by four multiplied.
Give thanks for the blessings we bring you
Our foibles, though comic, are small,
If you're ever in trouble
Just come, at the double,
To The Lordship, Moor Place, The Palace, The Hall!

That was the problem in a nutshell, as far as Mummy was concerned. Between them, these families ran the village. They sat on the Bench, organised fetes and fund-raising, read lessons in Church, chaired the PCC and, crucially, they owned the land, which they had no intention of selling off in dribs and drabs. It wasn't as if they didn't welcome newcomers and make use of what talents they had, but until someone had lived in the village a long time and thoroughly understood its dynamics, there was no way he or she could exert much influence.

After seven years of frustrating scratching around to find grazing for her ponies, and without a single field she could use as she pleased, Mummy longed for broad acres of her own. She had taken a correspondence course in agriculture, and become fascinated by the new breed of farming specialists and entrepreneurs, clever, educated men, scientifically literate, unfettered by tradition, who were changing the face of farming. Monoculture, intensive rearing of livestock, high-tech nutrition, economies of scale were the new buzzwords. Always an enthusiast, she longed to be part of this farming revolution, which promised fortunes to be made by those quick and clever enough to get in on the ground floor.

Money was the problem. Even if the land had been available, buying a few hundred acres in Hertfordshire simply wasn't an option. Casting around for something more affordable, she heard of two farms for sale in Radnorshire, and persuaded Daddy to look at them. One was on good red soil and in pretty sound nick, but with only eighty acres. The other was called Fforest Farm – well named, too, since Fforest in Radnorshire does not mean woods, but a place where nothing much grows, and in 1948 its four hundred acres of sour, boggy land were in the last stages of neglect and unproductive decrepitude.

However, it had possibilities. The farmhouse was substantial, and it had a romantic history which greatly appealed to my parents, having been built on the site of Colwyn Castle, from which the Norman baron William de Breos had subjugated William the Conqueror's rebellious new subjects on the Welsh Marches. His wife, Maude de Ste Valerie is still remembered in local legend, and a large rock near Painscastle, another de Breos stronghold, is known as 'Moll Wollby's Stone,' having allegedly been removed from her shoe and tossed from one castle to the other.

At Fforest Farm, some of the ancient square-cut stones from Colwyn Castle had been incorporated into the house, and it was still surrounded by the remains of a dry moat. The farm had grazing rights on the hill and was, besides, only nine miles from Chapel House

Back and forth swung the debate. The Brunant was a compact, credible working farm which might even, given good luck and good management, be run at a profit. The Fforest looked like a black hole of effort and expense but, no matter what follies and mistakes the apprentice farmers made while learning their craft, whatever they did there must be an improvement on its present condition. In the Spring of 1948, my parents decided to rent it for two years with an option to buy if they managed to raise a mortgage, and on the first day of the summer holidays Mummy and I forded the Wye on Micky and Taffy, and rode over the hill from Chapel House to inspect our new domain.

CHAPTER FOUR

Fforest Farm

'THERE IT IS – look!' said Mummy, pointing from the top of the hill.

I was short-sighted though no-one had yet suggested that I needed specs, and stared vaguely round for something resembling a farm. 'Where?'

'Straight below the wood. The house is to the right.'

Viewed from above, the Fforest looked more like an extension of bleak, barren moorland than a farm, not at all what I had expected from her enthusiastic descriptions, and my heart sank.

Only one field was fenced or even recognisable as pasture. The rest was a greyish khaki patched with gold-tipped rushes and great swathes of dull green bracken. Overgrown hawthorns and brambles showed where there had once been hedges. Black pools of stagnant water spilled out on either side of the stream that bisected the land laterally, and the presence of a second brook was suggested by a line of alders on the far side of the road that ran past the short drive up to the tall grey house. Coming straight from flourishing well-maintained Leicestershire farmland to this bleak example of the Welsh Marches at their most impoverished was quite a shock.

Radnorsheer, poor Radnorsheer,
Never a park, and never a deer,
Never a squire of five hundred a year
But Richard Fowler of Abbeycwmhir

Grandfather used to tease his friends across the river from the relative affluence of the Breconshire bank. Never had the lines seemed more appropriate.

It was a damp, sticky, muggy July afternoon. The sweating ponies fidgeted and tossed their heads, longing, as I did, to get somewhere cool and dark where the horseflies could not torment them but Mummy, surveying the view with pride and pleasure, seemed in no hurry to move.

'Well? What do you think?'.

'It's lovely,' I said wanly, forcing the words out through my bitter disappointment. I had hoped for – even expected – something completely different, a pony-mad child's paradise with flat ground for schooling and long grassy gallops, plenty of stabling and above all, lots of obstacles for Taffy to jump. Building cross-country fences was my major obsession. I searched for and collected poles and cast-off tyres, and painted oil-drums in red and white stripes. Where once I had looked on wooden hurdles or stray bits of four-by-two as useful for making rabbit runs and hutches, now I saw them as potential jump-material and in imagination had already constructed a sort of mini-Badminton course at Fforest Farm.

Just a few months earlier, Mummy had fired this ambition by hiring a caravan and taking Gerry, Olivia and me to the first running of what is now the world's most famous three-day horse trials. We had parked in the avenue leading to the kennels of the Duke of Beaufort's hounds, who serenaded us with melodious baying, slept three in the caravan's very small double bed, kicking and complaining all night long, and watched in awe as super-schooled, superfit horses galloped and jumped an amazing variety of obstacles. Mummy had even encountered the Queen and Princess Margaret in the archway leading to the Orangery and, despite her surprise and corduroy trousers, managed to drop a respectful curtsey. It had all been very relaxed and informal. Ever since I had dreamed of having my own cross-country course (a good deal smaller, naturally) and inviting Jo and Cilla and Tessa to come and stay, bringing their ponies– a dream that now evaporated like a puff of smoke.

In silence therefore, mouth tight shut against the flies, and I'm afraid in no very good temper, I dragged open the disgraceful hill gate and followed Mummy down to the farm.

Mr and Mrs Davies, and their daughter Eva, thin as a rail from doing all the work, outside and in, were waiting to welcome us with tea and Welshcakes. As Mummy went inside, I got a glimpse of a dark, gloomy parlour, with a stone-flagged floor.

'Put the ponies in the shed,' she called over her shoulder.

Which shed? The muddy farmyard, fringed with nettles, broken implements and bits of rusty metal, was surrounded by sheds and barns in a state of advanced decrepitude, and dominated by a vast, sprawling midden which steamed gently despite the muggy afternoon.

I pulled open one shed door after another, but either they were deep in muck or full of sacks and bales. At the far end of the yard, backing on to the moat, I found some depressed-looking cows chained to stanchions, and beyond them an empty pen with a broken hayrack, into which I managed to lead the suspiciously snorting ponies. The door had been much chewed and there was no bolt, but I found some twine and tied it shut. Micky greedily stuck his nose in the manger, whereupon a hen which had been nesting there suddenly erupted in a cloud of squawking feathers. He shot backwards in alarm, knocking over a stack of tins, put his foot through the reins which I had failed to knot up properly, and snapped them near the bit. It was all a far cry from Badminton.

Nor did it get any closer to that ideal when the Davies family moved out to their modern bungalow on Hundred House Common, a couple of miles away, and plans for altering and rebuilding were discussed and drawn up. With so much to do to the house, there could be no question of moving immediately from Much Hadham, so my parents decided to install a bailiff who would take over the day-to-day running of the farm in the more habitable rooms to the left of the staircase, and spend most of our school holidays camping by the Colwyn brook while building work started on the house's righthand side.

Any thoughts I may have had about galloping Taffy about the hills from dawn to dusk that summer were swiftly dashed. In Radnorshire child labour had survived the Victorian era – schoolchildren of all the local farming families worked in the fields – and Mummy thoroughly approved of it. The trouble is that the jobs you can entrust to children are usually tedious, repetitive, mind-blowingly boring, and hard on the back, and stone-picking – or 'pucking' as it was known – fulfilled all these criteria.

Both fields immediately below the house were absolutely carpeted with stones, which had worked their way up through the thin soil and did machinery no good at all, and clearing these became our hated holiday task. It was very simple. A grownup drove a tractor and trailer out to the field. Each child was given a bucket and told to clear a certain area. Grownup then walked up to the house to confer with builders/ drink coffee/ plan farmwork, while the sullen, bolshy, complaining child labour-force toiled back and forth tipping buckets of stones into the trailer for what seemed hour after hour before the grownup finally sauntered back to see how the job was going.

Our French cousins, whose work-ethic had always been suspect in Mummy's eyes, downed tools on the second day of their visit and declared that this wasn't their idea of how to improve their English. Nor would they wear the denim jeans they were given to work in. *'Ca fait paysan,'* they said contemptuously. Maman wouldn't approve.

In this they were undoubtedly correct. There was always a degree of needle between Mummy and her intensely chic, beautiful French sister-in-law, a high-maintenance female whose Gallic love of self-pampering went almost beyond parody.

Temperamentally, they were chalk and cheese. You could see Mummy grit her teeth when Marianne wafted down to breakfast in full make-up and a lacy negligee when everyone else had been up for hours, drank a leisurely cup of coffee, nibbled a piece of toast, then announced importantly, *'Alors, je vais me soigner...'* and that was the last you saw of her until lunchtime.

I guess that by inviting her nephews and niece to visit us without their parents, Mummy hoped to instil in them the love of outdoor life and hard unremitting toil which she was attempting to impose on her own brood, but found to her disappointment that their resistance was, if anything, stronger than ours. I only remember them risking a single visit, and thereafter the Christmas card from their little chateau near Rouen tended to be inscribed, tongue-in-cheek, *From the Castle to the Farm...*

Burning rushes was much more fun than pucking stone, and equally necessary. After years of neglect grass had more or less given up on the sour acid soil, and in its place reeds had spread from the many small boggy patches into great camouflage splodges, covering most of the lower fields.

Neither sheep nor cows eat reeds with any enthusiasm so their grazing value is nil, but in July and August they were as dry as they ever would be in the damp climate, and we found that a long dribble of TVO – Tractor Vaporising Oil or, as Mummy called it, Life-Blood of Modern Farming – judiciously spread along the windward edge of the reed clumps and ignited would flare thrillingly into a wall of flame. Too thrillingly, sometimes. If the wind changed, the flames would veer with it, threatening vehicles, dogs or, on one very frightening occasion, surrounding the sheltered spot where two-year-old Miranda had been parked to sleep off her lunch.

In the nick of time, Mummy remembered her youngest daughter and Gerry, with great heroism, dashed through the billowing smoke to rescue her, leaving the rug, Thermoses and rest of the picnicking equipment to be blackened and burned. It was, as everyone remarked, a near thing.

It took several years of intensive burning to bring the reeds under control, after which my parents embarked on an ambitious programme of 'mole-draining' – dragging a small anvil-shaped block of metal just below the turf to create lots of small tunnels diagonally across the slopes, to remove the worst sogginess, and at the same time slathering the starving grass with a black powder called Basic Slag, to correct the chemical balance. Spreading – or, as it was known, 'sprodding' – basic slag was the dirtiest job we children were ever asked to undertake, beside which moving the muckheap paled into insignificance. From hair to feet the fine silky-feeling powder blacked you up like a Nigger Minstrel, and the rim round the bath afterwards was a grim sight.

However the result of all this effort was deeply satisfying, as even a child of my in-built laziness had to acknowledge, because quite rapidly the khaki fieldscape which had so appalled me on first sight turned a beautiful delicate green, and when the few depressed cows were replaced by a carefully selected handful – you could hardly call them a herd –

of Uncle Geoff's highly-bred Guernseys, the Fforest looked well on its way to becoming what Daddy (in imitation of Uncle Remus) called, 'A sho'nuff farm.' .

It was time, Mummy decided, that we all learned to milk. A gaunt, patient, elderly cow named Eva was chosen for me to practise on, but it took me so long to extract enough milk even to cover the bottom of the bucket that Sal, an agricultural student from South Wales who had come for a few months' work experience, usually took pity on us both and finished the job. When hand-milking, you have to squat awkwardly on a stool, tucking your head right into the angle of the cow's leg and flank, simulating the posture assumed by a calf, so inevitably your hair smells powerfully of cow for the rest of the day. Once settled, you have to work away with a firm steady rhythmic pressure, never pausing in case the cow thinks you have finished, pulling and squeezing until hitherto invisible veins spring up in the backs of your hands and never-used muscles in your forearms begin to ache intolerably.

If you are rough, or take too long, the cow is quite within her rights to swish a heavy and frequently muck-laden tail across your neck and cheek, or even resort to the ultimate sanction of kicking over the bucket that you hold between your knees, and there is not much you can do to prevent it. Though I loved bringing the milkers in from the field, seeing them choose their accustomed places, tying them up and feeding them, I was never a competent milkmaid, and where Sal would hang a foaming full bucket on the cow-shed scales, my own contribution would seldom amount to more than a few pints.

Guernsey cows were not well suited to the cold wet conditions in Radnorshire, and had to be cossetted with rugs and special rations in a way that swiftly ate up any profit from the sale of milk. Mummy persevered with them for years, because they looked so pretty and their butter and cream was delicious – bright buttercup yellow, glistening with beads of moisture, well worth baking bread to go under – but even she had to acknowledge that milking cows, particularly in winter, was long-term servitude.

No matter how early you started, it seemed that no sooner would you have fed, milked, washed up and mucked out on a dark November day than a distant bellowing would give notice that the cows were queuing at the field gate, wanting to come in and restart the whole cycle. After that first experimental summer twice-daily milking gradually and inexorably slid into the hands of a succession of landgirls, found in the *Situations Wanted* columns of *The Farmers' Weekly* and *Horse and Hound*.

Their employment followed a predictable pattern. A honeymoon period when they were hailed as perfect angels – cheerful, efficient, energetic, eager to work – would be succeeded all too soon by a slow slipping from favour as their weaknesses were discovered and productivity tailed off. Few of them stood it for long. Finally they would do something completely unacceptable, miss a milking, top up the churn with water, be found hitting an animal or in a compromising position with a local Lothario. Tears and recriminations would follow, off they would go, and soon a new advertisement would appear in the *Situations Vacant* columns of the farming press.

Mummy was an optimist and always hoped the new girl would be better than the last, but Daddy, whose approach to the servant problem was the classic mixture of fatalism and sloth, knew that if any real paragon was answering advertisements in the agricultural press, it probably meant some other employer had .discovered a pretty intractable Achilles heel.

Some had intriguing backgrounds. There was Rosamond, a nun who had lost her vocation, found life as a telephonist too stressful, and sought the supposed peace of a Welsh farm – little did she know, and precious little did she learn before deciding on a further career change. There was the unfortunate DP (Displaced Person) named Anna, a gloomy middle-aged Ukrainian peasant with no English and just a smattering of German, who wore heavy boots and a triangular headscarf in all weathers. The war had driven her from one country after another until she fetched up in England in 1946. She had no friends, no homeland, her family was scattered and she had no-one at all to love except our Wessex saddlebacks on whom she lavished titbits and affection, treating them more like dogs than pigs.

'Komm spazieren,' she would say, opening the doors of their sties and leading them off for a walk in the wood as no doubt she had done before she was chased from her home. We all did our best to cheer her up, but when she developed a hacking tubercular cough the doctor sent her to hospital in Hereford, and we never saw her again.

Sadder still was the history of Valerie, thin, tense, and brittle, who had been married to a German and trapped in Berlin throughout the war. In a terrible week of violence that nearly unhinged her mind, her husband had been killed, her baby murdered and she herself raped by the invading Russians.

Mummy treated her with great kindness, but I used to hear her sobbing at night in the room next to mine, and very early one morning she appeared staring-eyed at my door, telling me to wake my parents because she had taken poison by mistake.

I think that in fact she had tried to commit suicide, deliberately swallowing a number of the bright blue tablets containing arsenic which were then used to protect the turkeys from a disease called blackhead. These tablets were so big that you couldn't possibly take them by mistake – or, as she later claimed, confuse them with aspirin. Whether she then regretted what she had done, or whether it was simply a cry for help was never clear, but the hospital flashed into action with a stomach pump, and she survived, but the incident had broken Mummy's nerve and Valerie, too, vanished from the farming scene.

Now and again, though, a girl would take to life at Fforest Farm like a duck to water, marry into the neighbourhood, and become a friend for life. One such success story was sweet-natured Liz, who came to work for us less for love of farming life than the tempting words *'own horse welcome,'* in the advertisement in *Horse and Hound*.

We all goggled when the horse in question backed stiffly down the ramp of the enormous lorry Liz had hired to transport her, because unquestionably no less suitable animal for riding on the hill had ever been seen at Fforest Farm. King's Bounty was an enormous bony dark-brown thoroughbred mare of impeccable lineage, incurably lame, and disfigured by a swollen hock with a weeping, granulated wound on the front of it. With a cynicism which did him (or her) no credit at all, the stud owner who had been Liz's former employer had made her a present of this poor wreck of a once-great mare.

'They were going to put her down, so I said I'd have her,' Liz explained, but Mummy said to me privately that she thought it disgraceful

Top left: I could only just be squeezed into the family christening robe in March, 1938.

Top right: Playing with toy soldiers as war clouds gather, summer 1938.

Left: Insecurely perched on the flighty Blackbird above the Whee-air jump.

Below: Fforest Farm in 1949. It had been built on the site of Colwyn Castle where the Norman baron William de Breos once held sway.

Top left: With Clarissa and armfuls of the Angora rabbits we bred at Gaytons during the war.

Top right: Hanging on tight to fiery Mincepie (aged 25) a star of the VWH Pony Club with former owner John Oaksey.

Left: Wet weather gear – suitable for a Welsh summer.

Below: On our favourite mounts: *(L to R)* Stag (Gerry); Sally (Olivia); Dustyfoot (Miranda, half hidden); and Taffy (me) with George in au pair Sylvia's arms and Scot the border collie.

Top: Miranda inspects a fine potato crop in the 16-acre.

Right: A family portrait taken at Tenby where we stayed with Cousin Geraldine most summers.

Below left: My younger brother soon became a dab hand at bottle feeding orphan lambs.

Below right: No pets were allowed at Lawnside, so I can't think why Brag let me keep Mr Ham there for several terms.

Above left: A walk with our Nanny-to-be, who was saved from colic by, and named in honour of, the actress Celia Johnson.

Above right: With Boney, the sausage-stealing, selectively-deaf Dalmatian, who was killed by a car in 1939.

Below left: A handy rock to rest on after a long walk to the Begwns.

Below right: Restraining my sister Miranda with long-reins in the garden at Much Hadham.

Top: Family tea at Gaytons just after the war.

Left: Mummy with some of Lucy the labrador's nine-strong litter.

Below left: Siesta for Mrs White, stroppiest of sows, with her young family.

Below right: Lord of the farm-yard and bane of small children: Whimsical Walkern the turkey.

Top left: Helping (or possibly hindering) neighbouring farmers who were gathering their flocks for dipping.

Top right: Mummy feeding Jemima, the Jill ferret – so free with her teeth that she was best handled in gloves.

Below: Welcome break for haymakers *(L to R)*: Bill James, farm manager, John Anderson, his stepson, Madeleine James, George, and farmhand Jack Howells.

Left: More suitably dressed for Ascot than farmwork, my grandmother Lady Barstow turns hay with a pikle.

Top right: The geese that escaped the fox come racing for morning corn.

Below: Wartime haymaking at Abernant.

Bottom: Merry, the shire horse, pulling the gambo.

Above: Perfect going on the short-cropped turf of Aberedw Hill; me on Warrior, and Gerry on the Smatcher, with young Nesta running free. Summer, 1951.

Below: Clarissa and me with Judy the spaniel's half-grown puppies outside the front gate at the Fforest.

that anyone should have foisted such a burden of worry and expense on to a girl of eighteen.

Bounty took up residence in the temporarily empty bullpen, standing there patiently all winter with her aristocratic head propped on the gate, and her bony rump protruding from the biggest New Zealand rug the saddler in Builth could provide. Every day Liz would carefully dress the wound on her hock, but it never healed, nor did the swelling go down. She was a sad sight. One holidays when I came home from school it was a relief to find that Bounty was gone from the bullpen, and I guess that at last either Mummy or the vet had managed to persuade Liz that it was kinder to have her put down.

With four children at different schools and another on the way, Mummy needed help indoors as well as out, and for five years a loosely-connected string of Swiss au-pairs, each of whom introduced her successor, did much to keep the show on the road .

Neat, bustling, downright Hanni, first of the line, had a strong sense of self-worth. '*Madame, dans la maison, je sais tout faire,*' she announced unequivocally when questioned about her domestic skills, and we soon discovered this was no idle boast. She could cook, wash, iron, clean, teach, draw, knit, sew, whip up a costume for the Nativity play or a soufflé for supper with equal ease, and speak four languages fluently.

A hard act to follow, we all thought, but her willowy brunette friend Lisa who replaced her was nearly as competent and a junior ski champion to boot. And so was lovely lively Engadin-born Nellie, and her more bookish cousin Anita who came the following year.

The only Swiss au-pair who didn't quite come up to scratch was Dora, clumsy and short-sighted (or perhaps clumsy *because* of her short sight) whose major drawback was a problem with BO – she was what Daddy described as 'a bit pouffy.' But by the time Dora was due to leave, Gerry and I were away at school and childcare had returned to an acceptable level, so she was not replaced and thereafter both Gaytons and Fforest Farm were nanny-free zones.

While reconstruction work went on in the farmhouse, we camped by the Colwyn brook, which was agreeable but midgy. Hours were spent damming the narrows with stones and sods of turf, expending vast amounts of energy in the hope of creating trout-pools, but in vain. No matter how carefully the dam was plugged, water always managed to find a way through and the level remained unchanged.

So much time is spent in simply maintaining life – by which I mean keeping warm, dry, clean and fed – while camping, that there never seemed to be a moment's peace. Toiling up the steep fields between camp and the farm buildings in order to fetch milk and other supplies was a chore which we were supposed to do in rotation but all tried to escape, with the predictable result that Gerry, who was not only the strongest but had the keenest sense of duty, ended up doing most of the fetching and carrying.

Inside the tents was cool and dark and after a morning milking or pucking stones I would have liked nothing better than to lie on my campbed and read for the rest of the day, but that was not an option. Though Mummy's maternal ancestors had been glamorously bohemian artists and craftsmen, on her father's side she descended from a line of sporting parsons and missionaries, and it must have been one of these who instilled in her the conviction that reading novels in the daytime was so deeply – even wickedly –self indulgent that it amounted to a sin.

This was a problem, since I was already hopelessly addicted to reading. Books were my *feste Burg*, my certain refuge when real life became boring or difficult. Quality didn't matter. I could be just as happy with the most unutterable rubbish as with a good novel, but without a book on the go I felt – and still do feel – incomplete and uneasy.

'All right, darling?' Mummy had once asked when I was quite small, coming to tuck me up when we were staying in a strange house.

'Yes, but I aren't awfully interested in the Oxford English Dictionary,' I am alleged to have answered, so evidently the rot had already set in. Now I was eleven she would have much preferred me to spend my holidays engaged in vigorous physical activity rather than lolling about reading.

'Just going to clean my saddle,' I would mutter, stuffing a fat Enid Blyton under my jersey and heading for the dark stables. Above the stalls was an old loft with a few musty haybales, and there I would take refuge, ears pricked for a scrunch on the chippings which had replaced the mud round the house, and keeping a wary eye on a knothole which commanded the yard.

Sometimes several of us went up there to play Monopoly, a game for ever associated in my mind with grit and hayseeds, but this was risky because any outburst of giggling or chat might give away our position, and there weren't many secret yet relatively comfortable hideyholes about the farmyard. It was a wet summer, and reading out of doors was hardly possible, while reading by torchlight after dark soon made my eyes ache.

Our camp by the stream came to an abrupt conclusion. After a day of relentless drizzle, it was Mummy's agreeable habit to check the money in her bag, say decisively, 'When all else fails...' and bundle us into the Hillman shooting brake for an evening of smoky, blissfully warm entertainment at the Castle cinema in Builth, then a fuggy fleapit of the first order but with a good line in cowboy films.

Munching fish and chips off our laps, we would sit in the prim and proper single seats of the third row, occasionally turning to watch the antics of snoggers in the double-seated back rows, where stifled squeals and wild bursts of hilarity were referred to in family-speak as 'slap-and-tickle in the two-and-ninepennies.'

The programme started with a warm-up B-film of extreme banality, followed by a roll of drums heralding, *The Gaumont British News – presenting The World to The World!* Stiff, clipped, voices would then deliver a few uplifting stories – new tankers launched by Royalty, politicians on the stump, the result of major sporting events – the pictures accompanied by a series of dreadful puns to show the Gaumont news-editors were not entirely devoid of humour, then the lights would go up in the auditorium, the back-row snoggers would adjust their clothes, and we would race down the aisle to be first in the queue for ice-creams and Smith's Crisps. At long last, when the lights dimmed again, the main feature would begin to roll.

That particular evening, there were water-splashes across the road in several places as we drove home, but it wasn't until Mummy's torch picked out the shine of water below us that we realised quite how much it had rained since we left. All the tents were awash to the brailing, with our bedding, clothes, books and campbeds floating about, and what had been a tranquil meandering brook had turned into a raging white-capped torrent.

Soaked and shivering, we grabbed armfuls of possessions and stumbled back up the hill to the Fforest, where we slept on sacks and car-rugs on the bare boards of the upstairs rooms, with the spaniel puppies, Punch and Judy, curled in the angle of our knees like hotwater bottles.

Another blissful year at Old Dalby followed, but alas, with no-one older to squash me I was growing ever more bumptious and naughty, and every term was marred by at least one disgraceful episode.

At Hallowe'en I waited until everyone was in bed, then stole out to the stables, draped Taffy in sheets with a pillowcase with holes in it over her head, and led her up the dimly lit wide shallow double-staircase to the half-landing.

There, even her iron nerve broke. She flung up her head and gave a wild whinny that brought the grown-ups out of their bedrooms, then swung round and slipped stumbling down the stairs, skidded across the polished boards of the hall, and disappeared through the front door. She might easily have broken her leg, and I was severely scolded.

'You just don't *think*, do you,' said Polly.

Even worse was the shameful occasion when, for some reason I can't recall, I lost my temper with Tessa, wrestled her to the floor of my bedroom and, seizing her by her thick fair plaits, began banging her head against the carpet. The more she screamed at me to stop, the harder I thumped in a berserker display of violence that I could not control. The memory makes me feel quite sick.

Polly happened to be away, but Miss Smith came to Tessa's rescue, pulled me away, and told me to stay in my room until she had decided what to do with me. I remember sobbing until the spit in my mouth was thick enough to blow into bubbles, and wondering miserably what Polly would say. In fact, she took it very calmly – partly, no doubt, because she hadn't actually seen the attack – but kind Miss Smith left on my pillow that night an envelope marked *Read, Mark, Learn and Inwardly Digest*, containing a two-page letter of sensible, measured, valuable advice on what would now be called Anger Management.

In the summer term we had the great pride and pleasure of seeing Magic and Mariner, the harum-scarum hound puppies we had 'walked' the year before – walking being a purely technical description of galloping frantically after them every time they disappeared after rabbits into the wide blue yonder – win their respective classes at the Quorn Puppy Show but, as the end of term drew near, I blotted my copybook yet again.

It sounds absolutely absurd, but I persuaded Jo to hide with me under the chintz flounces of the long window-seat in Hubert's study, where he and Polly used to sit in the evening, in the hope of seeing them make mad passionate love there after supper. We had a long, long wait in dire discomfort, lying cramped on our sides with knees doubled up, listening to the clink of glass and murmur of voices from the dining-room, and serious doubts about the enterprise were already in our minds when at last we heard footsteps approach the study door.

By then it was too late to abort the operation. We lay doggo, holding our breath. Was the romantic scene about to unfold?

There was a long silence, broken only by the rustle of paper. Peeking out, I could see Hubert's polished shoes but not a sign of Polly. The silence went on and on until, predictably, I began to want to pee. In vain I tried all my lasting strategies, but it was no good. My bladder was about to burst.

'Come on!' I hissed at Jo, rolled out from under the valance and staggered to my feet, hardly able to move from cramp.

Polly and Hubert were reading newspapers on either side of the fire, and looked up in mild astonishment.

'What *are* you doing? It's high time you were in bed,' she remarked as, feeling unutterably foolish, as we slunk out of the room. The episode was never referred to again, but can't have enhanced my reputation.

Near the end of term a few weeks later, Jo and I were in the big square tackroom, cleaning our saddles and bridles before Sandford took the ponies to the station for the journey home. We were talking idly about the holidays, and she happened to mention that next term she was going to share my room with Tessa.

'Then where'll I sleep?' I asked, and she looked surprised.

'Oh, but you won't be here. You're going to boarding school. Didn't you know?'

I hadn't, and the calm certainty with which she broke the news hit me amidships.

'But – but *why*?'

'Surely you know?'

'No. Do you?'

She thought about it, head bent as she polished her curb-chain so I could see nothing of her expression, only her centre-parted red-gold pigtails flicking back and forth as she rubbed.

'Well, yes,' she said at last. 'But if you don't, I can't tell you.'

'But I want to know. *Please*, Jo.'

'No.'

I went on nagging, and eventually she gave an exasperated sigh. 'Well, OK, but I warn you, you won't like it.'

'I don't care. Please tell me.'

'Well…' She hesitated, then said in a rush, 'Cilla told Polly she can't stand you any longer.'

To say I was flabbergasted is an understatement. I could hardly believe that gentle, slow Cilla, who had so often been the target of my taunts and teasing, should have the power to banish me from this Garden of Eden just by telling Polly she didn't like me. Couldn't stand me. It just shows how successful Polly had been in treating us all alike that it was only now fully brought home to me that she was Cilla's *mother*, and no mother is going to stand by and see her daughter made unhappy by the cuckoo she has welcomed into her nest.

So the decision had been taken, my parents contacted, the usual euphemism trotted out. Phyllida had outgrown Miss Smith's teaching. It was time she moved on.

And for the past month while I in blissful ignorance had been galloping about on Taffy, bossing the others as usual, thinking myself the cat's whiskers, Mummy had been frantically writing and telephoning headmistresses of boarding schools, trying to persuade them to take me at short notice by offering to send them Olivia and Miranda as well in due course. She had delayed telling me until she had secured a place at one of them, but thanks to Jo I now knew the real reason behind my banishment.

It was a shock that changed me profoundly. For the first time I began to worry what other people thought of me, and what they said behind my back. How could one possibly tell? Though I remained *au fond* the same bossy little know-all I had always been, I adopted a humbler alter ego, and tried to be less contrary and curb my critical tongue. It wasn't quite a Damascene conversion, and sometimes the mask slipped, but although my improved behaviour must have come as a relief to my parents and siblings, I was too ashamed ever to let on what had goaded the leopard into changing her spots.

That summer we had a much better organised camp, with big Army bell-tents pitched among the trees of the spinney flanking the drive, very close to the farm buildings and house where the alterations were now well advanced.

Since most of the family still spent term-time at Much Hadham, only bringing the younger children and ponies for the holidays, Mr and Mrs Watts were in charge of the Fforest most of the year, and I got the impression that she, at least, resented being superseded when the boss-lady swooped in with orders and new plans.

It is quite possible that her husband did, too, but the permanently melancholy, downtrodden expression on his sallow face made his state of mind difficult to read. He looked thoroughly costive, and no wonder for – as Mrs Watts revealed in an unguarded moment, and Mummy instantly passed the fascinating information on to me – his bowels moved only once every ten days. Ever after, I could never look at him without wondering if this had been *the* day or one of the other nine.

He had been a farmhand working for her father on the splendidly named Pen-ys-yr-plwydd, (which apparently meant nothing more exciting than The Top End of the Arable Land) and was seventeen years younger than his domineering wife. She had inherited the farm and definitely wore the trousers: a strapping, florid woman with a quick tongue and an air of barely suppressed indignation.

Between them they had produced a single daughter Eunice, a dark, delicate child of about seven. She had her father's sly, treacly eyes and a wistful expression, and reminded me of an Arthur Rackham fairy.

Some months earlier, Olivia and I had both been given golden hamsters, which we called Hannibal and Hamelcar. Hannibal soon succumbed, but Mr Ham – as mine became generally known – was a most engaging and enterprising little chap, very tame and with a strong homing instinct. I carried him wherever I went, and so long as I wore my shirt tucked well into my shorts he was perfectly secure, though going to the loo in a hurry was dangerous because it was easy to forget about him. More than once I found him clinging desperately to my shirt, with his feet hooked in the holes of the Aertex, when the elastic snake-belt that supported him was suddenly undone.

His closest brush with the Grim Reaper, however, occurred one evening at camp, when Mummy had gone to the station to fetch Daddy from the London train, and the rest of us had been chivvied into tidying up for his return.

It was my turn to empty the bucket of the Elsan, a portable loo which was a great improvement on the Army-style latrine, a stinking trench surmounted by two bars, which we had used (not without a good deal of protest) the year before. A dark brown tarry liquid called Elsanol was sloshed liberally into the bucket to keep the smell within bearable limits, and about twice a week some child was detailed to take a deep breath, pull out the bucket by its wire handle, carry it at arm's length across the farmyard and empty it on the muck-heap.

I had lifted the lid and was leaning forward to catch the handle when Mr Ham, with lamentable timing, climbed up to the V of my open-neck shirt and peered out. A second later, to my horror, he plummeted straight into the noxious contents of the bucket, balanced for an instant on the morass of paper and excrement, then vanished below the surface.

I plunged both hands in, fished around for what seemed an age until I felt something wriggle, and pulled him out, stinking and bedraggled but still alive.

The car's headlights were coming up the drive as I rushed with him cupped in my hands into the kitchen tent, which was lit by a Tilly lamp, and started to clean him with a wet handkerchief, but the tarry chemical clung to his fur and I was afraid it would blind him.

'Put him on the table,' said Mummy, jumping out of the car and instantly grasping the gravity of the situation. 'Bring me your tooth-brush.'

She sloshed gin into a glass, and very gently sponged poor shivering Mr Ham all over with it, then brushed the resulting sludge off him with the toothbrush, while I stood uselessly by, grizzling that he was going to die.

After what seemed an age, however, he perked up and opened his bright buttons of eyes. Mummy suspended her cleaning operation and to our astonishment he sat up and began to lick fussily at his fur, possibly enjoying his first-ever taste of the hard stuff. We put him in a nest of dusters, observing him closely all evening, then returned him to his cage overnight. Next day he spent curled in his sleeping-quarters, but by evening was quite himself again, stuffing his pouches with nuts and storing them in his larder as if nothing untoward had befallen him.

The only long term result of his near-fatal immersion was the loss of his fur, and that was only temporary. A naked adult hamster is a rather revolting sight, but before I went away to school, leaving him in Olivia's care, he had begun to grow a fine silky coat once more. I hardly need add that never again did I risk taking him to the loo with me.

That summer I fell in love again, this time with a black, rough-coated Border collie called Scot, with thin legs and a foxy profile, a white bib and one white paw, whom I thought the most beautiful and beguiling dog in all the world. He followed me everywhere, and lay on my campbed at night. He seemed to know what I wanted him to do before I even asked him to do it, whether it was blocking a gateway to stop sheep escaping, or pointing out where the ponies had taken themselves to hide from the flies. If I went where he could not follow – in a car, for instance – he would lie down at the top of the drive, put his nose on his paws, and wait for my return. The only fly in the ointment of this perfect idyll was that he belonged to our bailiff, Mr Watts.

In retrospect, I can see that it must have been extremely annoying for Watts to have such a vital tool as his working sheepdog shanghaied in this way for the whole of the summer holidays, but at the time I thought him a cruel slave-driver to call Scot away and make him drive sheep here and there when he would rather be with me. No sheepdog can serve two masters, and given the choice between hard work on a diet of flaked maize and milk with Watts, and tins of Chappie and an idle life with me, Scot voted with his feet and began to take his professional duties ever more casually.

He was only three when I first knew him, but had already adopted the old dog's trick of using his voice to save his legs. He was far too canny to be blindly obedient, and instead of racing off like a bolt from the blue when ordered to, 'Get out round!' a bunch of ewes, he would run halfway then glance over his shoulder for confirmation of the command, and only frenzied whistling and shouting would impel him to keep going in the right direction. Nor did he favour the well-trained sheepdog's classic technique of snaking back and forth behind the flock, hustling them if they tried to stop and lying flat if they looked like bolting.

Scot's method was to bark until they went the way he wanted, and if one ewe split off from the bunch nothing on earth would make him go back for her. 'Good riddance,' he seemed to be saying as he trotted bossily behind the ewes he had managed to round up. 'That one's nothing but trouble – better left behind.'

But if his shepherding work was less than perfect, he was a marvel at driving cows, anticipating every breakaway move they might make on their twice-daily trudge from milking-parlour to meadow, and bringing them back to the straight and narrow with a well-judged nip on the fetlock; and he would run tirelessly on the hill behind the ponies – silent, interested, and always there when you wanted him. From time to time as you walked, you would feel a nudge from his sharp nose. *Here I am. What do you want me to do?* He was the perfect companion.

Compared to such a *preux chevalier*, my father's dogs scored pretty low. Punch and Judy were springer spaniels, liver-and-white, obsessed with hunting, not much use shooting, smelly, disobedient, just the sort of animals that inspired that cruel old couplet:

A woman, a spaniel, a walnut tree,
The more you beat 'em the better they be!

It wasn't in Daddy's nature to beat a dog (or anything else, for that matter), and once they grew out of charming puppydom, they rapidly got out of control. My nightmare was to be told to take them for a walk, because nine times out of ten they would wait until one was well away from the farm, then exchange a glance full of meaning and simply vanish into the bracken. Distant yapping might give you a rough idea of their direction, but you could yell their names until your throat felt like splitting without a hope of getting them back.

Daddy would say forgivingly that they were probably making too much noise to hear me calling them, but I knew the true cause for their deafness was sheer bloody-mindedness combined with the knowledge that they could run rings round me.

They also knew they'd be in trouble when they came back. Sometimes a couple of days would pass before hunger drove them to slink back up the drive, their tucked-up tummies and long ears caked in mud, their expressions literally hangdog. They would be scolded if it was Daddy who saw them first, or beaten in a half-hearted way if they encountered Mummy, and put in the kennel to reflect on their sins, but it was never long before their pleading whines secured their release.

When Punch began to show incestuous desires towards his sister, he was sold to a sporting neighbour, a keen shot but alas, not a good dog-man. So habitually did he roar, 'Damn-you-Punch,' that the unfortunate animal must have supposed that was his name, and their short partnership ended abruptly when Punch, running-in after a winged pheasant, was shot dead by his owner.

Judy, however, had a long and happy life. Once she no longer had her brother to egg her on, she stopped sneaking off to hunt in the Fforest wood, and steadied into a respectable matriarch after producing a first litter of puppies. She had a remarkable nose, and would go on diligently searching for a lost bird long after other dogs had given up, her plumed white tail wagging excitedly as she worked. We kept one dog puppy of hers and named him Flash, from the forked-lightning zigzag on his back. He was heavy and handsome, rather slow-witted, with a distressing propensity for releasing stealthy sulphurous farts as he lay on our camp-beds while Daddy was reading aloud to us. Like Granny, he read beautifully and never skipped, and these evening sessions were a highlight of camp life, but sometimes even he would be stopped in mid-sentence by one of Flash's silent-and-deadlies.

'Achtung! Broadside!' someone would hiss, and we would all vanish into the depths of our sleeping-bags until the foul miasma dissipated.

Evenings in camp were idyllic that long sunny summer. We ate from wooden plates, sitting round a glowing campfire, and sang music-hall ballads like *Abdullah Bubul Emir*, and *Pretty Little Polly Perkins of Paddington Green*. Gerry had picked up a number of pseudo-political songs from a Scout camp: I remember him grinding through all the verses of *Harry Pollit was a Bolshie* while Mummy watched to see how much the smaller children could understand of the off-colour jokes.

But if evenings were full of mirth and jollity, during the daytime the prolonged spell of good weather (for Wales) brought a new horror for natural layabouts like me – haymaking.

This was always a major worry for the Welsh farmer. To make decent hay that would neither heat and 'fowst' – go musty in the middle – or turn black and inedible, you need at least five days and preferably a week of dry weather, and naturally as soon as a suitable high showed on the weather charts, everyone in the neighbourhood cut his hay-crop and worked flat out to turn, ted, row up, bale and finally carry it.

Since the routine servicing and maintenance of machinery took a low priority at Fforest Farm at the time – there was always something more urgent to do – it was not unusual to find vital bits of implements worn out or missing when the moment came to use them, and since every agricultural engineer for miles around would be furiously busy during the dry spell, it was likely that when a mechanic did finally turn up to fix the machines, the weather would break that night and the haycrop be ruined.

There must, my parents thought, be a better way.

Earlier that summer, they had been invited to Austria, where the Caccias were now en poste, with Uncle Harold the British High Commissioner. In the course of wandering about the country in Aunt Nancy's little car, they penetrated remote valleys where the sun shone only briefly between beetling mountain peaks and were interested to see how, in this difficult farming terrain, the sturdy mahogany-faced peasants hung their hay on wooden tripods in order to dry it in the shortest possible time.

Perhaps this was the answer. If the method produced delicious-smelling dry mountain hay in Austria, why not in Wales? Always ready to jump in the deep end, Mummy measured and sketched the tripods and, on her return to Wales, commissioned Mr Morson the carpenter to make a large stack of them from unbarked larch poles. I watched the process with interest, wondering how I could recycle them later into jumps, but alas they were both too high and too flimsy to use for anything but their stated purpose.

Halfway through August, word zipped round the Wye valley: high pressure was building. A fine week was on its way. Out came the cutters, round and round drove the little grey Fergie 20, and by dusk that evening two fields lay in flat swathes waiting for the predicted hot weather to 'cure' the grass.

For three whole days the high held steady. Not a drop of rain tainted the thick greeny-silver rows as they were turned once, turned twice, thrown up in the air by a curious triple set of spiked wheels known as a Whiffler, and raked into long sausages by Darkie the cart-mare pulling the tedder, but the hay still wasn't quite dry enough to bale, and the presence of midges and an ominous heaviness in the air warned of approaching thunderstorms.

It was time to try the Austrian method. The big larch triangles were driven to the hayfield on a trailer, and we were set to work to prop them together into tripods which would act as drying-racks. As the rock-bottom job for children, this left stone-pucking standing. For a start, it was very difficult to get the brutes to stand up. Time and again we would have two propped correctly with the apexes touching, only for the third to collapse them all. In retrospect I think they ought to have been notched at the top, or even lashed together, but in their natural unwieldy state it was practically impossible to set them firmly on a sloping field. The rough bark tore our hands – no sissy gardening gloves in those days – and it was deeply disheartening to look back along the rows you had just erected and see how many had already fallen down.

More difficult still was the second stage when we tried to hang hay on them because it simply refused to lie in place. Either it fell between the widely spaced slats, leaving you with a damp little haycock surrounded by larch poles, or it blew off the tripod at the first puff of wind. I guess that the Austrian peasant farmer would have cut his hay with a scythe and didn't toss it about so much before putting it on the racks, but although her exciting new method was clearly not going to plan, Mummy (who could be a slave-driver at times) kept us toiling away at it until darkness put an end to our misery.

We woke rather late, tired and stiff, to a morning of brooding clouds and the threat of rain, and found a note from Mummy. *Come to the hayfield as soon as you've had breakfast.*

Oh, not again! I thought, and if I'd had the nerve, I would have refused to go because I had a very clear idea of what we'd find there. When we finished washing-up and had no further excuse for delay, we all straggled up to the Upper Committee, as the hayfield was grandly known – Gerry, David, me, Clarissa and Olivia, a puny workforce by any standards – and sure enough, of the thirty-odd hayracks we had left standing, at least twenty had collapsed overnight.

I hardly dared look at Mummy for fear of being ordered to start re-erecting them, but when I did steal a glance I was surprised to see her smiling. 'Well, obviously that hasn't worked,' she said cheerfully, 'but after you went to bed last night I saw an article in *Farmers' Weekly* about in-barn dryers. It sounds a marvellous idea. You bale the hay still green and stack it in tunnels, and this big huffer blows in warm air… There's a place in Leominster where you can hire them.'

Oh, the relief! Our spirits rose like gas balloons. Mr Watts, who was no keener on manual toil than the rest of us, embraced the huffer proposal with enthusiasm. He had seen at a glance the drawbacks of the Austrian hayracks, and distanced himself from helping put them up, but a tractor-powered in-barn dryer sounded like the kind of technology he approved. Better still, as soon as he had baled the green hay, he persuaded a cheerful bunch of neighbours to help us load it onto the farm waggon – the 'gambo' – since the wet bales were too heavy for children to lift.

By Friday night, when Daddy returned from London, all was safely gathered into the big asbestos barn at the Committee Dump, where once Radnorshire's snowploughs and other municipal machinery had been stored, with the tractor engine thundering night and day to drive the last of the moisture from the bales. It didn't make the hay any cheaper, but in every other way in-barn drying was a complete success. The bales retained their colour and delicious smell throughout the winter and, proof of the pudding, the animals hoovered up every scrap.

Towards the end of the long summer holidays, my new school uniform arrived from Debenhams in a large cardboard box, and since there were no full-length mirrors in the tents, we went over to Chapel House for a ceremonial trying-on of white flannelette shirt, brown-and-gold tie, pleated tunic and Sunday dress in a hideous milk chocolate shade – deeply unflattering to one of my sallow complexion – gold sash, brown cardigan, and handsome pinkish-beige overcoat, beautifully cut and seamed, a miniature version of the Army officer's famous British Warm.

'Now the hat!' crowed eight year old Olivia, secure in the knowledge that there were three years to go before the shades of the prison house closed on her.

The brown felt hat depressed my spirits still further. It might have been designed to make me look ridiculous. But if the outer garments were strange and constricting, those underneath were truly weird. White knicker linings with thick dark brown pants to go over them. (*For gym* explained the Clothing List.) A suspender-belt from which hung little bobbles to which you secured brown lisle stockings, two fore, two aft. Petticoats, pyjamas, hockey boots, gym shoes… the list seemed endless, and I crammed myself in and out of them as instructed in a daze of unhappiness, not so much because I was being sent away to school, but because of a scene I had unwillingly witnessed earlier that week.

Mummy had been in the dairy, washing the endless little metal cones of the separator before putting the cream to set in a big shallow crock, when Mrs Watts bustled up to her with flaming cheeks and blazing eyes, in a high state of indignation.

'Where's my butter, then, Mrs Barstow? That's what I want to know,' she began aggressively.

This put Mummy on the spot. Churning butter was a long, heavy job which she and Mrs Watts undertook on alternate weeks. Since there were always seven and often more in our household, we kept two thirds of the home made butter, with the remaining third going to Mrs Watts, who was in the habit of selling part of her share, something Mummy had learnt by chance and which was, she considered, against the spirit of the agreement.

We had had visitors to stay that weekend, and when we ran out of butter, Mummy had told me to fetch the last two pats from the dairy – pats which technically belonged to Mrs Watts.

'I'm afraid we've eaten it all,' she said with a conciliatory smile, 'but I'll make some more tomorrow. Perhaps you could make do with margarine till then.'

If she had suggested that the Watts family spread yellow phosphorus on their bread she could hardly have had a more explosive response. Mrs Watts seemed to swell like an enraged turkey.

'So it's margarine now, is it? You've eaten all my butter and you want me to make do with margarine? Let me tell you, Mrs Barstow, I've never in my life eaten that stuff and I'm not starting now, whatever you may say.'

'Not even during the war?'

'Never!'

'That was very unpatriotic of you, Mrs Watts,' said Mummy, recklessly burning her boats. 'We all have to make sacrifices at times, and I think it's disgraceful that you should make such a silly fuss just because there's no butter.'

'Patriotism, is it? You can keep your old patriotism, Mrs Barstow,' said Mrs Watts in a fine fury, 'and as for calling me silly, I tell you now I won't stand here to be insulted by you or anyone else. I'm giving you my notice this minute, and taking my family where I won't have to beg and scrape for every morsel I put on my 'usband's plate.'

'Well, if that's how you feel, Mrs Watts, I won't stand in your way,' said Mummy, and my world rocked. A sudden cold chill enveloped me as I realised the implications. I didn't care two hoots whether Mrs Watts stayed or went, but if Watts left the Fforest he'd take Scot with him, and I might never see him again.

I spent the next few days in an agony of worry, and at the weekend, after Daddy had talked to Watts, my fears were confirmed. The Watts family were leaving and we were to have a new bailiff.

'What about Scot?' I asked fearfully. 'Will he go with them?'

'I'm afraid so, darling,' said Mummy. I turned and rushed into my tent, flung myself on the bed, and burst into a storm of weeping.

Along with short sight and a long memory, Grandfather had passed on to me his embarrassing tendency to greet any moment of high emotion with tears. The emotion wasn't necessarily sorrow. Noble deeds, evocative sounds, even excessive happiness brought on the waterworks in just the same way, choking speech and reddening the nose. I could feel the tell-tale symptoms coming over me well in advance, and would try desperately to deflect my thoughts, but in vain. Once the first tears welled up and began to slide down my nose, I was done for.

'You're so lucky to be able to cry,' a sympathetic vicar once told me as I gulped and blubbed in a way quite unsuited to my age and station. 'It does much less harm than bottling up your emotions.' Be that as it may, I have usually found this inability to control my tears a great drawback, and only very rarely has it worked to my advantage.

This, however, was one of those occasions. After a whole weekend of torrential blubbing, Daddy – before he left for London – had another talk with Watts and next morning I found an envelope on the breakfast table by my place.

Inside was a postcard which I still treasure. It said:

To darling Phyllida, 1 sheepdog named Scot, on condition:
a) He remains a sheepdog and helps Weale when needed
b) He doesn't come into the house beyond the porch
c) He doesn't bite Miss Barrows

CHAPTER FIVE

Lawnside

MISS WINIFRED BARROWS, whom Scot was pledged not to attack, was my new headmistress. She was generally – and generally affection-ately – known as 'Brag,' because she was a name-dropper *par excellence* and – perhaps on the Can't Beat 'Em, Join 'Em principle – appeared to revel in the nickname and do her best to live up to it.

No-one loved a lord, an ambassador, a five-star general more than Brag, and among her parents she had collected an impressive assortment of Establishment figures. Not that she treated their children in any way differently from the offspring of lesser mortals. It wasn't because of social snobbery that Mummy had difficulty getting her to accept me as a pupil at short notice – simply that Lawnside was booked solid that year, and it would require juggling of beds and classes to squeeze an extra girl in.

She was short, stocky, and dynamic, with a fine rosy complexion and long ski-jump nose; a benevolent autocratic who had never taken an exam in her life but more than made up for her lack of qualifications by her energy and imagination. She was brilliant at bringing out the best in girls, worked extremely hard, and took great pride in the school which she owned and ran without reference to a board of governors or educational inspectors or any interfering body from outside.

Photographs of her in the Lawnside hockey team circa 1920 showed a rather beautiful oval-faced teenager with waist-length plaits and large, dreamy eyes. By the time I met her in 1949, most of the dreaminess had been submerged by the practical demands of running her school, but she

111

retained the big blue eyes and long hair, now greying and wound into a complicated arrangement on top of her head to give her much-needed height. She also retained a strong romantic streak, becoming misty-eyed and assuming a quite different tone of voice when talking of poetry – (she pronounced it 'poyetry') or literature, music, painting, theatre.

Drama was her major passion, and every summer she produced ambitious outdoor plays involving every girl in the school – no mean achievement, particularly since a run of wet Julys meant that they had sometimes to be transferred at short notice to the stage at the Winter Gardens.

Great Malvern was then a hotbed of private educational establishments. There was the Boys' College, the Girls' College, St James's and The Abbey, and lots of boys' prep schools. Lawnside consisted of five or six separate houses, some with adjoining gardens, others loosely grouped across a T-junction in quiet residential streets which only came to rowdy life at closing time on Saturday nights, when revellers poured out of the pubs down near the station, and staggered up the road with linked arms, bawling '*Goodnight, Ireen*' in painful disharmony.

The garden of the main house, Lawnside itself, made a fine setting for plays, the long lawn in question being flanked by mature Wellingtonias and other specimen trees which formed wings from which the actors could make their entrances, and a natural grandstand was provided by a pronounced ledge, almost a ha-ha, at the top. A croquet lawn acted as the main stage, and the long lawn then sloped gently down to the shrubbery which concealed props and make-up paraphernalia.

All the whole-school plays Brag produced while I was at Lawnside – among them *The Vision of Piers Plowman*, a very free adaptation of *The Return of Odysseus*, James Elroy Flecker's *Golden Road to Samarkand*, and a splendid blood-and-thunder in rhyming couplets about the British freedom fighter Caractacus's heroic struggle against the Roman legions – relied heavily on chorus-work, and here Brag was in her element. She would listen carefully to each girl's speaking voice, grade it high, medium or low, and use the different pitches to dramatic effect as the chorus explained and moved forward what would otherwise have been most confusing narratives.

She was a resourceful producer. It was traditional for the head girl to play the starring role, even when she was ill-fitted to take centre stage. Corrie, head girl when I arrived, was required to open *The Vision of Piers Plowman* with the heavily alliterative lines,

On a May morning on Malvern Hill,
A marvel befell me. Sure from faerie it came.
I had wandered me weary, so weary…

But being afflicted with a pronounced stammer, when she opened her mouth nothing came out but an agonised, 'O-o-o…'

Again and again she tried, but it was no use. It began to look as if tradition would have to be broken and her deputy play the part of Piers Plowman, but Brag still had a trick up her sleeve. At the signal of a dropped handkerchief, she made all the other actors, hidden among the trees, accompany Corrie through the opening two lines, then leave her to carry on alone, and to my astonishment, it worked. She recited the rest of the speech without a tremor.

During the next few rehearsals, Corrie's 'jumping powder' was gradually whittled away, until for the speech-day performance itself she needed no more than three words from the rest of the school to get her going, and the audience scarcely noticed the prompt.

But these plays lay far in the future on the sunny September afternoon just short of my twelfth birthday when Mummy drove me over from Fforest Farm, giving me a cigarette to quell my habitual car-sickness as the Malvern hills rose up out of the lush, red-soiled Herefordshire farmland. I felt itchy and foolish in my brown tunic and blazer with a golden rose embroidered on the breast-pocket, but it didn't seem so bad once I met all the other new girls similarly kitted out – unflattering as it was, the uniform gave me a comforting sensation of being one of the crowd.

I was quite used to being dumped in strange places, and hardly noticed Mummy drive away. At the time I thought it a bit of a swizz that new girls should start the term a day earlier than the rest of the school, but after a friendly welcome and tea in the Small Dining-room, Brag kept us so busy that there wouldn't have been time to be homesick even if one was that way inclined.

First we had to unpack, carefully lining our chest of drawers with newspaper before stacking in all the stiff new clothes – a first for me, because I usually dropped everything on the floor. My dormitory was the biggest in the house, an eighter, overlooking the drive, with flimsy cotton curtains on rails dividing it to give the big girls a bit of privacy. My new friend Mary Jane, a brisk little person with a turned-up nose, chose the bed nearest the window, and I hastily bagged the one next to her. Then the trunks were taken away by the school handymen, and the realisation hit me that the dark shadow of menace that had hung over me all the summer was now translated into reality, and I really was at boarding school. It was not at all what I had anticipated.

These expectations were largely based on the adventures of Teddy Lester, hero of a number of rip-roaring Edwardian school stories by John Finnemore. *His First Term*, a battered copy of which had passed from hand to hand of the Barstow family until the spine had broken and half the first chapter was missing, opened with a pillow fight in the dorm, and the painful retribution inflicted on the offenders by a sadistic flogging prefect. In a perpetual game of Tom Tiddler's Ground against bullies, sneaks, drunken gamekeepers and furious housemasters, the gallant Teddy and his chum Ito, a plucky little Jap who was a dab hand at ju-jitsu, came within a whisker of being unjustly expelled time and again, but right always triumphed in the nick of time. (The Japanese were in high regard when the books were written around 1905, though my generation, which naturally regarded them as demons incarnate after their atrocities in the Second World War, had to make a considerable mental adjustment to look approvingly on Teddy's choice of chum.)

However much I had dreaded facing the same sort of conditions, I must admit that, compared to the exciting shenanigans at Slapton School, Lawnside seemed decidedly tame as, without so much as a pillow fight, Mary Jane and I watched Matron turn out the light and went quietly to sleep.

Next day, however, I was glad we had been given the chance to find our feet before the other boarders swarmed into their houses and the school echoed with voices and laughter. Just as you should always put a strange pony into the field to settle down before letting the home team join it, so Brag's strategy of summoning new girls a day early ensured that we knew at least some of our classmates and were not overwhelmed by the sheer, boisterous energy of the returning habituées, many of whom had come up from the Junior School.

I remember feeling quite dazed when I first walked into the big dining-room with its high ceiling and long tables covered in oilcloth, and found it absolutely crammed with girls – more girls in a single room than I had ever seen in my life – all clattering and chattering and shouting across the tables, and if there hadn't been kind Mary Jane waving from the seat she had bagged me next to her, I would have been tempted to turn tail.

Since it was only tea, and a pretty boring tea at that, consisting mostly of fish paste sandwiches supplemented by bread and marge, because the weekly butter and sugar-rations had not yet been doled out, everyone sat where they pleased, and I was soon mesmerised by the party at the table next to ours, where one girl was effortlessly dominating the conversation while all the others craned to hear what she was saying. She was clearly a well-known wag, since her stories were punctuated with bursts of laughter and shouts of, 'Go on, what happened next?'

'They're Fifth Form,' said Mary Jane, following my gaze. We had learnt enough by now to know that the whole of Remove separated us lowly Upper Fourths from these glamorous beings in the Fifth, fourteen-to fifteen-year-olds and traditionally the wildest, naughtiest girls in the school, having outgrown their youthful respect for authority without yet acquiring the gravitas of the School Certificates, who would themselves mature in the fullness of time into the demi-goddesses of the Sixth Form.

Certainly the Fifth Form table was having a wonderful time, and making more noise than the whole of the rest of the school, but I had eyes for no-one but the principal raconteuse. She wasn't beautiful, far from it, having a pale, freckled, wedge-shaped face and untidy sandy hair, and was square-built rather than fat, so that her neck seemed to vanish into her shoulders, but so powerful a magnetism radiated from her that I could feel myself blushing as I darted covert glances across the table.

'Who's that?' I murmured.

'Which?'

'The one talking.'

'I think she's called Leesa.'

It seemed the most alluring name I had ever heard. I finished my tea in a daze, half fearful that she might notice me, half longing for it, and wholly baffled by the effect she had on me.

Leesa would have been astonished if she had ever known of my instantaneous enslavement. She was, as it turned out, a very down-to-earth girl, neither particularly clever nor athletic; in fact apart from a certain artistic talent she was entirely average in every way, and why I should have fallen for her at first sight remains a mystery. She was my secret idol, but I would have walked over hot coals rather than let anyone else know. Lots of girls flaunted their 'pashes,' which I thought silly, even vulgar, and I went to great lengths to conceal my feelings for Leesa.

For breakfast and tea you sat where you pleased, but there was a weekly draw for places for the more formal meals of lunch and supper. It was a sensible way of mixing seniors and juniors, and meant that Brag – who sat with us, but ate different food – talked to a whole range of more or less tongue-tied neighbours in the course of a term. You were supposed to kick off three different topics in the course of a meal, which was a good preparation for dealing with dinner-table bores in later life, and actually she was easy enough to talk to unless her mind was elsewhere. This would become apparent if she started glancing from side to side, her mouth twitching as if trying to reorganise her dentures, then suddenly rapped on her glass. An apprehensive silence would fall because there was no way of telling whether we were about to be blasted for bad table manners (this happened frequently); praised for special effort (rarely) or simply informed of arrangements for the following day. She had a quirky sense of humour and twice I remember her telling us to scream as loudly as we could for the next two minutes.

A long queue would form outside the dining room before lunch on Monday, and one after another we would draw our lunch and supper places from a waste-paper basket full of numbered slips. The odds against sitting next to a particular person were quite long, but during my first term the worst happened and I found myself next to Leesa at lunch for a whole week. Was she, I wonder, puzzled because I turned scarlet and stammered when she spoke to me? Did she think I was either very stupid or very dull?

Over the next two years as we rose up the school in our separate forms, I gradually learned to maintain at least a semblance of composure in her presence, but it was never easy, nor could I understand why she had this peculiar effect on me which no-one else seemed to feel. It certainly wasn't love in any sense I recognised. If anything, I was ashamed of my reaction to her presence – how I was always aware exactly where she was in a room, and the strange way her name jumped out of team-lists as I ran my eye down them.

After taking School Certificate she left and I never saw her again, but when I heard that she had died, unmarried, in her thirties, just as her artistic career was taking off, I felt a powerful pang of loss despite the fact that I had never really known her at all.

Although I missed Taffy and Scot, and sometimes thoughtlessly stretched a hand behind me hoping to make contact with that sharp, loyal nose, boarding school was much more fun than I had expected. Apart from the gaping hole of maths, my various governesses had taught me enough to hold my own in the Upper Fourth, and it was actually a pleasure to have a bit of competition, with fortnightly grades and class placements, and stars awarded for good work.

There were also, inevitably, stripes for bad behaviour, and you had to read out the reason for these to the assembled school at Prayers, and often face a public rocket from Brag. Rudeness, answering back, untidiness and resentment of criticism were my principal failings, and received more or less run of the mill opprobrium, but any hint of cheating or deceit would send Brag ballistic. She would rage at the culprit with really frightening fluency and often reduce her to tears.

I was never on the receiving end of such a tirade and rather enjoyed her volatility. You never quite knew which way she would jump. She had favourites and bugbears, and if you were one of the latter it was all but impossible to change her opinion, which she expressed so loudly and publicly that some girls – some parents too, particularly fathers – admitted to being scared of her.

However, she had a compensating sense of fun. When Brag gave the school a party, which she did every term, she really went to town. In the Spring, St Valentine's Day was celebrated with hearts and flowers and love-bird decorations, plus competitions for love-poems, Valentine cards, and imitation bird-calls. Most people blew on their thumbs to produce owl-like hoots, but a more enterprising approach was taken a particularly plain stout girl called Susie, who brought the house down by seizing her own pendulous jowls and flapping them as she quacked to produce a most realistic imitation of a duck.

On Midsummer Eve we were taken in big buses to the foot of Midsummer Hill, and regaled with a splendid picnic on the summit. On a tree-lined bank above a little dell, we feasted on sausage rolls, cheese triangles, fruit cake and apples washed down with fizzy lemonade, and then sprawled on the grass to watch short original plays put on by each form in turn, with the Worcestershire plain slowly darkening below us until the sun finally set in the west and the magical evening ended with a wild race downhill to the buses.

Best of all the parties was Hallowe'en, which was held in the big hall of the Malvern Winter Gardens, decorated with cut-outs of black cats, skeletons, cauldrons, ghosts and googlies galore.

Dressed in a black cloak and pointed hat, with her long grey locks streaming down her back, Brag would supervise the lighting of candles in jam jars in the Lawnside drive before the whole school set off up the hill in crocodile, with prefects swathed in white sheets running up and down the line making spooky shrieks and trying to blow out the candles.

A couple of weeks earlier, a van-load of large turnips and swedes would have been delivered to the Art Room, and every odd moment since we would have spent carving them into fantastical masks and monsters. These would now have been numbered and arranged on long tables, and it was a great thrill to come in from the wild, dark night to the hall lit with lanterns and candles, and find a card next to your cherished creation showing that it had found favour with the judges.

Paper bags full of party food were handed out by Sixth Formers dressed as witches, and we formed a circle round the hall, each with her jam jar and candle planted before her, and ate watching first the teachers, then the sixth form compete at apple-bobbing in the middle of the room, cheering as the highly competitive English mistress plunged her whole head with its coronet of plaits into the water-tub and emerged, spluttering and gasping, with a Cox's Orange Pippin gripped in her teeth.

Then it was our turn with the apple-bobbing, form by form, after which we moved on to the even more taxing feat of eating a currant bun threaded on a string while kneeling with hands behind our backs. There were rowdy games and fortune-telling organised by the prefects, and finally prize-giving before the head girl made a graceful little speech thanking Brag for the party, and we went out two by two into the lamp-lit streets.

In the bleak post-war years when so many foodstuffs were still rationed, I was always amazed by the lavish scale of these parties, and the care and thought put into planning them. I am sure Brag enjoyed them as much as we did, though she was particularly strict and acerbic in the days that followed them – probably tired out.

Lawnside was not a brainy school. Only one girl from my form made it to Oxford, and one to Trinity College, Dublin: the rest took a single A-Level in their Sixth Form year and then left at the end of the summer term with no plans for further education beyond finishing school in London, Paris or Rome. In fact in some respects the school motto: *Knowledge is no more a fountain sealed* was a bit of a joke, since although the humanities were well taught, science remained a closed book. Either Brag couldn't recruit a suitable teacher or she considered physics, chemistry, botany, biology and all but the most basic mathematical subjects of little use to girls. During the four years I spent there, my form toyed with nothing more in the scientific line than the alimentary canal of the rabbit. We had just begun teeing ourselves up for exciting revelations about its reproductive arrangements when the so-called Science Mistress married and left. She was never replaced.

There was a rapid turnover of geography teachers, too, and several other staff were hardly up to the job of controlling teenagers. We used to mock Miss Twiss for her tortured Northern Irish vowels, pretending we couldn't understand her, and also played up shamefully when an ineffective old lady with a quavering voice tried to maintain order during Needle-work.

'Keep the room *still* !' she would beg as the noise-level rose, and in response we would run to hold on to the door and walls as if in the throes of an earthquake. She was too downtrodden to carry out her threat of complaining to Brag, but we would have been given a merciless tongue-lashing if she had.

Mademoiselle Courcou, aka Mammy, was one long-serving mistress who never had the least difficulty in commanding respect. She was a big, lumbering flat-footed woman who wore a mannish tweed overcoat indoors and out. Her complexion was so pale it might have been dusted with flour, but her eyes were quick-moving, shrewd and cynical. She had heard every excuse known to the schoolgirl mind for handing prep in late, and knew exactly how to deal with it.

Her lessons were as rigidly structured as the Liturgy and she was a great believer in learning by rote. We would leap up as she huffed and puffed into the classroom and dumped her heavy hold-all by her desk.

'*Bonjour, mes enfants, asseyez-vous.*'

'*Je m'assieds. Je suis assise,*' was the correct response and woe betide anyone who varied it.

Every lesson included verbs, dictée, vocabulary, reading French aloud, and ended with the whole class chanting the poem she had chosen for that term, until we could have recited it in our sleep. The result was that when we faced up to School Certificate Oral French, as well as a few minutes of stilted question-and-answer conversation, we could offer the examiners a choice of at least a dozen short poems with absolutely no fear of forgetting a line, so deeply were they embedded in our memories.

For my first two years at Lawnside, Mammy seemed to me a ferocious tyrant, then as I accepted her rules, she gradually morphed into a teacher whose lessons I enjoyed, and finally a friend whose determination to get me through French A-level was if anything greater than my own. She seemed ancient as the hills to a Fourth-former, but younger and livelier – even prepared to let us argue with her – when we were in the Sixth Form.

There were hints of some mysterious sorrow that had blighted her life, forcing her into the slavery of teaching cloth-eared English teenagers how to murder the French language. On her birthday she was given (as we all were) the opportunity to chose the hymn for Prayers, and since the

Tsarist anthem *God the All-Terrible* was her invariable selection, we speculated that this tragedy was connected with the Russian Revolution. Her family exiled? A lover who died? I shall never know.

Yet if Lawnside was decidedly short on intellectual rigour, it was nevertheless an intensely civilised school. I never saw or heard of any girl being bullied, and when seniors had occasion to talk to juniors, they did so in a friendly, reasonable way – there was nothing like the open enmity between age-groups that lent such spice to *Teddy Lester's Schooldays*.

We didn't exactly shine at games, either. Being in the middle of a town, we had no playing-fields near at hand, and had to walk, slouch, run (depending on your state of keenness) a good mile and a half to some roughish pasture behind the Technical College, where there was a rudimentary pavilion and hockey pitch. I was a slow runner, and not a natural team-player. Once I had the ball I tried to hang on to it, deaf to the Captain's shouts of, 'Pass, you nitwit! Pass!' Being left-handed I was comfortable playing left half, a position from which one took part in most of the game without the heroics of bullying or shooting goals. Hockey sticks were longer and heavier in those days, and we wore studded leather boots which could make mincemeat of an opponent's unguarded shins, but as Mummy remarked philosophically it was better to have battered legs than missing front teeth, like so many lacrosse players.

In summer we had the use of four tennis courts belonging to the Manor Park Hotel, but again the school's approach was somewhat lackadaisical. The coach concentrated on girls who showed promise, and left the rest to play pat-ball with minimal instruction. Since we had no special sports clothes – hockey was played in shirts and tunics, gym in shirts and brown knickers, and tennis in the same dresses we wore for class – by Friday the smell of adolescent sweat could be pretty punishing.

Still more uncomfortable were the arrangements for swimming. Across the road from Lawnside Gables, the Sixth Form house, were the municipal swimming baths, open-air, unheated, grubby and unappetising, the changing-cubicles dank and smelly, with slimy slatted floors. Between 7.15 and 8.30am, before the pool was opened to the public, any girl who could not produce a convincing excuse was obliged to swim for quarter of an hour, three times a week.

A more grisly start to a summer morning would be hard to imagine. Roused from your warm bed, you staggered downstairs and, under the gaze of Nurse Painter, aka Nanny P, who looked a dear old softie with pale blue eyes and fluffy grey hair but was actually a good deal tougher than old boots, were forced to choke down a slice of bread and marge which had been cut the night before and was curling at the edges, very difficult to swallow. It was an article of faith with Nanny P that a girl who swam without eating would sink like a stone, and she refused to let anyone past the door until she had finished chewing.

Across the garden, perhaps with a minor diversion to snatch a few ripe gooseberries off a bush, across the road, and in through the creaky door to where the chilly heavily-chlorinated rectangle of water awaited the first brave soul's honeypot jump. It was far too cold to linger on the concrete surround. The only hope was to immense oneself quickly and swim up and down as fast as possible until released by the merciful order to come out.

My bathing dress was a dark-green wool one-piece, on the close-fitting side and difficult to stretch far enough to get the straps over my shoulders. It was an even worse struggle to get out of it in the dank, dark changing-room without tramping on discarded and no doubt verruca-infested bits of band-aid.

I had never swum in a heated pool – up till now total immersion had been either in the Wye, the tooth-chattering sea at Borth, or a neighbour's green and slimy pool at Much Hadham – so I already looked on bathing as an ordeal rather than a pleasure, and found conditions at Lawnside much as I expected. For girls who had learned to swim in sunnier climes, though, the municipal baths at daybreak were a horrid shock. Jenny and Gill, identical twins who had grown up in India, knocked spots off everyone else with their aquatic skills and always won the Diving Cup, but even they looked pinched and grey by the end of the Swimming Sports and when, after an outbreak of polio at Eton, Brag told us that she was with great reluctance cancelling swimming for the rest of the term, I for one sent up a silent cheer.

This announcement, like others of its kind, was made during 'Prayers,' as the morning assembly was called, though so much school business had to be crammed into the twenty-odd minutes between breakfast and our first lessons of the day that unless a girl was sick unto death or a major calamity had befallen the nation, precious little actual praying took place in the big hall at Lawnside Grove, the only space large enough to seat both senior school and The Lodge, as the junior house was known.

When the prefects had everyone seated to their satisfaction – tiddlers in front, Sixth Form at the back – and shushed us to silence, Brag and the staff would stalk on to the dais, bid us good morning, and call out the name of any girl whose birthday it was. Up you would stand, shuffle along the row and approach the dais, to be presented with a tissue-wrapped, ribbon-tied book, a card, and a white box containing a very decent birthday cake with your name iced on it, big enough for the whole form to have a slice. Nor did the special treatment stop there. You were also allowed to choose the day's hymn, and to go up the town that afternoon with your special friend to buy sweets.

I turned twelve just a few days after term started and, knowing myself the veriest squit in the school hierarchy, felt too shy to mention my birthday, so was astonished when Brag called out my name. I couldn't think how she knew. Invited to choose the hymn, I hastily opted for the all-time Barstow family favourite, *Guide Me, O Thou Great Redeemer*, and got a much less agreeable jolt when Miss Parke, at the piano, struck up *the wrong tune*. I was unaware that any tune other than Cwm Rhondda even existed. Nor did the other girls seem to know the words. Hot with embarrassment, I listened to them stumble and mouth through all three verses and decided there and then to choose something really hackneyed next year.

A few brisk prayers came next on the agenda, followed by the daily two-minute Newsflash, presented by each girl in the school in turn and, I seem to remember, in alphabetical order. This was our single regular brush with current events and window on the outside world, and had to be recited from memory, which some girls found easier than others. After listening, roughbook in hand, to three consecutive BBC bulletins on Nanny P's wireless – at 6pm the previous night, then 7am and 8am, you scribbled a précis of three or four stories that made the headlines, memorised it as best you could and, with heart thumping fit to choke you, marched up to the front of the hall and gabbled it out to the assembled throng.

A succinct account, clearly delivered, might well be rewarded with a star from the dais, rather like being knighted on the battlefield. I remember being thus honoured when I memorised a story about the exiled king of Nepal, sonorously repeating his full title Maharajadirajah Tribuvana Bir Bikram Shah, which made everyone laugh; but the great thing was that no matter how badly you did your Newsflash, no-one ever scoffed since they knew full well their turn was in the pipeline this term or next, and the relief when the ordeal was over made one quite light-headed.

Then Miss Parke would crash into the opening chords of some stirring march – Wagner's *Meistersingers* was reserved for Speech Day and Prize-giving at the Winter Gardens – and out we would file, row by row, to begin the day's work.

Gwendolyn Parke was Brag's special friend, and in the holidays they shared a cottage somewhere up in the Malvern Hills, whose location they kept deliberately vague. She was a concert-standard pianist, and took only the most musical girls as pupils, while the rest of us shared a series of run-of-the-mill music teachers who never, poor ladies, managed to get me beyond a Pass at Grade 2 with a thumping finger-stumbling rendition of *Gathering Peascods* after which, to everyone's relief, Mummy agreed that I had no talent for the piano and let me give it up.

Miss Parke's star pupil was a very pretty and gifted girl one form up from me. She was called Diana – known as Tiddly because she was tiny – had fair bubbly curls clustering all over her head and was living proof of the power of ante-natal suggestion. Her mother told mine that although she and her husband were completely unmusical, she had so longed for a daughter who could play the piano that she had spent her entire pregnancy listening to Mozart, morning noon and night and, lo and behold, when Tiddly was born, she was soon revealed as a musical prodigy.

She had no inhibitions about performing, and was often put on parade to show prospective parents the quality of Lawnside's music, her fingers fairly flying over the keys of the grand piano on which Elgar himself had once played in Brag's drawing-room while the 'Cook's Tour' – as such visitors were known – balanced tea-cups on their knees and murmured appreciation. Sometimes she even deputised for Miss Parke at Prayers, an honour none of the other music teachers were granted.

Choral singing was another art-form dear to Brag's heart. As a child she had known not only Elgar but several of the friends represented in his *Enigma Variations*, and Sir Ivor Atkins, one of the last survivors of that circle, still came weekly to teach Lawnside's Special Singers, as the choir was known. (He was pretty old and doddery by then and I am sorry to say that irreverent schoolgirls that we were, we mocked his stiff gait and shushing Churchillian speech, and referred to him as 'Saliva Napkin').

It was a very different matter when his place was taken by the brilliant young organist at Worcester Cathedral, David Willcocks. Not only young and brilliant, either, but also handsome, friendly, full of jokes and charm. There was a concerted gasp from a hundred-odd adolescent female throats when he strolled into the Hall in Brag's wake, sat down at the Piano-Which-Elgar-Played (which the school handymen had trundled across the road from Brag's drawing-room in his honour), whizzed up and down the keyboard a few times in sheer exuberance, then started putting us through a series of musical exercises before launching into the setting of the Magnificat which we had learnt with Sir Ivor the previous term.

How we sang! How we tried to catch his eye and pitch our voices ever louder in the hope of making an impression! More work was done in a single lesson than poor Sir Ivor had managed to get through in a whole term, and there was a spate of applications to join the Special Singers and get the chance of singing lessons at even closer quarters.

Pretty soon he began coaching us to take part in the Cheltenham Festival of Music, which involved a lot of intensive practice, lesson-missing and hair-washing in order to do the school credit. With our blue summer dresses starched so stiff they could practically stand by themselves, we were bussed into Cheltenham to perform in the Regency Town Hall, and after a fearful battle with Westonbirt and St Mary's, Ascot, scraped second place in the Schoolgirl Choir class with two set-pieces chosen by the judging panel, followed by Handel's aria *O Had I Jubal's Lyre*, full of long, fast, showy runs that left us gasping for breath.

Brag was delighted, and rewarded the whole choir with the unheard-of double treat of a shopping trip up the town on Saturday afternoon, plus permission to sit in the chancel of Malvern Abbey for Matins on Sunday. The latter was usually a privilege accorded to those who accumulated more than six stars in a single week, but it was a bit of a poisoned chalice as far as I was concerned, because under the eyes of the whole congregation as well as the Abbey's regular choir it was impossible to read the paperback thriller I had concealed between the hollowed-out covers of a Prayer Book.

I had – and still have – a problem with long sermons. It seems so unfair to subject people who have come to church (thereby making a large hole in their precious Sunday) to a long harangue about their supposed faults and wickedness without giving them the chance to speak up and refute the charges. I never found it easy to accept criticism with good grace – a recurrent theme in my Behaviour reports – being inclined to sulk or answer back, but those were personal, recognisable faults and, however unwelcome, I would know in my heart the criticism was justified. The priest in the pulpit, on the contrary, couldn't possibly know whether or not his congregation deserved his strictures, and I would sit in the pew either grinding my teeth and mentally refuting his argument, or staring around at the memorial tablets trying to see how many words I could make out of a single name.

The Rev. Ronald B. Lunt, though a learned and kind man as we later discovered during his Confirmation Classes, was extremely verbose and never said a thing once if he could say it three times. I longed to slam my prayer book shut the moment he went over the statutory eleven minutes and say, 'Amen!' very loudly, as Sir Roger de Coverley used to.

In Lent he stretched services almost beyond endurance, and we tried every trick in the book to make ourselves come over faint, so that we could be taken home early by a prefect and made to lie down for an hour. Stuffing the soles of your shoes with blotting-paper was said to be infallible, but never worked for me; while holding my breath while the second-hand of my watch made a complete circuit merely brought on a fit of coughing.

However there was one panacea for boredom in church that never failed me, for it was only when we were wearing our smart overcoats that I had the chance to locate and secretly crinkle the crisp white £5 note which Mummy had slipped between the right-hand pocket flap and its lining, and stitched in place. 'Mad-money,' she called it, meaning that if I ever felt mad (in the American sense, i.e. angry) enough to want to bolt home from school, I should have the wherewithal to buy a train ticket to Hereford and a taxi back to the Fforest.

It was a great comfort to know it was there, and when the coat passed on to Olivia and then Miranda they, too, were told where to find it in case of emergency. Only at the last minute before the trusty garment was handed over to Lawnside's Second-Hand Uniform cupboard when Miranda grew out of it did she remember to take the note from its hiding-place and put it to more conventional use.

Another big name in Brag's pantheon was that of Sir Barry Jackson, who had founded the Birmingham Repertory Theatre. He had been part of the charmed circle which included Elgar and Bernard Shaw, and had often stayed at Lawnside, besides playing a large part in establishing the Shakespeare Memorial Theatre at Stratford-on-Avon. Several times a year we were given the opportunity to go by bus to this huge, strangely barrack-like building, to picnic on the river-bank and attend a matinee by the Royal Shakespeare Company, where so many famous actors began their careers. Then, as now, producers loved to shock, and some of the scenes got pretty steamy. I remember seeing Brag lean sideways to look anxiously along the row of innocent, ignorant schoolgirls as Antony and Cleopatra rolled about semi-naked on a large sofa, breathing out in hoarse, lascivious gasps the lines which we had plodded through in wooden monotones in English Lit.

There was always a rush to bag the back seat of the bus for the long drive back to school, but for me the combination of exhaust and exhaustion was a sure trigger for motion sickness. Quite suddenly I would feel hot all over, then icy cold and, before I could ask the teacher in charge to stop the bus, would project the remains of several meals over my unlucky seat-mates.

We were allowed three exeats or home visits per term, and since my parents lived too far away to make this feasible on still-rationed petrol, from time to time other girls would kindly ask me to go with them, and meet their ponies and dogs and brothers and sisters, and feast on Sunday roasts and delicious rich cakes which made the return journey something of an ordeal. Twice I disgraced myself by throwing up over the beautiful leather upholstery of Mr Pugh's treasured Bristol sports car and frankly it is something of a miracle that after the first episode I was invited a second time.

There wasn't much for visiting parents to do in Malvern on a Sunday, and since they were both happy and busy at home Mummy and Daddy were reluctant to waste such a major part of the weekend hanging around the over-heated Mount Pleasant Hotel making stilted conversation with their schoolgirl daughters, for by this time Olivia had joined me at Lawnside, though the three-year age gap meant we saw very little of one another. But the occasion of my Confirmation was a three-line whip they could not escape. A calf-length white dress was obligatory but difficult to find in Wales, and the one Mummy eventually bought was a twee little number in floppy crepe, horribly expensive, and impossible to wear in any other circumstances. I felt a fool in it, and the moment the confirmation service was over, thankfully changed into the comfortable red wool dress I wore as 'mufti,' after tea, whereupon family spirits revived as we all cast piety aside and dashed off to the cinema to catch the first sitting of *The Dam-Busters*.

Verse-speaking exams were mandatory all the way up the school. Though I had no difficulty in memorising the poems set by the Guildhall School of Music and Drama, when it came to delivering them to stony-faced examiners my harsh, rather nasal tones and plummy accent never impressed them enough to award me the coveted Distinction that my best friend Jane achieved in every grade. With her dark, dramatic looks and beautiful speaking voice she was, for me, a source of constant admiration bordering on envy, and though I knew very well I could never rival her effortless stage presence, where she led I usually tried to follow.

On one occasion, this was to the Cheltenham Literary Festival. A new Drama teacher asked for volunteers to compete in the class for Shakespeare duologues, and Jane and I and a stage-struck, curly-headed form-mate called Sue were duly entered in the schools' section of the Spring festival and set to learning our lines. Mrs Barraclough listened to us reading, then directed us to suitable short scenes. Jane chose Cleopatra's dream of Antony; Sue opted for Juliet immured in the tomb, and I rather unimaginatively followed suit with another scene from Romeo and Juliet, this time between Juliet and her Nurse – a poor choice since I entirely lacked the mercurial grace necessary to play Juliet, and was not helped by the lines which, like most of Shakespeare's comic passages, were woefully unfunny.

Mrs Barraclough toiled like the trouper she was to bring us up to standard. She had pasty, rubbery features and twinkling slits of eyes. Though heftily built, she concealed her corpulence in flowing dark dresses swathed with shawls, and could move about the stage with surprisingly speed and agility. She had, we learned, once danced in the *corps de ballet*. When she turned to drama coaching, her most famous pupil had been the comedienne Diana Dors, whom she had transformed from a mousy teenager into the world famous pneumatic Blonde Bombshell, Britain's answer to Marilyn Monroe.

The competition was held in a hall which seemed to me enormous, with rows and rows of empty chairs broken only by the three-strong panel of judges at centre front, with the couple of dozen schoolgirl competitors crowded humbly at the back.

We were called to the stage in alphabetical order, and being a B, I wasn't given long to develop stage-fright. Nor was I particularly worried, having known myself outclassed from the moment the first budding Beatrice embarked on her scene, and I gave my usual undistinguished performance, lumbering ridiculously from side to side speaking to empty air as I played the alternate parts, and getting only one laugh – unfortunately unscripted – when I plumped on to the chair which was my sole prop and all but missed it. (This gaffe was rewarded with the comment: *The candidate must learn to sit down with more grace and control,* which my parents found much funnier than I did.)

Back in my seat, glad it was over, I enjoyed watching the other contestants. Some were impressive, but when Jane took the stage it was plain to us all that she was in another league. She drifted a couple of steps towards the footlights, gazed into infinity, and as she began in her low, musical voice, '*I dreamed there was an emperor, Antony...*' the row of judges gave a little purr of content and relaxed in their seats, recognising a star.

She won by a distance, to her own apparent bemusement. Never before or since have I heard that speech delivered with more drama, dignity and pathos but Jane had no ambition for a stage career and it was Sue who later took to the boards.

As we inched our way up the school, Priscilla, whose powerful brain was beginning to flex its muscles, Jane, the good all-rounder, and I rotated top marks in whichever form we happened to be. I was usually second or third, seldom achieving first place, partly because of my Achilles heel in maths, and partly because I hated to be seen to try hard at anything. This was unfortunately part of the Lawnside ethos of the time. It was OK to win through natural brilliance but very infra dig to do it by making an effort – an attitude that led to endless complications, denials, and studying by torchlight under the bedclothes.

Our passage through the Fifth Form was scarred in traditional fashion with scandals and naughtiness, punishments and recriminations. Everything we did seemed to get us into trouble, whether it was walking on the hills and getting back late, sitting on radiators (guaranteed to give us piles), breaking things, losing things, forgetting things – there was no good in us. My 'attitude' was constantly criticised but I couldn't see what was wrong with it. Nor did I understand why Brag flew into a truly terrifying rage when two girls – yes, Leesa was one of them – were found in the same bed.

The whole house was summoned from the dormitories to sit on the stairs and listen to a lengthy harangue about their wicked behaviour and why it must never, ever happen again, but Brag didn't actually tell us why not and unless you happened to have heard of lesbians, *The Well of Loneliness* and related matters (which none of us had) the whole tirade was thoroughly puzzling.

Worrying, too, since it meant it would now be more dangerous than ever to creep into bed with Sally, who slept next door to me, to listen to *Saturday Night Theatre* on her tiny wireless, turned very low. This was a weekly treat I much enjoyed and increased my annoyance with Brag for making such a fuss about nothing.

Easter happened to be unusually early that year, and feeling ourselves hard done by because of spending it at school, we melted a lot of choco-late bars on the single form-room radiator, meaning to pour the resulting mess into the shells of our breakfast boiled eggs. Unfortunately several slipped between the radiator and the wall and began to drip slowly on to the floor.

We wiped up the spreading pool as best we could, but the choco-late burned on to the radiator bars was impossible to get at. The cleaner complained to our house mistress, a spiky, chain-smoking ex-police-woman called Mrs Moore, and she in turn sent us for a bollocking in Brag's study, an over-heated den dominated by a huge picture of St Sebas-tian looking like an agonised pin-cushion with arrows protruding from every limb, and full of small tables loaded with knick-knacks. You could hardly move without knocking something over, which did nothing to increase our confidence and was, I think, a deliberate weapon employed by Brag to keep pupils in their place.

Furious with Mrs Moore for putting us on the spot, we consulted Sue's *Guerrilla's Handbook* (such a curious publication to be doing the rounds in a girls' boarding school) for ways to disable the smart little car she kept in the garage outside the classrooms, and found what seemed to be a perfect method, requiring no special mechanical knowledge. By putting sugar in the tank, we could block up the filter and prevent petrol reaching the engine – or so the author claimed. Like butter, sugar was still rationed, and we each collected our personal allowance before breakfast and tea, carefully hoarding it through six days and mashing up the remains into a delicious extravagant spread to eat neat on the seventh when the pots were due to be refilled.

All those who had smarted under the lash of Brag's tongue were eager to contribute sugar to the fund, and there must have been well over a pound in the bag that Sally, Sue and I carried into the garage half an hour after lights out, after making sure that Mrs Moore was in her sitting room, puffing smoke over our clean clothes as she checked the laundry lists and listening to the late night news. Without some kind of funnel, however, it was difficult to introduce sugar into the petrol tank, and a good deal got spilt on the garage floor as we tipped it in, replaced the cap, and tiptoed away.

Breathlessly we waited at the windows next day as Mrs Moore, brightly lipsticked and high-heeled, got into her car ready for her day off. The engine started perfectly. With growing chagrin we watched her reverse smartly out of the garage and turn in a scrunching circle before driving out of the Lodge gates. No choke, not so much as a hiccough from the car.

'Must have been the wrong sort of sugar,' Sue suggested lamely. We regretted the waste of our rations and felt very much let down.

Our attempt to make cherry wine in the summer wasn't much more successful. After half-term, which had been timed to coincide with the Fourth of June at Eton because so many girls had brothers there, I salvaged from our al-fresco picnic two big screw-top bottles that had contained Bulmer's Cider. These we crammed with carefully-stoned cherries, added water and sugar, and screwed the tops on tight.

Unsure how long it would take the wine to develop into the delicious alcoholic brew we needed for our end-of-term midnight feast, I hid the bottles under an upturned waste-paper basket and forgot about them until about a fortnight later, when I walked into our form-room to collect books from my desk and found everyone staring in consternation at shards of thick brown glass on the lino. In the night the bottles had exploded, showering the walls and ceiling with pinkish gunge, but in this instance Mrs Moore was thoroughly supportive, saying it was an interesting experiment and helping us clear up the mess – just one more proof that it was impossible to know how adults would react in any situation.

I don't know how Mummy managed to persuade Brag to let me keep my hamster at school that year, since all pets were banned, but in Mr Ham's case she made an exception and he spent much of his time that winter and spring running round my waist between my shirt and tunic, firmly supported by the yellow girdle which gave even the most lissom schoolgirl figure a cottage-loaf outline, and occasionally popping his head with its bright buttons of eyes out for a breath of air.

Apart from shredding the kipper end of my school tie for nesting material, he behaved very well, though I spent one night in tortures of guilt and anxiety when I let him stray too near the steps leading up to The Grove, and he vanished into a crack between the stones.

It was a sunny afternoon and several of us were sprawling on the grass and chatting under the cool umbrella of the mulberry tree after tea, while Mr Ham ran about between us taking his daily outdoor exercise, and I didn't actually see him pop into the unnoticed hole, but Zinnia suddenly gasped, 'Look out!' and when I looked round, he was gone. Everyone blamed everyone else and I was in despair. Someone ran and fetched a torch, but you could only see a couple of inches into the crack, and there was no way of telling how far he had gone.

The bell rang for prep and we had to leave him, but I persuaded Nanny P, who was then our house mistress, to let me go out again to search for him between supper and bedtime. Back and forth I went, up and down the steps, looking for a sleek golden ball curled up in the tufts of grass that grew in the cracks, but it was hopeless. At last I gave up, certain that he had gone for ever, and in what seemed an entirely futile gesture left his open cage at the foot of the steps where he had last been seen.

I prayed, everyone in the dorm prayed, the whole house fairly pulsated with prayers for Mr Ham's return… and the miracle happened. When I looked into the sleeping compartment of his cage early next morning, there he was, tightly curled, exhausted by his nocturnal exertions. It was a copybook example of divine intercession that impressed me deeply.

In the School Certificate form, the tempo of work gathered pace and we were constantly nagged to revise by our teachers. Mammy was particularly gloomy about our prospects.

'Eef you do not know ze sobjonctive, *zair ees no 'ope for you!*' she would declare in doom-laden tones.

Relying on memory, as usual, I committed various algebraic formulae and geometric theorems to heart, but since I didn't properly understand Pythagoras, let alone anything more complicated, the chance of getting through O-level Maths seemed daily more remote. In other subjects I felt confident enough, because although being aware of the danger of hubris I joined in the fashionable complaints about the terrors of exams, in fact I enjoyed them. It made one feel proud and important to file out of prayers early, like gladiators marching to their doom, while everyone murmured, 'Good luck, good luck!' sounding just like a flock of hens.

Then the brisk, preoccupied walk to the big, flint-faced exam hall near the Abbey, eyeing groups of girls from other schools as we were ushered to our well-separated desks, each provided with a glass of water, a sheaf of paper, pens, blotting-paper, all fresh and crisp and enticing, while the invigilator stalked round dispensing the Oxford and Cambridge exam-board's small printed paper face down on each desk before retiring to her rostrum, barking out a few last instructions and warnings, then saying portentously, '*You may now turn over your papers!*'

When one emerged into the sunlight after concentrating furiously and writing frenziedly for one or two hours, one felt at first dazed and then delirious with excitement and relief. In a gabbling cacophony of giggles, moans and shrieks, the disorderly crocodile would tumble back downhill to school, probably attracting a few sharp remarks from Brag if she happened to notice, though in general she turned a blind eye to most misdemeanours committed by those engaged in exams.

Sure enough, I failed O-level maths that term, and again the following spring, despite Mrs Brown the nice maths mistress' heroic efforts to bring me up to scratch with extra coaching, after which my parents agreed there was no further point in flogging a dead horse and, to my great relief, let the matter rest.

Towards the end of my second term in the Sixth Form, I began to wonder why Brag had not yet suggested that I should become a prefect. Could she have forgotten? Prefects wore no distinguishing badge and were not given much in the way of special privileges, but nevertheless it was regarded as an honour to be invited to join their ranks and by this time most of my Sixth Form contemporaries and even a few notably worthy characters from the School Certificates had been quietly elevated. So why hadn't I?

It wasn't the kind of thing one could discuss with anyone else. Guiltily I searched my conscience but couldn't think of any particular wickedness. In fact, I had been making quite an effort to be good since arriving in the top form. It was a pity no-one seemed to have noticed. Brag liked me, I was sure of it. Had I, perhaps, a secret enemy in the Staff Room, that smoke-filled retreat – forbidden territory even to the Head Girl – where our teachers congregated to mark homework, let down their hair and blackguard their charges to their hearts' content?

Or could this mysterious failure to raise me to the ranks of the great and good be connected with those long-running complaints about my 'attitude' that still dogged my school reports? Recent phrases nagged at me. *Phyllida must develop more maturity and stability of character... she has powers of leadership but could make better use of them... I hope she will be a more positive influence next term... occasionally evades her duty... her manner has been casual of late... she should lead courageously rather than being led... take matters more seriously... individualistic attitude tends to make her unco-operative...* Oh, that wretched unpinnable-down 'attitude'! I couldn't see how to change what was essentially part of my make-up, but recognised that these were hardly ringing endorsements of my suitability for prefectship. Most of my friends already belonged to this select band, and Jane was also Captain of Games. Despite my inclination to mock authority and resist any manifestation of bossiness, I began to feel undervalued and left out.

Prefect or not, I still had access to the Sixth Form study, a small cluttered room under the stairs of The Grove, with a mains-powered wireless and comfortably sagging armchairs and sofa on which we rolled about, in paroxysms of laughter, at *Hancock's Half Hour* and *Take It From Here*, so much funnier in my view than *The Goon Show*, which reduced Gerry and David to the same state.

Here, too, amid gales of giggles, we minutely evaluated the looks, charm, intelligence or lack of it of our partners from Malvern Boys' College, with whom we were to give a display of Folk Dancing at the Winter Gardens towards the end of the summer term. It wasn't quite Morris Dancing – no bells – but not far off it, and I don't know how much pressure had been applied to the dozen or so boys detailed to prance and cavort with us once a week on the grass tennis court at the bottom of Lawnside garden, though possibly the lure of actually touching the hands of real live girls had overcome their natural reluctance to make fools of themselves.

Apart from David Willcocks and Sarge, who took Gym, Lawnside had no male teachers, and boys were generally regarded with curiosity and suspicion, alien creatures, possibly dangerous, to be treated with extreme caution. Brag used to tell us how lucky we were to have so much more freedom than the school's first pupils, who had to be escorted from room to room, and describe with more than a hint of approval how the headmistress would ride a white pony to church at the head of the school crocodile, and whenever they passed a man or boy she would hold up her hand and avert her head – a signal for all the young ladies to do likewise, so the fact that she had agreed to mixed-sex dancing was a bit of a turn-up for the books, and we were all keen to participate.

No question of choosing our own partners, of course. We were paired off briskly in height order by Miss Sherwood, who had an Egyptian profile and strong, thick black hair cut in a square fringe across her forehead. Her speciality was Greek dancing as pioneered by Isadora Duncan, whose pupil she had been, and instructing heavy-footed lads and lasses how to lumber their way through country dances was, she made clear, not quite her style. However, it would have been considered even more infra dig by Miss Parsons, the grandest of our dancing teachers, who wore a turban and flowing sleeveless robes, an unfortunate choice of garb that displayed more than was advisable of her sagging, crepey underarms, and was summoned over from Cheltenham only to solve the trickiest bits of choreography in the Prize-giving Day plays which involved every girl in the school.

Even at that age I recognised her skill in manipulating and balancing the large, unwieldy cast on those occasions, arranging entrances and exits and showing us just how to back up the principal players without distracting attention from them. She never seemed to shout, yet her voice was audible all over the garden, unlike poor Miss Sherwood, who was often quite hoarse by the end of a rehearsal.

Fortune smiled on me in the country dancing: to general jealousy I was allocated dark, hawk-featured Dai, whom everyone's feminine instinct had instantly identified as the best-looking of the bunch, which made me the target of much enjoyable teasing and innuendo.

'Never say Die,' people would whisper in my ear as we skipped and gallumphed about the smooth mown grass, linking arms and weaving chains to Miss Sherwood's orders. (It happened to be the name of that year's Derby winner.) 'He's Dai-ing for love of you,' and other such nonsense.

Good-looking he may have been, but his conversation was so banal as to be virtually non-existent. I suppose those poor boys had been so savagely browbeaten into good behaviour, so threatened with dire consequences if they stepped out of line, that they hardly dared speak. Until, that was, their headmaster and our headmistress decided to celebrate the success of the joint endeavour with an end-of-term party which I described in a breathless letter home.

> *'Last night we had the dancing with the Boys' College and although it was wet so we could not have it on the lawn here, and it had to take place in the College gym, it was a great success. We were the hostesses although they were on their own ground as it was supposed to be Lawnside's dance, so Brag was in her element, dancing with the headmaster, arranging the refreshments (and jolly good they were, strawberries and cream, sausage rolls, ice creams and meringues and samwiches) and generally carrying on.*
>
> *The bishop of Portsmouth, who is very keen on country dancing, said that he would turn up in his kilt, so I was looking forward to seeing if he would wear his gaiters as well. Unfortunately he funked it at the last moment and only came in ordinary clothes. He behaved ordinarily, too, except for one moment when he knelt down and started to say his prayers out loud: I believe he is a bit of an eccentric.*
>
> *There was lots to eat but as the seventh hell in Dante's Inferno would have seemed like a deep freeze beside the atmosphere in that gym, I did not get very hungry in spite of all the energetic dances, and as no-one else did either. Priscilla – who is a provident sort of girl – put all the food she could find into a large box, covered it with newspaper, and gave it to me to smuggle out to Lawnside under my coat... No doubt the usual flood of correspondence between the two schools will now begin again. We have to censor it and stop them from posting letters illegally, and this is a very boring job.'*

That 'we' reflected my new status. At the eleventh hour of the eleventh month – or, more accurately, in the second half of my last term – the tap on the shoulder had finally come and I finished my schooldays as a prefect. The words Serious and Responsible which I had avoided and mocked for so long suddenly seemed to fit me like a glove, and I revelled in the opportunity to boss others around and censor their love-letters.

Not that the censorship was very effective. Once the ice had been broken between us and the Boys' Coll, inter-school fraternisation took hold like wildfire. Rather to my disappointment, Dai was far too much of a goody-goody to follow up our dance-floor relationship, and I heard never another peep from him, but it was generally agreed that luscious, lollipop-eyed Rosemary had overstepped the mark by several yards when she was surprised in the coal-hole, sitting on the Head Boy's knee, and there were other small scandals and declarations of undying love to be stamped on by Brag before single-sex calm was restored at Lawnside.

'*We say goodbye to Phyllida with real regret... I only wish she could be Lawnside's Head Girl next term,*' declared Brag on my final report, which delighted my parents and made me both pleased and proud, though I have always wondered if she wrote the last words with her fingers crossed.

CHAPTER SIX

Farm Life

MEANTIME, BACK AT the Fforest, matters had not been standing still while I was preoccupied with school. For a start, the family had expanded. It seems incredible now that I should have failed to notice during our summer camp in the spinney in 1949 that Mummy was going to have another baby. I suppose she never mentioned it or thought I already knew, but I was extremely unobservant so it was a great surprise to me when, during the Christmas holidays, my brother George was born.

Being fourteen years younger than Gerry, and my junior by twelve years, all his needs and pastimes were out of step with ours and we regarded this new addition to the family with a certain detachment, like a toy, to be played with and then put away in his box while we got on with our busy lives. I have no doubt that this rather casual treatment contributed to his extreme adaptability and equable nature in later life, so different from me and Gerry who had been brought up to consider ourselves the hubs of the universe and reacted badly when we discovered we were nothing of the kind.

George – and to a lesser degree Miranda, then four – was expected to fit in with everyone else's arrangements without much consideration paid to his own wishes. Now Mummy had the farm she had always wanted, she was determined to make a go of it, and George was brought up a proper farmer's child, lugged here and there in his Moses basket, kept up late, dumped in odd corners and fed at odd times. He had a few narrow squeaks, as when he crawled into the bull-pen and was spotted by the tractor-driver heading for the manger, with old Heygrove, the Hereford bull, eyeing him suspiciously. He was knocked flying by a skittish foal, bitten by a jealous bitch when he tried to pick up a puppy, and spent so long aboard the tractor that by the age of six or seven he could probably have driven it.

Soon after George's birth we left Much Hadham for good and squashed into the side of Fforest Farm not occupied by the new bailiff, Ron Weale – compact and ruddy, with bright blue eyes and an open, direct manner – his slight, dark, elfin-faced wife, Milly, and their small daughter, Sylvia. As a family, they were friendly and accommodating, a different kettle of fish from the Wattses, but even so we were obliged to live at closer quarters both indoor and out than was comfortable for either side.

Though Daddy had taken over the big fourth-floor flat in Seymour Place which Grandfather had rented from the Prudential, and lived there during the week, commuting to his office in New Square, Lincoln's Inn, and Gerry and I were at boarding school in term-time, during the holidays Fforest Farm was extremely crowded. Gerry's bedroom – known as 'Arctic' – was right at the top of the house, and any helper, au pair, or temporary cook would be billeted in 'Antarctic,' just across the landing, next to the ever-gurgling water-tank.

A steep flight of stairs led down to George's tiny nursery, The Slot, next door to the room Miranda and I shared, with Olivia just through the wall in another narrow bedroom. A half-landing and more stairs separated us from the only bathroom and a loo so small that although one entire wall was papered with a map of England, you became familiar only with the counties at your own eye level whether seated or standing, since it was impossible to step back far enough to examine anything higher up. I got to know the geography of mid-Wales, Gloucestershire and the Home Counties, and points east as far as Norfolk pretty intimately, but anything north of Yorkshire was *terra incognita*.

A new bedroom had been added for our parents, icy cold because it lacked the thick stone walls of the farmhouse proper, but although they must have been very conscious of bathroom and loo doors constantly banging, at least they were out of earshot of the rest of us, who could all hear one another through the thin internal walls.

On the ground floor, three small rooms had been knocked into one to give a big, if oddly shaped, open-plan hall, living-room and dining area, with a small appendix just big enough to take an upright piano. Behind the little Victorian grate lurked an open fireplace, whose massive cut stones had probably been salvaged from the original castle by thrifty Welsh builders. The chimney was so wide you could see the sky from the bottom, and it took a great deal of tinkering with hoods and draught-holes to make it draw satisfactorily. The first year we were regularly kippered and smoke filtered up through the bedroom floor in a choking fog, but when at last the proper balance was established the fire looked very handsome and threw out a good heat – in that room, at least.

The rest of the house was unbelievably chilly, especially since the hot-water arrangements were both erratic and inadequate. A gas-fired geyser over the bath blew out clouds of steam as it released a thin trickle of tepid water, so you were usually colder after bathing than before, and had then to face the freezing dash back down one flight of steps and up another to regain your bedroom, lit only in those early, pre-electricity days by a smoky lamp or a couple of candles.

Filling the lamps was a chore nobody enjoyed, and we took it in turns. The paraffin was stored, along with anthracite nuts for the Aga, in a small hut adjoining the cow-shed. Dark, dirty, and smelling of oil, it was just tolerable in the daylight, but since all too often I forgot it was my turn until dusk had fallen, I would have to struggle with funnels and fuel-tins in the half-dark, inevitably slopping paraffin over and sometimes into my gumboots, as well as getting my hands filthy from the soot adhering to the lamp. Downstairs we used gently-hissing Tilley pressure-lamps, whose light was adequate to read by, but finishing a book in bed was out of the question.

The solid-fuel Aga was a capricious brute, too. You stoked it by lugging in a hod of anthracite which you set on the stone flags in order to use both hands to hook a kind of poker into the handle of the little solid round stopper in the middle of the hotplate, and lever it up. Then, holding your breath against the smoky fumes, you had to pour the anthracite into the open hole (which sent a cloud of black grit over every nearby surface), judge precisely how much fuel would keep the beast fed overnight without choking it, and quickly clap the stopper back in place before your lungs collapsed.

Finally, you had to riddle, for riddling was the key to successful Aga management. There was a little lever hidden by a door at floor level, and by pulling this from side to side you shook fine grey ash from the bottom of the fire-basket into the shovel-shaped tray below. When glowing cinders began to fall into the ash-tray, you had to pull it out and, again holding your breath, carry it outside and having checked the direction of the wind, fling it in a wide arc over the bank of the moat. It was a gritty, nail-breaking business, best done in gloves, and left you with a throat full of fumes.

Even with the greatest care, it was all too easy to let the Aga go out, and come down next morning to a bleak cold kitchen smelling of grease and soot. I don't know how Mummy managed to keep us all fed in such unpromising surroundings, nor can I remember the food we ate at a single meal. She was a dashing, inventive cook, but became bored by the relentless round of breakfast, lunch, tea and supper, and hurried through them as quickly as possible. Children who dawdled over their food tested her patience.

'Salt-pepper-mustard down my end!' she would say briskly as she sat down after serving us all. Then, clearing her plate while we were still munching, she would pick up the telephone and make a series of quick calls to fill the time before the second course. Having done all the cooking, she reckoned that someone else could deal with the aftermath, and would filter away to do something more important the moment she left the table.

Washing-up, however, was an enjoyable ritual, particularly after supper, when Daddy or Gerry would bag pole position at the sink, and kick off a singsong in which everyone joined.

I'm Nausea Bagwashio, Soapsuds I sloshio! Daddy's voice would boom to the tune of *La Donna e mobile* as he swished up a mountain of foam.

Give me your vestio, I'll do the restio.
Why grow so weary, when for ten lire
I'll be your wife and a mother as well to you
Be your wife, dear, be your wife, dear,
And a mother as well to you!

Then, mournfully:
Niente mangario, niente bovario,
O, niente vino! Niente ice-creamo!
Niente cigaretti, niente spaghetti,
'Cos the old Tedeschi have taken 'em all away!

And we would all chorus:
The Tedeschi, the Tedeschi, have taken 'em all away!
I'm Nausea Bagwashio, I hate the Boschio,
Their passions I freezes, by giving them diseases...

Belatedly he would remember the younger children's innocent ears. 'Come on, someone else choose a song.'

Off we would go: sea shanties, Elizabethan love-songs, folk, soul, Negro spirituals, rounds, and London music-hall and French café songs would rock the house until the last of the crockery was dried and put away, but I never did learn the more indelicate words of *Nausea Bagwashio*.

Freshly home from our expensive schools, where there was central heating, servants to do the cleaning, and meals appeared like magic, Gerry and I found it difficult to adjust to the home routine of constant hard labour and sometimes rebelled. My strategy was to mutter something about seeing to the ponies and disappear to seek out the book I kept in the stable. Gerry, who was at the tired, floppy stage of adolescence, habitually overslept, missed breakfast, and would then be in Mummy's bad books for the rest of the day.

'Why can't you be like Phylla, and do something useful?' she would demand. (Little did she know just how useful I was being, but in Mummy's eyes any outdoor activity was OK, while children sitting about indoors drove her into a frenzy.) Naturally enough, this did not endear me to Gerry, and I drew into a closer alliance with Olivia, who shared my taste for covert reading of pony books by Joanna Cannan and the Pullein-Thompson sisters, and Enid Blyton's Adventure series.

Dragging himself downstairs one Sunday, Gerry found all the break-fast crockery had been left on the table as the rest of the family hurried off to church, and was gloomily anticipating the rocket he would get when Mummy returned when he hit on a brilliant way to rehabilitate himself.

At last my thoughts begin to turn from contemplation hopeless,

I think again of water hot, think of detergents soapless, he wrote of this Eureka moment.

When Mummy came home, grimly prepared for a session with cold encrusted scrambled egg and be-ringed coffee cups, the kitchen was sparkling, the china washed and put away… and Gerry instantly gained Favourite Child status.

Being large and strong but lacking an eye for a ball, he had opted to become a Wet Bob at Eton, and his administrative skill earned him the job of Ninth Man in the Monarch, one of whose duties was organising the heats for the Bumping Races on the Thames and recording the results for the magazine.

I had been given an Olivetti portable typewriter for my birthday, and he bribed, bullied and blackmailed me into making fair copies of the fiendishly complicated charts of the heats, all arrows and crossings-out and illegibly scrawled names. The originals looked like page-proofs corrected by Balzac, so sorting them out cost me much time and effort, but when they were done Gerry was so pleased that he promised to take me on a three-day camping trip into the wild mountainous hinterland where Twm Shôn Katti – the Robin Hood-ish Welsh outlaw and brigand – once had his hideout.

All holidays Gerry had been longing to explore this area, and I was hugely flattered to be asked along, especially since on picnics past he had been inclined to mock my fire-making and foraging skills. It was to be a Survival exercise. We would take the smallest of bivvi tents and the lightest of equipment, snares and a tiny trout-rod. We would live on what we could trap or catch, and feast on mushrooms and blackberries plus iron rations consisting of 4oz oatmeal per person per day, half a bar of chocolate, 2oz raisins… and that was it.

For several days we packed and re-packed our rucksacks, bickering over what we'd need. Gerry's instinct was to take enough kit to cope with every possible setback, scenario, or vagary of weather. Mine was to carry as little as I could. I wasn't a great map reader, but the closely-packed contour lines on the country we were to cross looked ominous. Even unburdened, I found it difficult to hoist my own weight up steep slopes.

'Boots,' said Gerry.

'I'll be all right in gym shoes.'

'You'll get soaked.'

'I don't care.' The thought of climbing hills in clumping boots was far worse than three days of wet feet. In any case, Gerry made a practice of stamping in a puddle at the start of a walk, saying it was no use trying to keep dry, so what was the difference?

I won my point with the gym shoes, but had to concede that we'd need sleeping bags, extra clothes, a frying pan, mugs, plates, towels, oilskins (no gossamer-thin waterproofs, then,) torches, matches, iron rations, knives, kettle, trout rod... The final heap of kit was a dismaying size, and that was before we had each added a paperback.

Gerry had a big haversack on a frame, which took three-quarters of our equipment, and I stuffed the rest into Daddy's old army knapsack, whose straps were too widely set and kept slipping off my shoulders. On a misty early September morning, Mummy drove us forty-odd miles into the wild mountains west of Tregaron, the roads getting narrower and the hills steeper as we left the last villages behind, and put us out on a wooded slope just below the line of low cloud that hung over the Pysgwda valley.

'I'll come back on Saturday and meet you by the Deuddau Pool,' she promised. 'Sure you've got everything?'

Expecting a walk, Lucy, her yellow labrador, jumped out of the car and stood wagging her tail hopefully.

'Why not take her with you?' said Mummy on impulse.

Gerry hesitated. 'We haven't brought any dog-food.'

'Oh, it won't hurt her to lose a few pounds. She might catch a rabbit.'

Lucy was very much a one-woman dog, and as the car drove away, her ears drooped. She sat down by the roadside, evidently prepared to wait until Mummy came back. We set off up the hill, and when I looked back she hadn't moved.

'Come on,' I called. 'Walkies!'

With unconcealed reluctance she got up and followed, looking the picture of misery. Something must have warned her this walk was going to be longer than she'd bargained for.

When the mist burned off it became very hot carrying our packs, and the flies were terrible under the trees, but we struggled to the top and were rewarded with a breeze and a stunning view over ridge after rolling ridge of empty moorland, with orange-tipped rushes and deep cwms blanketed in the dull green of late-summer bracken. Never a farm, never a fence, never a tree in sight; just the occasional grey-white back of a grazing sheep, curlews calling, and pipits springing from the tough mountain grass.

'Oh, look!' I said. 'Ponies!' And there was a little group of mares flinging up their heads to stare at us before trotting purposefully away, their woolly-coated foals tittuping along as if welded to their sides.

I longed to be galloping across that vast landscape on Taffy myself rather than humping a heavy load on Shank's pony, but Gerry was in his element, consulting the map, showing me how to use the compass, telling stories and jokes, sometimes singing snatches of song and never for a moment complaining that he was carrying far more than I was. The only person who was truly unhappy was poor Lucy, trailing along fifty yards behind. We wished very much that we had resisted bringing her, but there was nothing for it now but to jolly her along as best we could.

In the middle of the afternoon we chose an idyllic spot beside the Pysgwda, a charming little river with sun-dappled pebbly shallows and deep dark pools, and set up camp. It took a surprisingly long time to get the tents and stores arranged to Gerry's satisfaction, build what I considered to be an unnecessarily perfect fireplace with unnecessarily large stones, dig a latrine ('Why can't we just go in the bushes?') and find a really clear-running spot to wash and fill the kettle. Lucy watched our activities with an expression of deep misgiving, then went inside the tent and lay on my sleeping-bag.

We gathered dry twigs and bigger branches and snapped them into usable lengths, and soon had a good fire going, though in the light, changeable wind smoke kept chasing me from one side to the other. I remained to stoke it and cook the sausages which Mummy had insisted we added to our ration while Gerry went upstream to try out the fishing. Presently he returned with two small trout and a face covered in red blotches.

'The midges are terrible,' he said.

They went on being terrible until it was dark, and to avoid them we crouched so close to the fire that we were practically in it. The sausages were charred but delicious, and we recklessly cooked both fish as well, giving the heads and bones to Lucy who wolfed them down and looked around for more.

'We'll get you a rabbit tomorrow,' I assured her – an empty promise, as it turned out for, in the whole three days, those two tiny fish were the only food we caught. Living off the land was a non-starter. There were no blackberries. No mushrooms, not so much as an edible fungus that looked anything like the illustrations in Gerry's pocket guide. The hazelnuts were still unripe, their insides more pith than kernel, while of rabbits, pheasants, pigeons, hares we saw no trace. As hunter-gatherers we failed abysmally, but I felt this was partly because we didn't devote enough time to searching for food. The trouble with camping is that it takes so long to keep yourself reasonably warm, dry, clean and fed that self-maintenance swallows up most of your waking hours, and there is precious little time or energy left to do anything else.

We did explore the wooded slopes of the river in a desultory way, but it was so hot that I was always glad to get back to the campsite and flop down by the remains of the fire on the pretext of getting it going again, while surreptitiously golloping down another chapter of my Ngaio Marsh.

Sheep occasionally grazed into view, and after sharing our porridge oats for meal after meal, Lucy would not have objected to eating one raw. There were even moments when I thought she might turn on Gerry and me. We were also getting hungry and increasingly tetchy by the morning of Day Three when we struck camp, loaded the haversacks, and set out to cross the dauntingly steep ridge that lay between us and our RV with Mummy on the road beyond the Deuddau Pool.

After two hot clear days the weather had become steamy and oppressive, with little black flies dancing maddeningly round our heads as we forced our way through deep bracken. Gerry set a slow pace and kept stopping tactfully to give me a breather, and although I suffered from the classic follower's resentment of the boots trudging steadily in front of me, for once I managed not to say anything disagreeable and we reached the top without a major bust–up.

We were sprawling in the sun on the rocks that crowned the ridge, with Gerry trying to pick out the rowan tree above the pool through his binoculars, when the turf on the hillside opposite suddenly turned a darker shade of green, lightning flashed overhead, and seconds later, down came the rain in torrents. It was so violent, so unexpected, that we were soused through before we had the wit to squeeze beneath the overhang of a big flat rock, evicting a startled ewe which had been enjoying a fly-free snooze there. She pronked downhill in great bounds, her back appearing and disappearing in the bracken, while we pulled the rest of our kit into the shelter and lay peering out through the downpour.

Nearly as suddenly as it had begun, it stopped, and the hillside began to steam in the sun.

'Better get across the stream before it starts again,' said Gerry, and we stumbled and slid downhill as fast as we could in our clammy wet clothes. But when we reached what should have been no more than a shining thread of water, a mere brook that you could practically jump across, it had become a foaming torrent, impossible to cross, and we were forced to set up camp on the wrong bank, out of sight of the road and our rendezvous.

'What if she comes and can't find us?' I whinged, keen to end the adventure asap and get home to hot baths, warm beds, and food, glorious food.

Unlike me, Gerry was positively revelling in adversity. Up till now things had gone altogether too easily for his taste. 'We'll just have to camp here and hope the stream goes down overnight.'

By late afternoon the rain had set in steadily, drumming on the tents, and we ate the last of our porridge, chocolate and raisins in our sleeping-bags, uncomfortably propped on our elbows, with heads out of the flap and Lucy lying lengthways beside me, edging me off the groundsheet. There was no wood so no question of getting a fire going, and though I had a couple of chapters to go in my whodunit the light was too poor to read easily. It looked like being a long night, and my spirits were at a low ebb when faintly in the distance I heard voices.

'What's that?' I was out of the tent in a flash.

'What's what?'

Before I could answer, Lucy had realised that her long long walkies was over and she could safely abandon us. With ears cocked and delight in every portly line, she bustled away into the murk, and a few minutes later led into sight the rescue party – Mummy, Daddy, Olivia, and her school-friend Jenny, carrying baskets of food and drink, with Scot bringing up the rear. Never was there a more welcome sight.

Finding the river in spate, they had backtracked to the nearest bridge some five miles downstream, abandoned the car in a farmyard and then followed along the bank to where they thought we must have set up camp.

Six humans and two dogs in two bivvies with a groundsheet draped between them was hardly a recipe for a comfortable night. Whenever you tried to move you found someone's feet or elbow or tail in your face, but well fortified with wine, pork pies and fruit cake and serenaded by one another's snores, we all managed a few hours' sleep, and woke so stiff that we could hardly crawl from our nests of rugs and blankets.

'I've been sleeping on the living rock,' groaned Mummy, combing her hair with her fingers and searching her pockets for a lipstick.

It was a beautiful morning. Overnight the stream had returned to its normal width and placidity, and as we loaded up our kit for the last time and made our way back to the car, I forgot all the low points and felt I would happily make the whole expedition again.

By degrees, two steps forward and one back, Mummy was learning the basics of hill farming, what could and couldn't be done on thin, poor soil in an unforgiving climate, but as usual she wanted to run before she could walk. She devoured books about animal husbandry, read *Farmers' Weekly* cover to cover, accumulated a shelf of teach-yourself manuals: pig-breeding, egg production, the proper management of turkeys.

A revolution was taking place in British agriculture which, since the war, was no longer the preserve traditional farming families. Businessmen, institutions and large companies were buying and amalgamating run-down farms, slapping up steel-and-asbestos buildings and, by applying business methods to livestock production, turning them into agri-factories in which cattle, pigs and poultry were intensively reared.

In the drive to cut costs, time, and labour, a good many corners were also cut in the matter of animal welfare. Beasts were crowded together, their movements restricted and any natural behaviour that interfered with the production-line's smooth running was ruthlessly eradicated. Chickens were de-beaked to stop them pecking one another. Calves were deprived of roughage to keep their meat white. Cattle and sheep were doused with noxious chemicals that not only killed parasites but did no good at all to the animals' nervous systems. Pigs were mutilated in a number of ways to facilitate handling and stop them fighting, while sows were confined in farrowing crates so narrow that they could not turn round. This prevented them from lying on their offspring, but often resulted in them having so many survivors in each litter that they could not rear them all.

The new vogue for high-protein concentrates enormously increased the yields of dairy cows, but the stress of carrying such a burden of milk also wore out their udders and placed a painful strain on their hoofs. Despite these obvious drawbacks, those who got in on the ground floor of this new style animal husbandry made a lot of money, and Mummy wanted to be among them.

She couldn't help being aware that Daddy was not – and never would be – a farmer. Though he was perfectly happy to drive a tractor at weekends and apply his mind to any problem she could not solve, his career lay elsewhere. He enjoyed the variety and complexity of his work as a London solicitor, the company of his colleagues and the mental stimulus of legal problems. Many of his clients were old friends who had been with Trower, Still & Keeling for generations, and given the choice he would not have lived so far from London.

He had bought the Fforest because Mummy wanted it so much, but as a realist he must have known from the first that far from ever paying for itself, it was likely to prove a bottomless hole of expense. This didn't worry him too much, because he saw it as a good place to bring up his family and besides, in those days losses made by the farm could be set off against tax on his income as a solicitor. He saw that to make money on a Welsh farm you had to live like a frugal Welsh farmer, forswearing life's expensive pleasures and luxuries, and to underline the point, he commissioned a cartoonist friend to illustrate an old verse on agricultural economics, which he hung on his office wall. It went:

> *Man to the plough, wife to the cow,*
> *Boy to the barn, girl to the yarn,*
> *And your rent is soon netted.*
> *BUT...*
> *Man tally-ho, Miss piano,*
> *Wife silk and satin, boy Greek and Latin,*
> *And you'll soon be Gazetted!*

What with private schools and hunting high on the winter agenda, our family was plainly embarked on the second course, but although there were sometimes edgy sessions with accountants and bank managers, it never prevented my father backing Mummy's new ventures, with each of which she was certain to earn a fortune, pay off the farm's ever-growing overdraft and incidentally make her name as an agricultural pioneer.

In-barn egg production was the first of these short-lived enterprises, entailing (as in every case) much upheaval plus considerable financial outlay. A brand-new deep-litter house was built, floored with layers of hardcore, sand, bark, and finally thick wood-shavings, and equipped with nesting boxes and tiered perches which the younger children enjoyed using as a climbing-frame before the hens took up residence.

It looked and smelt lovely for the first year, and brown eggs fairly poured out of the handsome hybrids, whose feathers glinted greeny-black in the sun since they counted among their mixed ancestry Plymouth Rock, Black Sumatra and Rhode Island Red genes. They pecked around in the litter and took dust baths in favourite corners in the most satisfactory way.

Unfortunately, as with all honeymoons, the glamour didn't last. Chickens have an astonishing talent for degrading their surroundings, and since poultry-keeping was in Wales traditionally women's work and Mummy was often too busy to attend to it, once again we children found ourselves landed with a particularly unattractive holiday job, which in this case meant scraping encrusted guano off the perches with long-handled hoes.

As the powdery calcified deposits came loose, they showered the toiling scrapers with feathers and mites, very itchy in the hair; and disinfecting the woodwork with a strong solution of Jeyes Fluid made our eyes sting. Very soon cobwebs had begun to blur the outlines of the shed. The straw in the nesting-boxes became glued into mats when soft-shelled eggs broke and, worst of all, certain villainous hens developed the depraved habit of pecking out the yolks. This was a hanging offence, but unless you actually caught the culprit red-handed – or in this case yellow-beaked – the difficulty was first to identify her, and then to force yourself to nab her and carry out the execution.

Nor did their vices stop at egg-eating. Despite the carefully balanced diet and relatively liberal house-room, the hens developed aggressive tendencies, pecking one another's bare patches during the moult until they became raw.

Mummy sent for a de-beaking instrument, but the diagrams showing how to use it were so reminiscent of the Spanish Inquisition that her nerve broke and she decided the hens' bad behaviour must be due to a lack of green fodder. Armfuls of bolted cabbages, hedgerow weeds, lawn clippings were distributed among them but made no difference except to befoul the hitherto dry deep litter, and at last she admitted defeat and opened the door of the shed – which of course was what the hens had wanted all along.

Out they poured, clucking and scratching all over the nearest fields but, being hopelessly naïve about predators, most of them soon fell victim to foxes and the survivors, rejoicing in their liberty, took up residence in the stables, laying eggs in the hayracks and mangers in the good old traditional way.

Though it was now clear that intensive egg-production was not a quick or easy way to pay off the farm overdraft, Mummy was not through with poultry-keeping yet. As soon as the deep-litter house had been thoroughly cleaned with blow-torches and its woodwork given a fresh coat of creosote, a large and handsome Broad-Breasted Bronze stag turkey with a pompous gait and flapping wattles whom she named Whimsical Walkern and his six meek wives were installed there instead, and this little flock settled down to raise their families and provide Christmas cheer.

Again all went swimmingly at first. The big buff-speckled eggs hatched, the chicks flourished and grew into gangling adolescents, the young turkeycocks ruffled their neck-feathers and began to fight, and then disease struck. Four were found dead one morning, six the next, eight the day after. It was like the Black Death. Birds that were perfectly healthy one evening were obviously unwell next morning, hunched and listless, and by dark would be stretched out cold. No-one could tell us what was wrong.

The vet hummed and hawed and sent samples for analysis. Turkeys were non-native, delicate birds, prone to heart attacks and nervous disorders, an easy prey for opportunistic viruses. Soon his fees and those of the laboratory swallowed up any hope of profit. Ever more toxic medicines were prescribed for the few remaining birds, and after poor Valerie's near-fatal run-in with the arsenic tablets, Mummy decided to pull the plug on the turkey-breeding enterprise.

'Would you really want to eat a turkey that had been regularly dosed with poison?' she demanded rhetorically, and threw open the deep litter house door. Out strolled the survivors, two demure turkey-hens and old Whimsical Walkern himself, who gobbled merrily as they asserted squatters' rights over the Dutch barn, roosting on the girders and spoiling a good deal of hay with copious droppings.

Soon Walkern was behaving as if he owned the farmyard, wantonly attacking cats and sheepdogs and any child under four foot tall – which of course included George. He was the perfect caricature of a choleric Colonel. When something displeased him, his feathers would ruffle up and his little blunt train fan out, then his wattles would glow bright red as he flapped the rather disgusting long floppy finger of skin sprouting from above his beak. His gobbling would reach a crescendo before he launched himself at his enemy, and it was a bold spirit who stood his ground before that furious charge.

Mummy used to arm George with a stick with which to fend off Walkern's sudden savage lunges, though he was strictly forbidden to hit the old bully. It made crossing the farmyard quite an ordeal and, though he survived his wives by nearly a year, in a way everyone was relieved when a night raid by C. Fox Esquire terminated his reign of terror and nothing remained to remember him by but a fine portrait showing him in full display on the farmyard wall, with which Mummy won the hotly-contested photographic competition at the Hundred House Show.

Apart from a brief flirtation with Khaki Campbell ducks, which swam away up the Colwyn Brook and were never seen again, that was the end of serious poultry-keeping, but hope – particularly hope of hitting the farming jackpot – springs eternal, and soon Mummy had a new enthusiasm: pigs.

Understandably wary by now of intensive rearing methods, she decided to keep them in the most natural conditions she could provide, sheltered but free to roam and rootle as they would in their wild state. No farrowing crates, no tethering of pregnant sows, nothing but a stout rail a foot from the floor all round the inside of each sty to stop the sows crushing their offspring.

The old farm pig-sties were renovated and re-roofed, their cobbled floors replaced with sloping concrete which could easily be swept down to the wide ramp that separated the line of sties from the muck-heap. The concrete troughs had drainage holes through which water could be sluiced. There were even self-fill water-bowls, into which a metal plate released water when pressed down by the drinker's snout, but unfortunately this brilliant innovation was not proof against the destructive power of pigs. One after another, the metal plates buckled and jammed open, flooding the sty, for the Wessex Saddleback sows were unbelievably strong, like little piebald tanks of muscle and wilfulness. When they wanted food or water, they wanted it now, and woe betide anything animate or inanimate that got in their way.

Old Rock King David the Forty-Eighth, a Large White boar of distinguished ancestry, was a much gentler character than his bustling, stroppy wives. His movements were measured, even stately, and he loved being scratched along the backbone with a stick. He also had the advantage of prick-ears, which allowed him to see properly. I always suspected that the Saddlebacks' tendency to jump and squeal and threaten stemmed from the fact that their floppy ears hung over their eyes, and they were often alarmed by humans whose approach they had not seen. Though full of fun and character, they were unpredictable in their response to any strange situation. You could never tell whether they would charge at or away from any perceived menace, and although Mummy approved of – indeed relied on – us giving her a hand with the pigs, she made it a rule that no child was to feed them on his or her own.

Adjoining the pig-sty complex was the spinney where we had camped before the house was fit to live in, and here the little foundation herd settled to an idyllic life, rootling and wallowing, scratching luxuriously against the rough-barked pines, and eating their high protein ration of pig-nuts from a shallow concrete tray which could be filled from the far side of the fence. They were such fun to watch that 'pig-gazing' became Daddy's favourite way of winding down after a busy week at the office.

There was no need to go in among them unless something was wrong, and if you did, you had to be careful, particularly when there were piglets running around, because one high-pitched squeal was all that was needed to bring the furious mothers galloping.

An attacking sow will slash backward, so you were allegedly safer in front of her than behind, though I never put this to the test. Mummy's cousin Pamela, however, a tall, athletic redhead, happened to be taking a shortcut across the spinney when my sheepdog Scot, following at a distance, failed to clear the fence cleanly. He caught a paw on the barbed wire and yelped as he landed. The sows raised their snouts, saw Pam, and in an instant they were after her.

'I ran,' she said breathlessly, 'as I have never run before, but they nearly caught me.'

In the nick of time she reached the stile and vaulted it in a flash of long legs, still anxious lest her pursuers crashed their way through and trampled her to pulp. Everyone agreed she had had a lucky escape, and pretty soon a decision was taken to move the pigs farther away from the house, letting them roam free on several acres of woods and boggy ground adjoining the common known as Hungry Green, and bringing them back to the sties when farrowing was imminent.

The first part of this plan was very successful. The pigs loved foraging in the wood, and ploughed up the bog like mechanical rotovators. The downside was that the trampled ground became so soft that it was difficult to feed their high-protein nuts without wasting half of them, and removed from the vicinity of humans, the pigs grew steadily wilder.

This made the second part of the plan hard to implement. Chasing heavily pregnant sows through deep mud was no-one's idea of fun. Perhaps, thought Mummy, it would be easier to give them individual shelters and let them bring up their families in self-selecting groups. There were bound to be more losses among the piglets, but that was Nature's way of balancing population against available food.

'After all,' she said, 'if every piglet that was born survived, the world would soon be over-run by pigs.'

A charming village of mini Nissen-huts made of corrugated tin sheets over wooden frames sprang up on the driest, flattest part of the pasture, each with its farrowing rail and plenty of straw, and the sows took to them at once like house-proud matrons, pushing the bedding into comfortable mats and carefully defecating out of doors. As far as we could see, there was no quarrelling over sites and, like his Biblical namesake, King David presided genially over this happy extended family, welcome in any hut he chose to honour with his presence.

Though it was far from easy to separate the weaners from their mothers when the time came for them to be sold, the system of outdoor rearing worked reasonably well until poor King David was struck down with erysipelas, which brought him out in blotches all over, paralysed his hindlegs, and in those days before broad spectrum antibiotics were widely available, soon proved fatal.

The son who took his place (Solomon, naturally) was a very different character, for whereas King David had been shown in his youth, petted and pampered and shampooed before his appearances in the ring, and therefore looked benignly on humans, Solomon was practically wild and potentially dangerous. Two-Legs, for him, were enemies. They harried his wives and stole his children, and if he got one in his power he meant to destroy it.

The pig-bog became a no-go area which we children dared to cross only by darting from the shelter of one tree to another, always ready to take to the branches if Solomon spotted us.

Even the wooded slope above the bog was treacherous soft ground, and I remember a terrible scene when a neighbouring farmer who was shepherding on the adjoining common noticed that a two-year-old chestnut filly whom Mummy had bought for ten shillings in a farm sale and named Fforest Fawr (The Great Fforest) was struggling in a bog-hole and sinking ever deeper. Why and how she had left her companions on the other side of the fence and broken into the pig-enclosure we never found out, but when we got there she was submerged to the withers and had given up struggling, only her desperate rolling eyes under her long fluffy forelock and occasional grunting whinnies to show she was still alive. Solomon the boar, with his sows in attendance, stood a few yards away, staring with baleful curiosity at this apparently legless interloper.

It was a hot muggy afternoon in July, just at the beginning of the summer holidays, and among the trees the horseflies were a constant torment. Daddy, who had hoped to spend a peaceful afternoon fishing on the Wye, instead took the situation in hand. He sent Gerry (who could drive but was too young for a licence) off in the old Land Rover to fetch spades, ropes, and everyone from the farm; instructed me and a friend who had come to lunch and was wearing rather unsuitable clothes to drive the pigs through the gate into the next field, and told Mummy to ring the garage in search of a vehicle with a winch.

They did better than that: they produced a caterpillar tractor, which crawled across the soft ground where our Fergie and Fordson would have got stuck. Our neighbours turned out in force and dug like heroes, and at last succeeded in getting ropes and a surcingle round Fforest Fawr. Slowly the caterpillar hauled her out on to a gate laid on its side, and thence to the ramp of the horse-trailer.

She was a pitiful object, black with mud, her sides heaving and one hindleg at an awkward angle, but an hour after we got her into a stable she was trying to stand up, and by the time the vet came she was on her feet and staggering about, no longer at death's door, though she was never properly sound thereafter. The pull of the tractor against the suction of mud must have snapped or dislocated something in her back or hip, and though she subsequently had a nice filly foal which we called Fforest Fiddlesticks, she was always lame behind and had to be sold as a brood mare.

Boggy patches were a constant hazard, despite the mole-draining programme. We lost two more ponies – a plain little black mare called Shân, and Dustyfoot's daughter Smoky II – in different fields the following year. Often you didn't spot the treacherous softness until too late. I remember once during a check out hunting I was sitting on my pony on what looked a perfectly sound bit of hillside just a few yards away from Mr Morris the Subsidy, a garrulous stout party in bicycle clips and trilby hat on a fiery little blood horse, idly listening to his flow of talk, when I noticed that his mount's legs seemed to be getting shorter.

'Hold up, horse!' he said impatiently as it fidgeted.

'Watch out, boyo, you're in the bog!' said his companion sharply, and next moment Mr Morris had flung himself off and was wading up to his knees while his horse floundered forward in great leaps to regain solid ground.

That summer, Gerry and I had an anxious few hours on Mynydd Eppynt, and once again Mummy's recklessness was the prime cause. Each year, the North Breconshire Show at Builth Wells (which eventually morphed into the Royal Welsh Show) was followed a week later by a smaller horse show and gymkhana at Erwood, only a few miles from Chapel House, and Mummy decided it would save time and trouble if, after the first event, we rode over the hill to Chapel House, parked the ponies there for the week, and rode them on to Erwood the following Saturday. Daddy, who rather detested horse shows, would spend the afternoon fishing the Chapel House water, then bring us all us back to the Fforest in his car.

As the light began to fade, we left the showground and rode up the network of lanes overlooking the Wye. I was riding Taffy, as usual, and as usual we had crashed our way round the Under 13.2 hands show-jumping course, collecting faults in double figures. Mummy was on her latest purchase, a leggy, 14.2 hands liver-chestnut half-bred who had competed in flapping races. She had named him Stag because he jumped like one – head up so that his nose was parallel to the ground, he would take a flying leap without bothering to check his pace or judge his distance – Gerry rode a sensible chunky grey cob with a hogged mane called Caradoc.

At the hill gate, instead of following the drovers' track which swooped in a wide arc round the edge of a shallow bowl in the hill, Mummy decided to take a shortcut across the middle. 'Much quicker,' she said briskly.

'I wouldn't go over that green patch,' Gerry warned.

'Nonsense. It's perfectly all right.' Mummy vigorously legged Stag into the dip, but hardly were the words out of her mouth than he snorted, jibbed with his nose stretched down to the ground, and tried to retreat – but too late, he was well and truly in the bog.

He plunged forward in a panic and, by a great piece of luck, located firm rock beneath a tussock, and heaved himself on to it. Mummy jumped off, and there they both stood, on a small island of rock and coarse grass about three foot across, with the disturbed bog quivering all round them and no way back that we could see.

The sun set, black clouds of midges danced around us in the gloaming, the harvest moon rose, and stubbornly Stag refused to leave his refuge. You could hardly blame him. He wasn't a hill pony. He had had a nasty fright and didn't want to repeat the experience. It began to look as if we would be on the hill all night.

 Endlessly we debated who should go for help. Gerry didn't want to leave me and Mummy stranded, but I couldn't be sure of finding the way down to Chapel House on my own.

While I held the horses, he patiently circled the boggy area, prodding with an old fence-post, trying to find solid ground, but although a human might – with care – tiptoe cautiously from tussock to tussock, a pony was too heavy. Just a couple of steps and Stag would be up to his girths again. The best hope was a flying leap, but we couldn't persuade him to attempt it.

Mummy buckled the full length of Stag's reins to one half each of each of the other ponies' and all our stirrup leathers, then tossed the end to me and Gerry and told us to pull while she harooshed Stag from behind. It was no use. He braced himself and threatened to kick, and we couldn't get enough purchase on the long thin 'rope' to pull him forward.

'Try taking the ponies out of sight!' she called.

So we led Taffy and Caradoc away round a shoulder of the hill, tripping and stumbling in the bracken, but as soon as we were out of sight Stag began neighing and of course Taffy answered, so he knew we hadn't gone far.

'He nearly went,' reported Mummy when we returned. 'I think if I hadn't been here either, he might have risked it.'

She knotted the long rein round her waist and, while Gerry and I held the other end, placed her feet very carefully on one tuft of grass after another until she was back on firm ground. Again we led Taffy and Caradoc away, while Stag's neighing became ever more frantic, and had probably gone about half a mile before to our great relief he came cantering after us, sweating and thickly plastered with black mud but otherwise none the worse.

It was nearly eleven o'clock before we reached Chapel House, to find Daddy pacing the drive, a shotgun under one arm and a bottle of whisky in his other hand. 'I didn't know which you'd need most,' he explained.

There is no more room for two bosses on one farm than for two cooks in the same kitchen. Though Ron Weale was a good, conscientious traditional stockman, he found it difficult to share Mummy's sudden enthusiasms for newfangled systems of management, let alone pigs and turkeys, and he tended to delay carrying out any orders she gave him until Daddy came down from London and confirmed them.

This annoyed Mummy, who felt herself sidelined. It used to make me uneasy to hear her bombarding Daddy with a litany of woe the moment he stepped off the 4.45 from Paddington. Whether she meant it or not, the implication was that while he lived in cushy London she had been abandoned to struggle alone on a bleak Welsh hill – which was far from the case. Though he would listen patiently and make soothing noises, the farm dramas must have seemed pretty small beer after the large-scale problems that had occupied him all week, but to her they were all-important and she was determined they should have his full attention.

While Ron was in charge of the sheep and cattle, and not too keen to accept her advice on how to manage them, Mummy directed her energies to the more congenial enterprise of horse-dealing. She had always been attracted to the beautiful little Welsh mountain ponies, with their Araby dished faces and floating action, and now that for the first time in her life she had plenty of land to accommodate them, she could hardly go to a sale without bringing back one or two. The colt foals were heartbreakingly cheap, just a few pounds each, since they were mostly destined for the plates of French diners. They would arrive miserable and traumatised, having lost their mothers and travelled for hours crammed into lorries and trailers, but after a week or so would form jolly, mischievous gangs who larked about on 'The Ranch,' as the fields across the road from the farm buildings were known, squealing and sparring, and making yearning eyes at any mare who happened to be in season. Since the fences were by no means all pony-proof, and the colts were often not gelded before they were sexually mature, this led to a good many unauthorized matings and the number of horses on the farm expanded exponentially.

The idea was that we should break and school them, show them at local gymkhanas, and sell them as well-behaved children's ponies. There were, however, a few snags to this plan. Although we could all ride after a fashion, none of us had a clue about schooling or systematically teaching ponies to jump. Our default position was what is rudely known as the Old English Lavatory Seat – firmly planted on the buttocks with legs well forward – comfortable and secure but far from elegant. By the 1950s the clap-on-a-saddle-and-hop-aboard approach was definitely out of date, but lunging, long-reining, flatwork, circles were alien concepts to Mummy, so all we ever did in the way of education was hack about the hills until the ponies could be relied on to behave reasonably, and then we put them up for sale.

Here Mummy's unshakable conviction that all her geese were swans proved a powerful weapon, and she generally managed to persuade the buyers that under the shaggy coat and unsophisticated manners the pony in question was a real treasure, with a perfect temperament, ideal for a child to handle and so on. During my school days ten or a dozen ponies passed through her hands in this way, and she acquired quite a reputation among our friends as someone who could usually produce a riding-pony to order.

Stag was sold for £90 – a very good price – in order to buy an oil-fired Aga, which was a great boon though I would rather have kept Stag, especially since Taffy was temporarily out of commission. The love lives of our ponies were getting steadily more convoluted, and although at the age of fourteen I was already too big for Taffy, like her previous owner I would happily have gone on riding her till my feet touched the ground.

I was looking forward to one last summer competing with her at local shows when I got the unwelcome news that she had foaled unexpectedly, thus securing herself six months of maternity leave.

Her scraggy bay filly Rico, father unknown, suffered the fate of many unwanted children. By the time I came home for the holidays, she was two months old, unhandled, and wild as a hawk – and so she remained for the rest of her life. Nominally she was mine, but I had neither the time or inclination to train her, and when she had produced two equally wild foals of her own, Mummy drew the line at keeping her any longer. Rather than condemn her to the sale ring and an uncertain future, I persuaded a marksman to shoot her in the field, and she remains a blot on my conscience.

Taffy's second foal could hardly have been a greater contrast. Sired by Sally's son Jock Scot (who had been born in the butcher's field at Much Hadham), the bay colt we named Pendragon combined thoroughbred, Arab, and Exmoor genes, plus Taffy's robust constitution and splendidly positive temperament. He was, by general consent, the best pony ever bred at Fforest Farm, and one of those rare animals who seems to realise what you want him to do without being told.

George, aged five, used to lead him about the farmyard as a foal, threading in and out of vehicles and other animals. Before Pendragon's second birthday, Miranda and George were scrambling on and off him with nothing but a halter-rope round his neck, and when the time came to put a saddle on him he accepted it with perfect grace, and calmly joined the party going off for a hack as if he had been doing it for years.

At 14.2 hands, handsome and robust, he was appreciably bigger than his mother, and everyone's favourite, carrying eight-year-old Miranda or Mummy herself with equal care and aplomb. For several years running he won the Best Trekking Pony at the Royal Welsh Show, and best of all, he jumped in Taffy's calm, uncomplicated way, appearing to gallop straight over his fences rather than take off and land.

In this respect he was completely different from Rhwstyn, a compact little ball of muscle whom Mummy bought after seeing him jump five foot over a plain bar at the Aberedw Sports. It was his party trick. He would trot steadily up to the pole apparently hanging in mid air without even a ground line to help him judge its height, and make a cat-like spring that took him clean over it. This he would do over and over again with no sign of resentment or boredom; the only trouble was that he wouldn't jump anything else. A course of coloured show-jumps would undermine him completely, and if you asked him to canter rather than trot at a fence, he would waver unhappily from side to side and finally slide into a refusal.

He, too, was a stallion when he arrived at Fforest Farm, and Sally – who was now in human terms Taffy's mother-in-law – further complicated our ponies' relationships by producing a foal by him whom we called Nesta, after an heroic Welsh queen. She had a mouth so sensitive that she couldn't accept a metal bit, and therefore wore a bendy rubber snaffle which gave her rider very little control. I remember trying desperately to stop her overtaking hounds on a steep downhill slope and eventually running her into the fat hindquarters of the Joint-Master's chestnut heavyweight, behaviour which did not escape a stinging reprimand.

Builth cinema provided us with a steady diet of cowboy films, and one holiday we were gripped by a craze for shooting a home-made Wild Western, using Mummy's 8mm movie camera. The storyline (as I remember it) required me on Taffy – Baddy – to ambush Clarissa on her black mare Victory – Goody – chasing her across 'The Ranch.' When she starting shooting, I would vanish from Taffy's back but continue to pursue while clinging to the saddle on the far side, finally overtaking the Goody and throwing her to the ground.

It looked so simple on paper, but the rehearsals were surprisingly painful. Time and again when I tried to cling to the far side of Taffy's saddle it would revolve and deposit me on the ground, and even when the girth was tight enough to take the strain, it was difficult to keep the pony cantering with her burden lopsided. Nor was it easy to unhorse Clarissa when she knew what I planned to do. Every time I seized her stirrup and jerked it upward, she would force it down again, and Gerry, operating the camera, became so weak with laughter that the resulting pictures were hopelessly jerky and blurred. No more than one short sequence of the film ever got developed, but our respect for professional stunt-riders increased enormously.

The filming did, however, give Mummy an idea for fund-raising for the Church in Wales, then in very low financial water. She painted eye-catching signs saying: *Danger! Highwaymen Operating* and underneath, in much smaller letters, *in aid of the Church in Wales*, which we nailed up at either end of the Fforest's stretch of main road, and Olivia and I, equipped with black tricornes and bandanna masks, spent a happy summer day galloping out of hiding on our ponies to hold up every passing vehicle and demand a contribution.

Great fun for us: rather less amusing for the tradesmen plying between Builth and Kington, who got stopped every time they passed. Many of them were Methodists anyway, and their comments became pretty terse. Nevertheless, we collected a respectable sum and had a really lucky coup when we caught the Bishop of Oxford, on his way to fish the Wye with a couple of friends, all of whom laughed and turned out their pockets, putting £8 in our tin – the equivalent of about £40 today.

While Ron Weale was responsible for the sheep and cattle on the farm, we children had no direct role in their management, and could make ourselves useful only on odd occasion when sheep had to be driven here or there or when, each summer, they were gathered off the hill for shearing and dipping. A huge cordon of pony- and motorbike-mounted riders with dogs would sweep the section of mountain where the Fforest had grazing rights, driving ewes and lambs from their hiding-places in the bracken and channelling them into the steep, rocky track that led down to the farm.

It was thrilling to gallop over the hill in pursuit of little bunches of sheep, yelling to stop them breaking back through the line, and a dramatic sight as all the little rivulets of moving fleeces coalesced into a single wide river which flowed down the hillside and through the gate to Beili Bychan common.

There sentries would be posted to turn the flock in the right direction, and more to turn them at the foot of the short, steep drive, at the top of which was the corral, strongly railed, with a wooden race leading directly to the dipping tank.

The next job was to sort out any sheep that weren't marked JB and chase them back to the hill – an operation marked, I am ashamed to say, with much casual brutality as we pounced on the struggling ewes and evicted them from the corral, then did the same for their frenziedly bleating lambs. In fact, the way we handled sheep in those days hardly bears thinking about. Pain and terror were inflicted on the poor creatures every time they came into contact with humans, and even then I always thought the livestock market in Builth where they were bought and sold was horrible beyond words.

There seemed to be a particular breed of red-faced, overweight, middle-aged men armed with sticks who gathered round the stock-lorries and trailers as they unloaded for the sole purpose of hitting every animal that came within reach, creating completely unnecessary terror, confusion and noise simply, it appeared, for their own gratification. Shouting, cursing, harrying animals this way and that, driving them into the sale ring under a hail of blows, generally all in pouring rain and with a background din of the auctioneer's barely comprehensible patter, made it a scene from hell.

On the whole the women who flocked into Builth on Mondays, when the main street jammed solid with traffic and shoppers, preferred gossip and stocking up with provisions to the livestock market itself.

Mummy used to go to watch her beasts sold, and made a brave stab at taking on the men at their own game, learning the names and farms of all our neighbours so she could strike up conversations, compare prices and pick up local news while making her way round the outside of the sale-ring, but it was uphill work getting them to talk, and really better left to Ron.

The life of a real hill farmer had always been both tough and harsh, so it was hardly surprising that many of them were chippy, secretive, and deeply suspicious of newcomers, particularly those with money to splash around. There is a big difference between farming because you want to and farming because you have to, and the fact that Daddy worked in London and paid the bills inevitably undermined her efforts to be taken seriously. They knew she wasn't really one of them, no matter how hard she tried to bridge the gap, so there was always a certain reserve behind their civility and occasional underhand behaviour that surprised and wounded her.

Daddy, who was even less at ease than Mummy when talking to

farmers, used to embarrass me by putting on a phoney Welsh accent to converse with our neighbours. I don't think he even knew he was doing it – or if he did know simply intended it to blur the distinction between us and them that bedevilled so many attempts at social interaction.

The result, unfortunately, was just the opposite. The person he was talking to would suspect he was being mocked, and clam up at once. Years later, I found myself doing the same thing in Co. Tipperary, putting on a cod Irish accent because I imagined it would make me less conspicuous, but when someone laughed and said, 'You're becoming more Irish than the Irish,' I squirmed and reverted to cut-glass Queen's English with all possible speed.

One annual fixture that did bring the locality together was the Hundred House Sports Day, which took place on the Fforest's big flat field known as the Sixteen Acre. In those days it was a rough-and-ready but very convivial hotchpotch of activities that combined sheepdog trials in the morning with children's races, games and agricultural competitions such as judging the weight of a sheep and bowling for a real live piglet, plus a few showing classes for ponies, and ended with hotly-contested 'flapping races' run round the perimeter of the field.

These were open to all horses and ponies of all shapes and sizes, and handicapped by distance rather than weight. Thus you would find a 12.2-hand pony allowed half a lap start over the lean 16-hand thoroughbred racing-machine with a tiny boy clinging to the neck-strap while two burly handlers held it in check, with half a dozen medium-sized, medium-paced horses spaced out between them.

At the starting pistol, off they would go hell-for-leather, and as the field was far from flat the smaller, nimbler animals often held their lead for a fair distance. Gradually, however, sheer speed would tell. One after another the ponies would be overhauled, and nine times out of ten as the race entered its final lap the thoroughbred would be in front. I remember intense excitement one year when we all thought a small black pony was going to flash past the winning post first, but it turned out that he still had a full lap to go, having been passed by the thoroughbred on the first circuit.

The race that engendered the most excitement, though, was the

Ladies' Cock Chase – a hangover, I now suspect, from some pagan fertility rite and with distinct echoes of the death of Orpheus.

Kicking off their shoes and tucking skirts into knickers, women of all ages, shapes and sizes from hefty, weatherbeaten farmers' wives to slim slips of teenagers would line out round the edge of the Sports Field while a man with a bulging sack walked into the exact middle of their circle. He would peremptorily wave back any over-eager ladies who tried to jump the gun by surging forward, then plunge his arm into the sack, draw out an indignant cockerel, and throw it in the air, and immediately there was a wild stampede of Maenads bent on catching the unfortunate bird.

Dodging and squawking, it would be chased until it was exhausted and finally captured and borne away in triumph with most of its feathers missing: definitely not a spectacle to appeal to the RSPCA or, indeed, to Daddy, who tactfully but firmly told the organisers that if they wanted to go on holding the Sports on his field they should consider dropping this particular competition.

Then, as if there hadn't been excitement enough, the day would end with a dance in the village hall. It would be scheduled to start at 8pm, but never did. For hours, it seemed to me, the men and teenage boys, unnaturally slicked and scrubbed, stood or lounged against one wall pretending to ignore the girls, curled and primped to the nines, who chattered and giggled in tight little groups against the opposite wall, stealing glances across the bare-boarded dance floor while pretending that such things as boys did not exist.

Forced by Mummy to put in an appearance, and unable to mingle easily with either group, I found this was pure agony until, after what seemed an interminable hiatus, that trusty old saviour of wallflowers known as the 'Paul Jones' would come to my rescue. Music would blare from a wind-up gramophone with a big horn, and at once the girls would join hands in a big circle and start to revolve clockwise, with the boys chivvied into circling anti-clockwise outside them. When the music stopped, you had to dance with whoever you were standing opposite, and although there was usually a bit of bunching to claim the most popular girls, by and large the boys played fair and each, however reluctantly, grabbed his allocated partner and manoeuvred her into the shuffling crowd, in a haze of Brylcreem and nervous sweat.

So, for the minute, the tension eased. It was not considered neces-sary to talk while dancing, which was just as well because in the first place neither I nor my partner could be sure of understanding what the other was trying to say, and in the second, we had no common ground on which to base a conversation. All too soon, though, the music would stop and one had to say something if he was not to skedaddle back to his mates, leaving one stranded in no-man's-land. At meals, family rules required us to make three attempts to talk to a neighbouring stranger, and only if these drew no response were you justified in abandoning conversation as a lost cause and devoting your attention to your plate. Applying the same principle at the village dance, I would kick off with a question about the day's competitions.

'How did you get on at the Sports?'

'Not so bad, ta,' was the usual unhelpful response.

Silence. He was about to ditch me. 'Do you live near here?' I'd ask desperately, but it was no use. He would mutter the name of some farm I'd never heard of and lumber off before I could even formulate a third question. It was disheartening.

An unexpected lifeline out of such social impasses proved to be televi-sion, which was slowly spreading to all but the most inaccessible farms. At last there was a shared interest we could chat about, and though I was always straining to understand the quirky speech patterns peculiar to Radnor-shire, with their carefree use of pronouns ('Us do know more about she than her do know about we,' was one of Mummy's favourite examples) it made talking to our neighbours – whether at shearing lunches, harvest suppers, or these stiff and stilted dances – very much easier for me.

During these teenage years, Fforest Farm was always crammed with extra children, many of them foreign and not slow to complain about hard work and minimal comfort. Since Ron and Milly Weale had left to run their own farm, Mummy had joyfully assumed supreme command, though she still had to rely heavily on the inherited lore of her newly promoted foreman, young Bill James, barely out of his teens but serious, hard-working, and well-liked in the neighbourhood. Between them they set to work to build up a herd of pedigree Welsh Black cattle, a tough, long-lived, dual-purpose breed far better suited to local conditions than the poor delicate Guernseys.

She also continued to rely a good deal on child labour, which came as a bit of a shock to town-bred teenagers from France, Switzerland, or Spain who thought they had come to improve their spoken English, only to find themselves roped into feeding, herding, and mucking-out farm animals, painting barns and repairing fences along with their hostess's children.

Beastly little snob that I was, I was wary of inviting my schoolfriends to stay, being all too keenly aware of the difference between our higgledy-piggledy life and their well-ordered holiday entertainments. When I stayed with girls from my form, our days would be filled with Hunt Balls and tennis parties, concerts and plays, whereas to any non-rider who came to us all I could offer in the way of diversion was painting the enormous roof of the covered yard which had replaced the midden as the farmyard's central feature.

Gerry was far more socially confident than me, and his friends made themselves useful about the farm, revelling in driving tractors with no nonsense about age or licences, and tinkering with farm machinery. Though willing, they were often naïve and failed to anticipate danger until it was upon them. Many a time the stripped-down, all-purpose Land Rover was bogged or overturned on the hill, and everyone had a scare when a big strong Etonian who had been assigned the job of stacking hay-bales at the top of the barn failed to respond to questions from below about why he had stopped unloading the elevator.

When Gerry climbed up to investigate, he found his friend collapsed and only semi-conscious, having been gassed by the fumes trapped under the roof, and had to drag him out double-quick.

Riding home on top of the hay-load in the warm, velvety dusk, with the sweet scent of honeysuckle wafting from the hedges, itching and tickling and aching all over after hours of heaving bales about, and looking forward keenly to supper and cider and singing, is one of my defining memories of summer in those years. Like all farmers, we kept a close eye on the weather, and an even closer ear to the predictions of our neighbours, and if a hot spell out-lasted the hay harvest we made the most of it with a visit to the sand-dunes at Borth, our nearest bit of seaside.

As soon as Gerry passed his driving test, he would drive us over the intervening hills in the open Land Rover, with a couple of us seated on the wide, square bonnet, clinging to the handles placed there for the purpose, and the rest crammed onto the bench-style front seat, legs entangled with the gears, or standing in the back, hanging on to the flimsy framework which normally supported the canvas top. Top-heavy and wildly overloaded, with arms and legs and flying hair in every direction, the jeep used to look like the illustration of police pursuing Mr Toad in *The Wind in the Willows*.

The only place Daddy refused to let us ride was on the tailboard.

'I've seen too many soldiers bounced off and run over by the vehicle behind,' he said very seriously. Though I couldn't see why we were more likely to be bounced off from the tailboard than from the bonnet, it was so rare for Daddy to put his foot down on a safety issue that nobody argued.

It was an exhilarating way to travel. We would wiggle up the mountain roads past Llangammarch and Llanyrtyd Wells, past Llwyn Madoc and Abergwesyn, and on to the open single-track, gravelly road that crossed the wild mountains, home to nothing but a few straggle-fleeced sheep and tangle-maned ponies, and finally creep down through narrow lanes flanked by high hedges until our noses caught the unmistakable tang of seaweed.

Bumping in low gear as near as we dared to the sea, we would abandon the jeep among the dunes and carry our food and rugs and towels to the edge of the beach, which was usually deserted, since Aberdovey, just across the estuary, drew most of the fledgling tourist trade. Bitterly cold though the water was, the exertion of getting there would keep me just warm enough for a brief dip and shoulders-under, but Gerry and Miranda were much hardier and would stay in – it seemed to me – for hours. No-one bothered with sun-cream in those days, and after sprawling about on the beach throughout a blazing August afternoon, most of us would return home with the shape of our bathing dresses or trunks clearly outlined in white against the rest of our lobster-red bodies and the prospect of several days of unattractively peeling noses, but given Radnorshire's usual dismal weather, we all regarded these as a badge of honour.

Now and again Daddy would prevail upon Mummy to join him in London for a few days, and the summer when I was fifteen I was proud to be left in charge at the Fforest while they were away. Gerry was in British Columbia with the British Schools Exploring Foundation, and the other children had gone with an au pair to stay at Chapel House.

Before she left, Mummy asked me to take Warrior, a young black gelding whom we were just starting to hack about the hills, over to the blacksmith – a boring job which I put off until his shoes were loose and clinking as he moved before reluctantly saddling him on a hot afternoon and riding the three miles to the smithy at Cregrina and waiting in the shade while the farrier put on a new set.

Warrior had a peaceful, laid-back nature and no great eagerness to exert himself in the heat, and we were slopping along the road on the way home, with me holding his reins in one hand and using a frond of bracken to swish away flies with the other when... I opened my eyes to find Mummy bending over me as I lay on the bottom bunk in the room I shared with Miranda, looking more frightened than I had ever seen her, saying, 'Can you hear me, darling? What happened?'

I tried to answer but my mouth was so swollen I could only mutter, and the odd thing was that although only semi-conscious I knew quite well I was lying when I told her I had been riding on Beili Bychan Common, which was right at the other end of the farm.

From that day to this I have no memory of what happened that afternoon, though I had ridden or led Warrior home and turned him out in his proper field, walked up the drive and put his tack in the stables before collapsing on Miranda's bunk.

Plainly I had fallen headfirst on the road. My face was a mess, nose broken again – 'Why can't you put your hands in front of it?' asked Mummy despairingly – and a semicircle of cuts on my cheeks and upper lip looked as if one of Warrior's new shoes had played its part. I still wonder what happened to scare him into such uncharacteristic behaviour, but the hours between 3 and 10pm that day remain obstinately blank.

The cuts and bruises gradually healed, but it was agreed that nothing much could be done about my nose until I finished growing.

Two years later, however, I was taken to the Middlesex Hospital to meet the New Zealander Rainsford Mowlem, who had learned from the pioneer plastic surgeon Sir Archibald McIndoe how to reconstruct damaged faces. He stared at me from every angle and explained what he could and could not do in the reconstruction line; then he and Mummy had fun drawing lots of noses within these parameters, all of which looked much the same to me.

I was booked in for an operation in which he scooped a sliver of bone from my hip, carved it into a suitable shape and used this to prop up the remains of my nose, with a neat seam at the bottom of the septum to add to all the other scars. Mummy warned me not to look in a mirror for a week, but of course as soon as I got out of bed I couldn't resist having a peek, and nearly screamed when confronted by a greeny-black-and-blue version of the Lord of the Flies, with tiny slits of eyes – definitely no rival for Helen of Troy.

The swelling took a good ten days to go down, and meanwhile I luxuriated in the undreamed of comfort of the Middlesex's Woolavington Wing, ordering my own meals, reading one trashy novel after another, and slowly losing the £5 per day which Daddy had thoughtfully provided for me to place bets on horses. It was an agreeable interval, though curiously my hip hurt more than my nose.

By the time I was ready to face the world again, everyone agreed that Mr Mowlem had done a good job.

'It'll do for a few years,' he said laconically. 'If it looks absurd when she's forty, we can do some more work on it.'

Forty seemed unimaginably distant to me then – a world away. Absurd or not, even when I reached and passed that age I felt no urge to tinker with his handiwork, though for fear of a repeat performance I have taken particular care to protect my nose from violent contact with hard surfaces ever since.

CHAPTER SEVEN

France

NOW I WAS over sixteen and had finished with school it was time to see a bit more of the world. Apart from two skiing holidays cosily cocooned among English-speakers I had never been abroad, so the thought of launching off among foreigners on my own was both exhilarating and daunting.

The first question was where to go, and for various reasons France seemed the obvious choice. Mummy loved the country and had spent much of her early childhood in Normandy where, before the First World War, her father had owned a flourishing textile factory near Rouen and cut a dash with his racehorses at Longchamps and Maison Lafitte. However, when France devalued its currency after the war, Grandfather lost his fortune overnight. From 24 to the pound sterling, the franc fell to 240, dealing his business a crippling blow. The racehorses were sold, the factory couldn't pay its suppliers, and in 1921 he fell victim to the Spanish 'flu epidemic and died.

Mummy was only seven at the time but her eldest brother, my Uncle Breynton, resigned his cavalry commission and, with one brother, Jack, at Dartmouth Naval College and the youngest, Giles, at school at Bradfield, set to work to learn the textile business so that he could pay off Maison Mills's debts and put the firm on a sound financial footing again.

My widowed grandmother, Elsie, was the third daughter in the large family of a fashionable portrait painter, John Hanson Walker, a protégé (and natural son) of Sir Frederic Leighton. She had been only 22 when she married her 44-year-old husband Robert Mills, who came of a line of Gloucestershire parsons and was, by all accounts, a clever, didactic and irascible man. He tried – not very successfully – to dominate his young bride and curb her extravagance, but during their marriage, Granny became expert at getting her own way while maintaining a pretence of demure obedience. When Robert died, leaving her to cope with his money troubles, she rose to the challenge magnificently.

Within months she had sold her Hampshire home and moved the family to Normandy, buying a house near the textile factory. Mummy, who was sent to a local school, therefore spoke fluent French, though she was always more secure in the vocabulary of the playground than of the corridors of power. I, on the contrary, was quite well-read in French literature and strong on grammar, thanks to Mammy's unbending regime at Lawnside, but could hardly stammer my way through a couple of sentences *viva voce*, and it was agreed that a year in France should put right this deficiency.

Then there was the question of how to pay for this French interlude, since currency restrictions were still tight in 1954. You were not allowed to take more than a pittance out of the country, so my father and Uncle Giles had agreed that each of them would pay for the other's children when they went abroad.

All my surviving grandparents urged me to seize this opportunity to spend the year in Paris, home of high fashion, culture, and the most delicious food in the world. 'The Louvre!' they sighed. 'Notre Dame! Dior! The Sorbonne!' but none of these (not even the food) held much allure for a determined philistine like me, and the thought of having to wear 'tidy clothes' – stockings, suspender belt, skirt and high heels – all day and every day was unappealing. Besides, Paris was full of former Lawnsidians who had been sent off to be 'finished,' and their letters made it plain that these establishments were just as strictly chaperoned and full of tiresome rules as any English boarding-school.

Over the next few months therefore, while I earned my keep after a fashion by helping at Fforest Farm and taking charge of the milking, my parents trawled their network of family and friends in search of an alternative to Paris, and eventually turned up a possibility in the shape of the Chateau d'Availles, a big country house ten miles from Poitiers in the heart of *la France profonde*. Here an enterprising and sociable spinster of impeccable *ton* and slender means named Marie-Therese Martel-Piault (no relation, as she said sadly, to the brandy distillers) augmented her income by welcoming small groups of foreign girls – never more than five at a time – to her home and introducing them to French life.

It sounded promising on paper, but plainly needed checking out. Mummy and Daddy cleared a long weekend, zoomed in their sleek black Riley 2½ litre over the ruler-straight but incredibly bumpy, poplar-lined roads to Tours, then wiggled along the white-gravelled country lanes to the miniscule hamlet of St. Julien l'Ars, where the Chateau d'Availles was the only house of any substance.

Tall, plain and elegant, with slatted shutters, sash windows, stone steps leading down to a long tree-lined avenue and an atmosphere of complete tranquillity, it was the quintessential French country house. They fell in love with it at once, and nearly as quickly with the sprightly, effusive little Frenchwoman who tripped down the steps to welcome them.

Like Brag, Mlle Martel was a pocket Napoleon who made up for her lack of inches by force of character, and it was difficult to judge her age. Her long hair, uncompromisingly dyed black with no hint of silver, was pulled straight back from her lined and wrinkled forehead, and her mouth was a garish slash of scarlet surrounded by pin-tucks, but her face was dominated by deep-socketed, fine large eyes, sparkling with enthusiasm and mischief. She spoke sonorous, patrician French, each consonant and vowel precisely enunciated, and this clarity was echoed on paper, for her handwriting was some of the most beautiful I have ever seen – bold, flowing and, though regular, possessed of an indefinable dash that made it wholly individual.

Effortlessly she charmed my parents into overlooking any drawbacks like primitive plumbing and the lack of tennis courts, swimming pool, or even drinkable water. All that could be found in Poitiers, she assured them, and as for company, any girl who stayed with her would meet the pick of the local *jeunesse dorée* – she gave regular bridge parties and small dances – and we would be invited to all the big houses in the neighbourhood, whose owners she had known since childhood.

It only remained to check out her claims with the Wimpole Street doctor and his wife whose daughter Sara had already been at Availles for two terms and, when Sara enthusiastically backed up Mlle Martel's account, to book my first-ever air ticket to Paris.

Heathrow was an eye-opener to me – so clean, airy, and spacious, with rich-looking, relaxed passengers carrying expensive suitcases and wearing light-coloured clothing of the sort you would never risk in a train. It was a world away from the smutty, gritty, crowded railway stations of those days and, it has to be said, a world away from the shabby, stressful places that airport terminals have now become. We kept an eye open for Sara, who was travelling on the same plane, but Mummy couldn't spot her, and finally waved me through to the departure lounge on my own.

I was already aboard and fiddling with my seat-belt, unsure how it worked but reluctant to ask, when a commotion in the aisle heralded Sara's approach. She had both hands full of carrier bags and cardboard boxes, far more than you were meant to take in the cabin, plus a bunch of flowers, and was calling out thanks to someone behind her, apologising to people as she forced them out of her way, flashing smiles this way and that, struggling with the overhead locker until every man within two rows leapt up to help her, and generally behaving like a film star.

I watched in fascination. She was like a tiny, delicate porcelain doll, with beautifully set hair swept back from her smooth brow and curled into little symmetrical horns above her temples, wide-set greeny-blue eyes and regular features that reminded me of nothing so much as a shop-window mannequin. Her supple, figure-hugging coat and skirt in soft green tweed were the last word in fashion, and her neat, narrow feet wore highly polished court shoes with stacked heels – again *dernier cri*. Beside her slender, glossy perfection I felt lumpish and badly dressed and could hardly believe she was only fifteen, nearly two years younger than me, because she looked at least twenty-five.

We introduced ourselves, and she astonished me again by ordering half a bottle of wine with her lunch. When the steward brought the trolley round she not only bought 200 cigarettes in a large carton, the whole duty-free allowance, but told me to do the same.

'I'll never get through them,' I said, laughing.

'No, no – they're for me. I smoke two packs a day, and blond tobac-co's so expensive in France,' she said with a kind of weary patience that something so obvious had to be explained.

Two packs a day? When on earth could she find the time? Was she showing off? I wondered. Joking? Not a bit of it. She filled her cigarette case and lit up as soon as the trolley moved on, leaning back in her seat and inhaling with a tremendously sophisticated air that I longed to emulate.

Porters, taxi, train to Poitiers – she dealt with everything in what sounded to me like perfect French, all the inflections just right. This was her third term at Availles, she told me, and I hugged to myself the thought of Mummy's surprise and delight if I could learn to speak as she did. What she didn't mention then and I found out later was that Availles was her second French billet. The year before she had lived *en famille* with friends of her mother's near Tours until the son of the house had become 'tiresome' – code for amorous, I suppose – and she had been placed under Mlle Martel's wing instead. It must have been during this first placement, when she was alone among foreigners, that her French had become so fluent.

The fatal flaw in sending me to Availles was the presence of other English girls, because of course being typical lazy teenagers, we used our own language not only to one another, but also to all the young men and women who came to Mlle Martel's parties and were keen to practise their English. Only at meals and in class did we make a real effort: even when we went to lectures at the University of Poitiers there were lots of other foreigners to undermine our attempts to speak French, and I never progressed beyond a certain point.

That was in the future, though. We were met at Poitiers by Mlle Martel's tame taxi-driver, small, squat, saturnine Didier, who had already fielded a third pupil for Availles, a dark, chic, exotic-looking girl wearing a striped pink shirt with a stand-up collar and big turned-back cuffs, tightly cinched by a wide shiny belt into a black hobble skirt. We had noticed her on the train, leafing through *Paris-Match*, but assumed she was French. She certainly didn't look in the least English. Her complexion was very pale, her lips and nails a daring frosted sugar-pink, and a narrow lock of her wavy black hair was carefully pulled forward on to either cheek in what Daddy rather coarsely called, 'Bugger's grips,' but others might describe as kiss curls. Long earrings like small warming-pans dangled to her collar. But what struck me most was her truly skeletal thinness. Cally's wrists and ankles looked as if they'd break at a touch, and it was no wonder her clothes hung so well because they had no bulges at all to contend with. She had a shy smile and a warm, soft voice, and men found her absolutely irresistible.

Didier was already charmed by the time Sara and I showed up. He shoved in our luggage any old how, and gallantly installed Cally in the favoured front seat of his black Citroen quinze. This quickly became the pattern with everyone we encountered. Male and female, young and old took one look at Cally and fell over themselves to please, aid and protect her from the evils of the world and, most of all, from her naughty, obstinate, health-destroying self.

Nowhere did they try harder than at meals. It was the first time I had encountered an anorexic and seen the curious effect produced on others by someone who steadily refused to eat. It seemed to give Cally a particular power and interest with which Sara and I – ordinary hungry teenagers – could not compete.

Though painfully thin, she would gently decline the offer of the most tempting foods, and instead of saying, 'Well, don't blame me if you're hungry before supper,' or words to that effect, Mlle Martel would send down to the kitchen for something different – an omelette, perhaps, or a little individual cheese soufflé – in a way that would ordinarily have sent Celestine, the grumpy, work-worn cook, into screaming hysterics – but no. Minutes later she would plod up the stone steps from her basement kitchen with some delicious offering on a tray, and Cally would thank her, and cut it in half and then in quarters, and add salt, and push it around her plate until it was leathery and cold (and every eye at the table was on her) and then perhaps take one or two tiny bites before saying that was plenty.

Left to herself, she would have survived on cigarettes and black coffee. Like Sara, she was a chain-smoker, lighting a fresh one from the still-burning stub of its predecessor, preferably a gold-tipped Balkan Sobranie, though these were hard to come by in Poitiers – and she became animated on two subjects alone: fashion and jazz. 'Classical jazz,' she always insisted solemnly, as if there was any other kind, and though I knew nothing and cared less about Sidney Bechet, Louis Armstrong, Jelly Roll Morton and the rest of the great New Orleans jazzmen, I would encourage her to talk about them because I found it marginally more interesting than analysing fashion.

Her brother Russell, another jazz freak, used to send her records which we played on Mlle Martel's little wind-up gramophone in the big salon with its double doors and polished floor. We would push back the furniture and carefully lower the needle – it was inclined to jump unless you had a steady hand – and then as the blare of sax and trombone stirred her blood, Cally would take her only exercise, swaying to the music in her hobble skirt and spike heels with some favoured swain, a rapt, dreamy expression on her face, while everyone else jived wildly.

Mlle Martel had in no way exaggerated her claim that Availles was a social hub. We often had two 'surprise-parties' in a week, besides bridge with the neighbours and endless spontaneous droppers-in – generally ravenous young men round about tea-time when Celestine's famous galette might make an appearance.

Because the telephone was generally defunct, these callers were seldom expected but always made welcome and urged to stay for whatever meal happened to be nearest. Old or young, priest, doctor, landowner, visiting nephew, aged aunt, they would sing for their supper by regaling Mlle Martel with local gossip, and inviting her to bring her bunch of '*belles jeunes filles en fleur*,' as they charmingly referred to us, to lunch or tea or play tennis with them whenever she pleased.

Poitiers society – what one might call the dinner-party set – was then small and tight-knit, with all sorts of class distinctions of which we were ignorant, but Mlle Martel was rigorous about admitting only the scions of families she considered beyond reproach to consort with her jeunes filles at Availles. She had no objection to our meeting boys of less distinguished backgrounds at the University or the riverbank café known as the *Fleuve Lethe* – the River of Oblivion – but if we encouraged them to visit us in her house they were quickly shown the door.

'You never know what to expect from people like that,' she would say decisively.

'Beastly old snob,' Lisa would mutter *sotto voce*. She was the fourth

English pupil and had arrived by car with her parents two days after the rest of us. From the first she made it plain that she was at Availles under protest. She had no interest in France or the French, she thought we were all ridiculously frivolous (she might have had a point there) and that literature and art were a waste of time. All she wanted was to go to technical college in Bournemouth and learn shorthand and typing. Though she was not unattractive physically, we found her difficult to like.

She had mousy-blonde hair cut in a boyish crop, and strongly marked dark eyebrows above a narrow, pointed nose, which gave her the look of a bird of prey. Her lower legs were thickly covered in hair. In class she made absolutely no effort to speak French, keeping a little book of shorthand symbols on her lap under the table and copying them on to paper when Genevieve, a lecturer from the university who gave us history lessons twice a week, wasn't looking. (I don't think she would have dared if Mlle Martel had been teaching.)

We led a peaceful, well-ordered life with infinite leisure to gossip and giggle, to paint our nails and dream, or lie on the lawn listening for the scrunch of wheels on gravel that heralded the arrival of a visitor.

As it grew hotter, the mournful cries of the peasants driving oxen – *'Bayard! Bayard!'* started at dawn and ceased in the middle of the afternoon, when the whole of Nature seemed to close down under the searing sun. I found it amazing that oxen-powered machines with a man trudging behind could plough, sow, reap and carry the corn off the enormous fields surrounding our château. They lumbered forward at a snail's pace, but they kept going hour after hour, and by mid-July the stubbles were bare and the harvest safely stored.

Every morning began for me in exactly the same way. As the whiff of coffee wafted up from the terrace below our bedroom, Sara would stagger out of bed and throw back the shutters. Then she would pad across the polished boards to examine her pretty petal-fresh face in the mirror over the fireplace and utter a sepulchral groan.

'God! I look a wreck!'

After breakfast, morning lessons took place round the table in the small salon. Genevieve or Mlle Martel would talk about history or French literature while we took notes, but it was all quite light-hearted and the lesson often degenerated into a discussion of last week's film or last night's party.

Twice a week we took the bus into Poitiers to attend lectures at the university, and if we missed the last bus home there was never any difficulty about hitchhiking. A hopeful thumb, a pleading look, and some little Renault or Citroen Deux Chevaux would draw up, cram us in, and deliver us to the end of Mlle Martel's tree-lined avenue.

Towards the middle of term, we were all invited to the Summer Ball at St Maixent, the military academy at Niort where several of Mlle Martel's favourite droppers-in were officer cadets. This promised to be a really slap-up party, marquees, bands, a funfair, dancing until dawn... Mlle Martel hired a small bus to take us there and back, and summoned her sister, Madame Germaine, from Paris to act as auxiliary chaperone.

The two sisters could hardly have been more different. Whereas Mlle Martel was the epitome of good breeding and good behaviour, a pillar of respectability, Madame Germaine was distinctly raffish in appearance, and had led a bohemian life. She claimed to be an artist, though the idealised puppies and kittens with bows in their hair and little girls with enormous eyes that decorated various tiles about the house were hardly High Art, but she was on friendly terms with many well-known intellectuals of the Left Bank, Jean-Paul Sartre among them. She had an illegitimate son, Guy, who worked as a journalist on the *Figaro*. Her hair was as starkly orange as Mlle Martel's was black, with no pretence that it was anything but dyed, cut in a heavy, straight, Cleopatra fringe only just clear of her long green eyes, and her complexion was dead-white, like an absinthe-addict.

For our part, we went into a frenzy over what to wear. Cally flew back to England and returned with an immense cardboard box, out of which she drew a dream of a ball-gown: midnight blue net with spangles, strapless, with an enormous skirt, and a matching stole with which to soften her sticking-out collarbones. She put it on and twirled gravely for our inspection, beautiful, ethereal, a very hard act to match.

Sara and I wrote passionate letters home, and both our mothers came up trumps. She went into Poitiers and returned triumphant with a slinky, silky, greeny-blue creation that matched her eyes, and I was taken in hand by Therese Lefevre, a chicly chignoned young woman who sometimes helped Mlle Martel. Together we visited her dressmaker, and with her devised a striking black strapless number, with fuschia flying panels attached at the hip to create a tulip-like effect. These panels caused me a good deal of trouble at the Ball, because they caught on the tops of little spindly gold chairs as I sashayed past, and the frequent sudden tugs as I was brought up short, plus the crash of the falling chair rather undermined my attempts to glide about with becoming grace.

And Lisa? She produced a letter from her uncle, asking her to join him in Paris for the very same weekend as the St Maixent Summer Ball – such a pity, but she really couldn't refuse his invitation – and on the Friday evening while we were primping and curling and nearly hysterical with excitement, Didier duly drove her to Poitiers to catch the Paris train.

None of us could eat much of the early supper Mlle Martel provided, and the moment the little white bus she had ordered appeared on the drive, we teetered out in all our finery, taking a double-seat each and carefully spreading out our precious skirts. After long thought, Cally had tied a black velvet ribbon round her white throat, and together with the spangled gauze stole the effect was stunning. Throughout the drive she sat silently, calm and serene, while Sara and I twitched and chattered nervously, and Mlle Martel and Mme Germaine made teasing remarks from the front seat just behind the driver.

We gasped when the Ecole Militaire came into sight, an enchanted castle all flood-lit and spot-lit and under-lit, with fountains flinging sparkling streams of diamonds into the air, and a huge marquee banked with flowers and pulsing with music.

The moment I got out of the bus I realised that my tight skirt and high heels were going to be a nightmare on the cobbles, but no matter: there were our three cavaliers – teasingly dubbed *Les Trois Moustiquaires* by Mlle Martel – looking incredibly glamorous in what I suppose was their mess-kit, tight trousers, gleaming buttons and shimmering epaulettes, waiting to greet us: proud, fiery, dark-haired Christian, who had a handle to his name and was Mlle Martel's favourite; his tall, fair-haired, good-looking friend Michel, and Bernard, whom they called 'Le Professeur,' short, balding, and with owlish spectacles.

No prizes for guessing who had been assigned to look after me. Christian bowed and smiled at Cally, who drifted away with him as if in a dream. Michel clicked his heels and asked Sara to dance and, after a few minutes' standing rather awkwardly on the cobbles while Bernard chatted to our chaperones, Mlle Martel took her sister's arm, said firmly, *'Allez, mes enfants, amusez-vous bien!'* and vanished into the crowd.

I felt a momentary panic, but there was no need. Bernard may not have been glamorous but he was good-natured and extremely polite, and took his duties as host very seriously. We danced, he brought me a glass of wine, he introduced me to other officer cadets who danced with me, and though from time to time he returned me to Mlle Martel, he always came back before I could feel a wallflower.

Now and then we caught glimpses of Cally and Sara whirling away with their beaux and around 2am, when I was beginning to wonder if my toes would ever regain their normal shape after being forced into points for so long, I noticed that they had swapped partners. Michel was holding Cally very close, his cheek pressed to the top of her head and his big shoulders bent protectively over her, while Sara and Christian danced with exaggerated formality at arm's length, his hand barely touching her waist, and both their heads well back as if to avoid contact. Sara looked annoyed, and Christian had a red mark on his cheekbone.

Bernard chuckled as he pointed out the new pairing to Mlle Martel, whose expressive mouth turned down at the corners. *'Oh, la la! Il est jaloux comme un tigre, le pauvre,'* she said. She shook her head and gave him a beseeching look. 'Be an angel and calm him, chou-chou.'

Bernard rose and took my hand. 'Come, mademoiselle.' I was far from pleased that they had chosen to feed me to the tiger, but Christian was too much of a gentleman to let his feelings get the better of him, and when tapped on the shoulder and offered me as a substitute dancing partner, he accepted the situation with good enough grace, while over the other side of the dance-floor Cally, eyes half closed, drifted serenely on, tightly wrapped in Michel's embrace.

On the way home in the breaking dawn, Sara was full of indignation. 'They had a fight! When I tried to stop them Christian pushed me away and I fell over and tore my skirt. Serves him right if he got a black eye.'

Though grateful for Bernard's protection throughout the long evening, I couldn't help regretting having missed this drama.

On Monday, however, when we surfaced round about midday, we found that Lisa had returned in an agitated state of mind. For some reason she chose to confide in me as we walked down the long avenue to the main road in the cool of the evening, and what she told me entirely altered my view of her.

She had not, it appeared, spent the weekend in Paris with her uncle. The letter purporting to be from him which she had shown Mlle Martel had actually been written by her boyfriend Nathaniel, whom she had arranged to meet in London. On arrival at the Gare de Lyons, therefore, she had crossed Paris by taxi, which made a large dent in her savings, taken the train to the coast and bought a ticket for the ferry from Calais to Dover. Another train deposited her at Waterloo station, where Nathaniel was waiting.

So far, so successful, but after this the story went steeply downhill. They had booked into a hotel in Sloane Street as man and wife, but after making love – first time for either of them – she had been gripped by such an agonising pain in her down-belows that she had forced Nathaniel to go out into the street to find an all-night chemist and explain the problem as best he could. The pharmacist, no doubt sniffing irregularity, had not been sympathetic or helpful, and poor Nathaniel, hot with embarrassment and without a prescription, had not been able to obtain anything stronger than aspirin.

All the next day had been spent holed up in the cheap hotel, Lisa doubled up with cramps and Nathaniel hovering anxiously. She had blamed him, snapped at him, and when finally he left to go back to St John's Leatherhead, where he was in the Sixth Form, told him she never wanted to see him again – words she now bitterly regretted.

By degrees the cramps eased, and she made the return journey without incident, but now – inevitably – she was terribly afraid she might be pregnant. The whole adventure had been an unmitigated disaster, and she wished very much that she had come to the St Maixent Summer Ball instead.

I made soothing noises and longed to tell the others the whole story, but unfortunately she'd made me promise not to, though from then on I regarded her in a very different light.

Much more frequent visitors than the glamorous officer-cadets were the three sons of a neighbouring landowner, all in their early twenties and unashamedly looking for wives. The eldest was Paul, the Vicomte, who wasn't actually deformed but nevertheless always reminded me of Toulouse-Lautrec, with a big head on top of hunched shoulders and thin legs. Next in line came fair-haired, silent, wooden-featured Pierre; and the youngest – our favourite – florid, jolly, roly-poly Hilaire, who looked like a peasant farmer and, being the proud owner of one of the very few tractors in the neighbourhood did, indeed, spend most of his life on it.

Though none of us had yet thought of actively looking for husbands and scoffed at the very idea, the mere fact of being eyed up as wife-material lent a certain spark to the banter over the bridge-table. Late, late into the night, in a thick fug of cigarette smoke – Sobranie, Virginia, and the Gaullois I pretended to like although they made me feel dizzy – we played rubber after rubber before tiptoeing down the stone steps to Celestine's cavernous kitchen and raiding the larder for galette and deliciously runny Brie.

We also drank heroic quantities of wine and pineau, but despite Sara's morning ritual at the mirror, it never seemed to do much harm. I suppose it wasn't particularly strong.

The only bathroom in the house adjoined our bedroom – a gloomy place smelling strongly of drains with a deep, greyish basin whose enamel was so scratched and scarred that it never looked clean, and a narrow bath with a complicated arrangement of taps that produced tepid water impartially from each head. There was also a stove. One Sunday morning I met Celestine toiling upstairs with a basket of logs, and presently the smell of woodsmoke filled the house.

'*Mademoiselle va se baigner,*' she explained.

'Se' baigner turned out to be a very loose interpretation. When Mademoiselle Martel took a bath – once a term – she liked everyone in the household to be in attendance, just in case…

When the stove had heated a big copper jug of water near to boiling point, Celestine poured it into the bath and ceremoniously diluted it with cold until the temperature was pronounced *'convenable'*. Then she and Madame Germaine helped Mlle Martel to remove her clothes and lower herself gingerly into the water. Sara and I stood by the door, ready to sound the alarm if she should come over faint, and Gaston, the gardener, stationed himself at the foot of the stairs, all prepared to dash up and fish his employer out of the bath at a moment's notice.

Cally – who had a gentle, soothing voice and was less inclined to giggle than the rest of us – was co-opted to stand in a corner of the bathroom to pass the soap and face-cloth and, ultimately, the carefully warmed towel. The whole performance was highly choreographed, with messages passing up and down the chain of command.

'She's in the water.'

'She's having her back washed.'

'Madame Germaine is cutting her toe-nails.' (That was the point at which I quit, never having been keen on foot-care.)

Finally, with maximum hullabaloo, she rose from the bath like Venus from the foam, was swaddled in several fluffy white towels and given a restorative nip of brandy. She spent the rest of the day lying down to regain her composure, while Celestine and Gaston cleared up the bathroom.

I was so happy at Availles that I would have liked to spend the rest of the year there, but over the summer holidays a new plan was hatched, and this time the Paris-touting culture-vultures had their way.

It so happened that Aunt Nancy's former governess, Mlle Roblin, with whom she had kept in touch over the past thirty years, had invested all her savings in buying a small modern flat in the 6th Arondissement, not far from the Jardins de Luxembourg, 11 rue Joseph Bara. Her idea was to board English pupils, who would enrol in the 10-week *Cours de Civilisation* run by the Sorbonne as a nice little money-spinner, and introduce them to the delights of French culture.

Aunt Nancy had loyally booked a place for Clarissa in Mlle Roblin's initial intake, and leaned heavily on my parents to do the same with me. It was absurd, she said, to spend a year buried in the depths of la France profonde in the company of a lot of country bumpkins when all the glamour and glory of Paris was there for the taking, and so persuasive was she that finally they agreed.

So it was that Clarissa and I, along with her school friend Rosemary and the daughter of a vague connection of Uncle Harold's named Gina found ourselves that autumn cooped up in extremely tight quarters with tall, severe, black-haired Mlle Roblin, whom I'm afraid I disliked on sight. It wasn't that she was in any way unkind, far from it, but she was strict and humourless and made all sorts of pettyfogging rules about keys, and using the telephone, and when you could or couldn't use the shower. It was worse than being back at school.

Right from the start Paris was a disappointment to me. I have never been happy in towns, hate the noise and smell of traffic, and feel uneasy among crowds. After the fun and freedom of the Chateau d'Availles, the cramped little flat with four strapping teenagers in it felt unbearably claustrophobic and I took to walking alone in the Jardin de Luxembourg like a prisoner in the exercise yard, *Les sanglots longs, Des violons, De l'automne, Blessent mon coeur/D'une langueur/Monotone...* pounding maddeningly in my mind. An equally depressing song popular at the time, *Les Feuilles Mortes*, seemed to echo my mood. The last line, I remember, was '*Et la mer efface sur le sable/Les pas des amants desunis,*' and I tried to whip up self-pity and emotion by imagining myself cruelly parted from a lover, but without success since the poor chap simply didn't exist.

Unlike Lisa, Sara, and particularly Cally, my life so far had been quite remarkably free of lovers, and the prospect of finding one in Paris seemed remote. Mlle Roblin didn't have the kind of social network that had made Availles such a lively, friendly place. If she had young friends and relations, she didn't risk introducing them to us, and our male fellow-students at the Sorbonne's *Cours de Civilisation* were a scruffy lot of the beards-and-sandals tendency, many of them German and Italian, their ages ranging from the teens to early thirties. It was difficult to imagine falling madly in love with any of them.

We attended lectures in the huge Amphitheatre Richelieu, a domed and cavernous hall with galleries on two levels. Even the twelve hundred students on the course made a thinnish audience in such a space, but the lecturers were first-class, spoke extremely clearly, and held our attention effortlessly – no mean feat with such a mixed bag of foreigners. Every morning there would be three lectures with a fifteen-minute break between each, during which time we would dash out to the corridors and courtyards for a drag.

The proper students – the French ones – seemed to be in a permanent state of fury with the authorities, and because we had very little interaction it was hard for us to make out exactly what was bugging them; but I thought money – or rather the lack of it – was the root of the problem. One exciting morning a flying mob came pelting up the steps from the cobbled courtyard, some limping, some with blood on their faces, shouting out that the riot police were after them.

'*Prenez garde! Ils tappent sur n'importe qui!* They hit first and ask questions later!' one was good enough to warn us as he dashed past.

The university authorities locked the doors and we had a long wait before we were allowed home for lunch. Historically the Sorbonne had a name as a home-from-home for subversives, and over the next years relations between students and police continued to deteriorate until they came to a head in the full-scale riots of 1968.

Mlle Roblin did the cooking herself, and fed us like fighting cocks. Once she asked me to collect the money for her weekly shopping from the Bank, and I was appalled to discover that she spent the equivalent of over £70 a week on meat and groceries for us – this when Mummy could feed the whole family for a tenner. I had never handled so much money in my life, and scuttled home on the Metro with my handbag clutched in a death-grip, feeling sure that the X-ray eyes of every thief in the arondissement could see what was in my purse.

When we returned to the Sorbonne after lunch, sleepy and well-fed, we would be dispersed into classrooms for written work. Thanks to Mammy, I could cope with this pretty well and found myself assigned to the top set where our teacher was the stout, sardonic Professeur Laval, a tremendous roller of Rs who, with one blistering comment, could pulverise the self-esteem of even the most bumptious student. In his presence I kept the lowest of profiles. He was an avowed egalitarian, very likely a communist, and when he took our names at the first lesson he was chagrined to discover among his pupils a face-grinding aristo – a Baron, no less.

Left: A lovely day's fishing at The Rocks, near Builth Wells, for me, Olivia and Gerry – but we caught nothing at all.

Above: Jumping Taffy in the Sporborgs' field, Much Hadham.

Below: Summer, 1948. Camping beside the Colwyn brook, which rose and flooded our bell tents. *Left to right:* Clarissa, David, Gerry, me, Olivia.

Above: Flash, who would go rabbiting with his mother Judy for days at a time.

Right: Mummy looking unusually pensive by the Chapel House lily pond in 1942.

Below: Mummy realising with annoyance that she is just about to shed a load of oats off the buck-rake, c.1952.

Above: I am unusually tidily dressed for tea with visitors in the Fforest garden overlooking the moat, 1953.

Left: Heygrove, the Hereford bull, weighed the best part of a ton and smashed through gates like match-wood.

Below: Romance for Heygrove, held by Ron Weale, farm manager, with his No 2, Bill James, holding the cow.

Above: The Radnor and West Hereford Hunt meet at Fforest Farm. On foot, Bridget Hart-Davis (among hounds) and my grandfather, Sir George Barstow, in mackintosh (centre).

Below: Picnic at Wolf's Leap, Abergwesyn. Gerry builds a scientific fire while Bonzo, the blacksmith's terrier, takes care of the food.

Above: Wild Welsh Mountain ponies greet tame ones above the Fforest.

Right: A long way to the top. Sylvia Weale and Miranda climb the haystack.

Below: Gerry, me, Olivia, Miranda and George on the garden wall, c.1954.

Bottom left: Jack Howells on everyone's favourite tractor, the Fergie 20.

Bottom right: Watkins, our ally against Mr Hadley, the head gardener at Chapel House.

Above: Winterscape: Beili Bychan common, enclosed as part of Fforest Farm, photographed by Olivia.

Below right: The best entertainment I could devise for visiting school-friends was painting the roof of the covered yard c.1952.

Below left: Scot, the best dog in the world – though certainly not the best sheep-dog.

Above: Summer holidays 1953. My first perm was deeply un-flattering and all my clothes had shrunk.

Left: Olivia and I take a break with Scot in the Fforest garden, summer 1953.

Below: Cowgirl Shirley exercising Smatcher and Ginger in the snow on our only flat field, once the castle's keep.

Above: My Coming-Out Dance during the Suez crisis was distinctly short of National Servicemen friends. Left to right: David Rutherford, me, my parents and Granny.

Right: My wedding to Duff Hart-Davis was on 22 April 1961, the wettest day of the year - but also the happiest.

Below: Full circle: our daughter Alice, born 1963, learns to rise to the trot on Nutty, with Preciway, retired steeplechaser, setting the pace.

'Perhaps Monsieur Celli would give us the benefit of his views on Voltaire,' he sneered, unable to bring himself to pronounce the title.

'Baron Celli,' the small, dark Italian murmured, gently but firmly.

'Your views on Voltaire, Monsieur Celli.'

'Baroncelli!' his friends chorused, because in fact the poor man's name was Agusto Baroncelli. The Professeur was far from pleased and thereafter seized every opportunity to needle him.

Because I was living among English speakers, my spoken French had hardly improved at all by the end of term, and though I felt confident enough that I had passed the written tests in French History, Philosophy, and Literature I was horrified to see Professeur Laval among the three examiners for the Oral section of the diploma.

After a bit of aimless chitchat, I was given a boring passage from an essay entitled *'L'homme qui sait tout'* to read aloud, and stumbled through it with the doom-laden feeling that I was making a pig's ear of the pronunciation and they were laughing at my accent.

'Eh bien, now tell me, what does it mean, *L'homme qui sait tout?*' asked one of the examiners, and I looked at him uncomprehendingly. What did it mean? Wasn't that obvious? The man who knows everything – how else could one put it? The Know-All? The Busybody? Was it meant ironically? Like a shorthand writer reading back what she has written, I had been too preoccupied with the words of the text to take in their sense.

'Well, mademoiselle?' he said impatiently.

Reaching back into my memory, I fished out a Latin word, hoping it was the same in French. 'It means *omniscient*,' I said tentatively. 'He thinks himself omniscient.' There was a short pause, then Monsieur Laval laughed. 'Good! *C'est trrrres bien, mademoiselle. C'est même savant.*'

To that one lucky word I therefore attribute scoring the second highest marks in the entire diploma course – the winner being none other than Signor Agusto Baroncelli. When the result was read out by the head of the department in the big Amphitheatre, I heard a whoop and saw out of the corner of my eye something drop from the gallery into the body of the hall as the winner abseiled down to collect his certificate without bothering to use the stairs, and I am glad to say that Professeur Laval had the grace to shake him warmly by the hand.

Life in Paris, with its emphasis on French culture, dignified behaviour, and tidy clothes may not have been entirely my cup of tea, but Mummy's brothers – Breynton and Giles – snapped into full avuncular mode as soon as they heard I was regretting the freedom of Availles. Not only did they take me and Clarissa to the Opera and the Crazy Horse, but also introduced us to the delights of the racecourses so conveniently placed on the capital's perimeter.

Longchamps, Maison Lafitte and Vincennes were all within easy Metro distance from rue Joseph Bara, and as soon as we knew the way we went there most Sunday afternoons. Race-meetings were often on Sunday, and after Matins in the English Church, which provided yet another opportunity to chatter in our own language, we would dive down into the Metro and rattle all the way out to the Bois de Vincennes for the equivalent of about two shillings. I never understood why the London Underground should be so expensive – the longer the journey the more you paid – while you could dart about Paris all day and all night on a single flat-rate ticket.

Vincennes epitomised the grubbier, grittier aspects of the racing scene and attracted huge crowds every Sunday, with many of North African and Middle Eastern aspect, and heavy emphasis on betting. The trotteurs who competed in harness races on a cinder track looked so completely different from the graceful thoroughbred beauties of Flat racing proper that they might have belonged to an alien species. Lean to the point of gauntness, long-legged and long-necked, with Frink-type big, plain heads, they appeared downright ugly in repose, their looks hardly enhanced by festoons of straps, hoods, blinkers and winkers, bandages and complicated devices to stop them breaking into a gallop.

In action, though, it was a different story. Pounding round the track with nostrils flaring and legs flailing, they became almost beautiful as they covered the ground with amazing speed, balancing their weight against that of the driver in his light, two-wheeled sulky. As the highly partisan crowd roared its favourites home, some of the finishes were thrilling, though like the Roman chariot-racing from which it derived, harness-racing was no stranger to questionable practices. I remember Clarissa and I were highly indignant when a gallant one-eyed trotter not much bigger than a pony put up a tremendous performance to beat the odds-on favourite driven by crafty Charlot Mills whose reputation was less than stainless, only to be relegated to second place purely, it seemed to us, to appease the fury of the crowd.

Going racing with Uncle Breynton was a very different affair. He believed in doing things in style, and chose for our first outing to Longchamps the first Sunday in October, the most glamorous date in the French racing calendar when the Prix de l'Arc de Triomphe attracted – as it still does – the cream of the world's middle-distance stars, colts and fillies three years old and upward, handicapped weight for age over the mile-and-a-half-long right-handed, horse-shoe-shaped course with its testing two-and-a-half furlong finishing straight.

We kicked off with a slap-up lunch in a restaurant popular with the racing in-crowd, Clarissa and me in our student best but outclassed in the fashion stakes by Uncle Giles's wife Marianne, in full war-paint, very high heels, and a most desirable pale linen ensemble with a provocative plunging neckline, her wrists clanking with gold curb-chain bracelets, as she flirted impartially with her husband and brother-in-law, tall and distinguished in their tailcoats and grey toppers.

As we wiggled through the tight-packed tables, Uncle Breynton stopped here and there to greet friends. His own horses were with George Bridgland, one of several French trainers with English names, and he was well-known to the racing elite. Clarissa and I both finished the sumptuous lunch with flaming Crêpes Suzette and while I was surreptitiously easing undone the top button of my skirt I noticed some of the noisy table of Italians over by the window were looking round at us and calling, 'Bertee! Bertee!'

For a time Uncle Breynton ignored them, but presently the waiter brought a note to our table and he excused himself to Marianne and went over to have a drink with the Italians.

'Why do they call him Bertie?' asked Clarissa, and I explained that when Daddy was looking for his brother-in-law during the campaign in Italy, he was told to follow the signs *'To Bertram Mills' Circus.'*

'Mario della Rochetta,' said Uncle Breynton, coming back, 'says his horse will win.'

'But of course!' Marianne laughed. 'Zat is what zey all say!'

Uncle Giles produced a list of runners and riders. 'Ribot,' he said thoughtfully, folding it up again. 'By Tenerani. Well, maybe…'.

And, a couple of hours later, Ribot it was, wiping the floor with the opposition in the most handsome style. He came flying up the brilliant green straight between the brilliant white rails without appearing to exert himself, leaving the rest of the pack struggling in his wake, and won the Arc by the then-record margin of six lengths while Clarissa and I shouted ourselves hoarse.

We had all backed him – quite heavily, I fancy, in Uncle Breynton's case – and returned to 11 rue Joseph Bara with pockets bulging. It was a different story when he won again the following year, but I shall never forget the glory of that first triumph on a golden October day.

By the time the *Cours de Civilisation* ended in February, all four of us were suffering from claustrophobia in the crowded flat. Quarrels between us grew noisier and more frequent. Someone was always on non-speaks with someone else, and we seemed to break something and be scolded for it every single day. Outside the over-heated flat it was cold and bleak. Sitting about in cafés watching the world go by was no longer an option: you had to keep moving, so we resorted to desperate measures like walking the whole way from Montmartre to Montparnasse in a couple of hours, or taking the train out to the Bois de Boulogne to ride very old, iron-mouthed, stiff-legged horses down its long tree-lined avenues.

Mlle Roblin did her best to propel us in the direction of plays, museums, famous sights and beauty spots, but she never came with us and, culturally speaking, I have always had a low threshold of boredom. There are only so many times that one can drift about the Louvre or rubberneck at Versailles on a cold winter afternoon without really understanding what you are looking at or for. The real root of the trouble was that by then we were sick of one another's company but unable to escape it.

Things improved briefly when Uncle Harold and Aunt Nancy came to spend a week with friends at the British Embassy. Nancy took me and

Clarissa with her to a dress-show, and then for her fitting at Balmain where, while waiting for what seemed hours amid the acres of pale carpet and little gold chairs, I was so horrified by the toffee-nosed staff and clientele that I made an easily-kept vow to wear ready-made for the rest of my life.

Uncle Harold's treat was far more appealing: a real blow-out of a dinner at The White Tower, where we ordered everything flambé from kidneys to our favourite Crêpes Suzette, and while we stuffed ourselves, he gave us a blow-by-blow account of how he had masterminded the King of the Hellenes' escape when the Germans overran Greece in 1941.

Like David, Uncle Harold was a splendid raconteur and brought the scene vividly to life. The King's reluctance to leave Greece, the difficulties of smuggling him aboard a caique and the dangerous voyage to Crete with German spotter planes swooping low overhead. Then followed the long rough climb along goat-tracks through the hills to a shepherd's hut which offered safety for the night, the difficulty of persuading the monarch to get a move on without offending him, trying to stop the villagers they passed from spreading the message that they had a royal visitor, and seeking to communicate by primitive wireless with the ship that was coming from Egypt to rescue them, without giving away their exact position.

A rendezvous was at last arranged – but so many things could go wrong. The ship would stand in to a certain small bay as darkness fell, and launch a boat to take the King off only after giving and receiving an agreed signal. During the long march across the mountains, Uncle Harold and his party checked their maps again and again, agonising over whether they and the ship were heading for the same bay. Above all, could they make the RV in time, before the rising moon made the vessel an easy target?

Then – disaster! A couple of hours short of their destination, the King announced that he had left his medals behind in the shepherd's hut. In vain Uncle Harold argued that they didn't matter, and that delay would put all their lives at risk. The King dug his toes in. He didn't want to leave his people and go into exile, but his capture would be a great propaganda coup for the Germans, which the British government wanted to prevent at all costs. Obstinate by nature and increasingly resentful of being hustled from pillar to post by foreigners, he seized on the loss of the medals as a delaying tactic, insisting that the orders they represented were, for him, inextricably bound up his notion of kingship and self-worth. Until they were recovered, he would not budge.

There was nothing for it but to send someone back. The fittest, fastest runner volunteered to fetch them, and for over two hours, while the sun slipped lower and the distant sea darkened, the King sat on a rock fifty yards from the rest of the party, smoking and brooding, refusing to go on even when it was put to him that the fleet-footed medal-bearer would catch them up before they reached the beach.

Spotter planes patrolled ceaselessly. The Greek royal family were by no means universally popular. Plenty of their disaffected subjects and communists lived in the mountains – so there was, besides, a constant danger that some goat-herd or woodsman would report their presence to the Germans, thereby making his fortune.

'Short of knocking him out and carrying him aboard, there was nothing we could do,' said Uncle Harold, grimacing at the memory, 'and I don't think his bodyguard and equerry would have stood for that.'

Darkness falls swiftly in the Mediterranean, and when the party, complete with medals, eventually stumbled and slipped down the steep path to the beach they could no longer see the walls of cliff that flanked the bay – so much longer and narrower than they expected that Uncle Harold began to worry whether any ship at its entrance would be able to see their answering signal.

For forty minutes they waited, straining their eyes into the blackness.

'You begin to imagine you see lights on the sea, and then realise it's just phosphorescence,' he said. ' I dared not use the torch until I was sure, because we hadn't got a spare battery.'

At last they all saw three distant flashes, repeated ten seconds later, and Uncle Harold responded with his torch. Breathlessly they waited – five minutes, ten – but nothing happened. What had gone wrong?

Again the ship signalled. Again they responded with the same result.

'They can't see us,' someone said.

The situation was now critical. It had been agreed that if three attempts at signalling got no answer, the ship could not risk staying any longer and would abort the mission. Uncle Harold told the tallest man in the party to wade out as far as he could with the torch, whose battery was fast failing, and try once more. Since their wader now had his back to the beach, the party could not see his flashed response when the ship made its final signal, but barely had he floundered back to dry land than they heard the low putter of an engine, and moments later a big rubber inflatable grounded gently on the pebbles...

Fourteen years later, Clarissa and I sighed with relief and looked with surprise at our empty plates. Immersed in Uncle Harold's story, we had eaten every morsel of the best Crêpes Suzette Paris could offer, almost without tasting them.

Despite such moments of interest and pleasure the charms of Paris – never strong for me – had faded to vanishing point and I was longing to go home to Wales. Mummy was a wonderful correspondent, but each of her letters brought news of changes that worried me. As her enthusiasm for Welsh Black Cattle increased, she had begun to thin out the ponies – it was true there were far too many of them, but even so I wanted to have some influence on who was sold and who remained.

Gallant Micky had been pensioned off after an ill-fated paperchase when I urged him to a final burst of speed on sighting the 'hare' and felt a sickening lurch as a tendon in his hindleg snapped. I was too heavy, he was too old: the whole thing was a disaster. That had been two years earlier and now I couldn't quarrel with the decision to put him down. Retirement didn't suit him and he had begun to look poor and unkempt.

Other favourites had suffered various vicissitudes. Taffy had lost an eye, probably from a blackthorn, and though she still jumped boldly, she had to hold her head on one side and found it hard to judge her take-off. Rhwstyn, the jack-in-a-box pole-jumper, had been sold to a happy home with a neighbour, but had the misfortune to put a leg through a rotten plank on a bridge while out hunting and he, too, had to be put down. Dustyfoot, fat and cussed as ever, had been bought for my godfather's children and was a great success with them – but then she broke into the shed where they kept chicken-feed and gorged all night with her nose in a sack until she foundered and died.

Ten or a dozen mountain pony mares and their foals had been sold *en masse*, but Mummy still found it difficult to come home with an empty trailer. As a result there were now several new full-size horses which I was keen to meet.

But over and above these considerations, I had a more compelling reason for wanting to hurry home. Now that my long and expensive education was complete, other excitements beckoned, the first of which was an arcane ritual known as 'Doing the Season.'

CHAPTER EIGHT

London

EVEN BEFORE HOMOSEXUALS gave the phrase an entirely different meaning, telling friends that you were Coming Out often caused bemusement. Coming Out? Where from – prison? And when you tried to explain, there were other questions. Why? What for? What was the point? It was hard to answer without sounding like an irresponsible flibbertigibbet.

For the truth was that Coming Out was less about being presented to the glamorous new Queen (though that was its ostensible purpose) than going to parties and dances non-stop for several months on end, buying lots of new clothes, attending the highlights of the summer season – Ascot, Henley, Wimbledon and so on – and involving your parents in considerable trouble and expense. This laid you open to accusations of fiddling while Rome burned, and better girls than you prepared for Real Life by working their way through secretarial college or university. Plenty of my friends from school and elsewhere had turned down the chance of Doing the Season for the eminently sensible reason that they thought the time and money could be better spent.

But though on the surface Coming Out was difficult to defend, it did serve the useful purpose of extending a girl's social network and giving her and her parents a chance to meet and take a good look at the kind of man she might eventually marry.

It was a kind of snowball. Having been introduced to the cream of the current crop of Debs' Delights (as the carefully-vetted young men invited to house parties, cocktail parties and balls were known) and, by

197

extension, to a wider circle of their friends, a girl was less likely to fall in love *faute de mieux* with the boy next door; and though some might claim that such a system was inherently restrictive, I would argue that a certain uniformity of background and outlook, shared interests and common aims gave these marriages a better chance of lasting than the modern matrimonial hunting-grounds of workplace or dating agency.

The ritual began early in the year with an application to the Lord Chamberlain's office. Since Mummy herself had been presented at Court – splendidly attired in brocade, train, and feathers – in the reign of George V, and had subsequently managed to avoid any scandal, divorce, or criminal conviction which would have scuppered my chances, her application to present me to the Queen was approved and, while I was still in Paris, letters and postcards began to pour through the letterbox at Fforest Farm as long-ignored, long-forgotten friends came back on the radar. *Hear you've a daughter coming out this year too… do let's meet… such fun to see you again…*

At the lunch party which followed, a dozen new acquaintances would swap names and addresses, add the names of well-behaved, well-connected young men of their acquaintance, if necessary adding the caveat NSIT (Not Safe In Taxis) or FI (Financially Insecure) to the semi-official List, and canvass suitable dates for parties and dances. These would be timed to avoid clashes as far as possible. After a month of giving and receiving these jolly lunches Mummy, whose high spirits and good looks made her seem years younger than her contemporaries, had an engagement book bulging with names and dates, and upon my return from France we slid gently into Stage Two of the ritual: Girls' Tea Parties.

Now we debutantes got our first chance to meet and, like strange ponies sniffing noses, we squealed and rolled our eyes and clumped into groups with people we remembered from school, anxiously analysing other girls' looks, dress sense, amiability, and degree of sophistication before tentatively becoming friends. Despite my year in France, I was painfully aware of my shortcomings in these areas, for besides being on the hefty side (all those crêpes) and naturally clumsy, I was uninterested in fashion and socially awkward. Short sight may have played a part in this, because I had never seen an oculist or admitted that I needed specs and therefore found it difficult to recognise people, particularly if I encountered them out of their normal setting. There were lots of In jokes I didn't understand, and I felt a country bumpkin when more trendy girls raved over actors and film stars, restaurants and nightclubs I had never heard of. Plainly there were adjustments to make and corners to knock off before I would feel one of the crowd.

It never occurred to me that other girls might find themselves equally out of their depth, and if Mummy hadn't already put in so much spadework (and hadn't been enjoying her return to social life so keenly) I might, in its early stages, have asked her to forget all about the Season and send me to secretarial college instead. But she had, and I didn't, so I blundered on down the prescribed track towards the next stage, which involved cocktail parties and, inevitably, a major revamp of my wardrobe.

'Some of these debutantes' underclothes are *grey*,' said the hoity-toity vendeuse at Debenham's as I stripped in front of a cruelly-lit full-length mirror. 'And most have heard of a slip,' she added disdainfully.

I wasn't wearing a petticoat, either, though my bra, pants, and suspender belt passed muster – just. But Mummy was more than equal to supercilious sales ladies, and gradually won her round as I obediently forced myself into a variety of day dresses, cocktail dresses, coats-and-skirts, and tight-bodiced, full-skirted ball gowns in taffeta, brocade, and chiffon. The final bill was staggering, but Mummy never flinched.

'Hair next,' she said. 'I've made an appointment at Raymond.'

Mr Teasy-Weasy himself, a great, greasy maestro with luxuriant black curls like an Italian tenor, dragged his comb through my uninspiringly floppy light-brown hair and gave a resounding sniff. Until recently I had worn it in short plaits which I chewed in moments of stress, and then the hairdresser in Llandrindod had cut it in an uncompromising bob. Now Mr Teasy-Weasy decided to layer it.

'No body,' he said contemptuously. 'Give it a cold perm,' he told an acolyte, and drifted off to schmooze a more important client.

The cold perm took hours and completely changed my appearance, the wiry curls ranged in such rigid rows that I hardly dared brush them. I bore it for ten days before attempting a wash which made every tightly-crimped hair stand straight out from my head until Mummy damped the whole thing down and rolled it into flat snails, secured with kirbigrips and firmly netted. So dense was the ironmongery that I could hardly get my head on to the pillow.

'*Il faut souffrir pour être belle,*' she laughed with what I considered a lamentable lack of feeling.

Such hiccups apart, the cocktail party stage of the Season was fun. Every day more invitations on stiff white cards dropped through the letterbox of Daddy's flat at 10, Wythburn Court, and I was kept busy writing acceptances and thanks in succession. There were two or even three separate parties every night and they nearly always finished with some agreeable young man asking what I was doing for dinner. Should we go to a restaurant? On to a nightclub? The Four Hundred in Leicester Square was a favourite place to dance, though you were mad to eat there because it was so expensive. I thought it the ultimate in glamour, with its red flocked walls and red plush seats, heavy with gilt sconces and mirrors, but on one occasion when I had lost a single pearl and amethyst earring which Mummy had given me, and went back to retrieve it the next morning, I was startled by how squalid it looked in daylight, all its glitter tarnished, the plush worn through, and reeking of last night's cigars.

I hate to think how much of their weekly earnings those agreeable young men spent on wining and dining girls like me, for no more tangible *quid pro quo* than a few hours shuffling round a dance-floor – far too crowded to do more than rock from foot to foot – followed by a chaste peck on the cheek at the outer door of Wythburn Court, since the mere mention that Daddy would be waiting up for me was enough to inhibit any request to come in for coffee. I liked them all but none exactly made my heart go pitapat, and though Mummy once informed me – in a tone so elaborately casual that it must have concealed acute embarrassment – that she'd been told only one debutante in three was a virgin at the end of the Season, as far as I was concerned she had little need to worry since I had neither the inclination nor the opportunity to leap into bed with any of these essentially callow young men.

In pre-Pill days, the danger of becoming pregnant was a powerful turn-off, too, simply not worth the risk of sleeping around. One heard stories of girls whose dances were postponed or cancelled because of 'emergency appendicitis', and people would nod wisely. Everyone knew what that meant.

We gave two cocktail parties ourselves, and I remember feeling proud that my parents – especially my mother – looked so much younger and livelier than the decrepit old wrecks other girls were burdened with.

It was a strange, topsy-turvy existence. After a flurry of high living, late nights, full war-paint and best clothes in London, we would dash down to Fforest Farm where Mummy would instantly slough off her society image and revert to being a struggling Radnorshire farmer, battling with the elements, absorbed in the welfare of sheep and cattle, as if hobnobbing with Duchesses and gilt-edged invitations to Buckingham Palace played no part in her life at all.

Three or four days of gumboots and heavy sweaters would follow, then back we'd whizz to London for more parties, more dresses to try on, appointments with hairdressers (I still couldn't handle my new perm), sessions with society photographers keen to fill the 'Girls with pearls' page at the front of *Country Life*, (I never made it there) and advice from beauticians (pretty futile, considering what they had to work on) while all the time my Presentation at Court stalked nearer like the hound of heaven.

Sad to say, after all the anticipation the whole business was a disappointment. Interminable waiting in our taxi in The Mall on a rainy Spring afternoon was followed by an equally slow and boring interlude while the girls to be presented were shoved and shuffled into alphabetical order in the long corridor whose double doors opened into the Throne Room. I was wearing a very beautiful square-necked cocktail dress of blue-grey shot silk, full in the skirt and so tight in the bodice that I dared not laugh or sneeze for fear of splitting a seam, and my shoes were so pointed that prolonged standing was agony.

Very slowly the queue advanced towards the dais where the Queen was sitting looking dutiful and remote, never a glimmer of a smile. As each debutante sank into her curtsey, the powdered footman at the door called out her name, but as he soon got out of step with his list, most were incorrectly identified. I was labelled 'the Hon. Harriet Barnsley,' who had actually curtseyed three before me.

The only moment of drama came when a very short, stout girl just in front of me, who was wearing unwisely high heels, skidded on the polished boards and fell with a heavy thud, flat on her back between the two footmen stationed either side of the door into the Green Drawing-Room. And did they rush to pick her up and dust her off? Not a bit of it. They went on standing rigidly, like a couple of stuffed dummies, while the poor girl struggled to her feet and crept away looking utterly humiliated.

That small incident seemed to me to characterise the whole performance: stuffy, pretentious, inhuman and sadly out of date. Even the famous chocolate cake by Joe Lyons tasted stale.

'Rather a damp squib, I'm afraid,' said Mummy, throwing her hat on the taxi's spare jump seat and fluffing her hair with her fingers. I was glad she'd said it before I was tempted to.

'Well, at least some of the girls were pretty, and that's more than you could say of their mothers,' Daddy said with a deep chuckle.

We were none of us surprised when a couple of years later the Queen decided to do away with presentation parties altogether. It must have been even less fun for her than it was for us, and thereafter debutantes made their curtseys to a cake at a charity ball.

Keeping the show on the road at Fforest Farm during these months when Mummy was so much in London was an agricultural student of a very different calibre from any who had come to us before. Bridget was in the middle of a farming course at Moulton College of Agriculture, and her mother had, at Celia Fleming's suggestion, written to ask if she could get a few months' practical experience working at the Fforest.

She had arrived while I was still in Paris, and in one of her letters Mummy described her as: 'not pretty but with a lot of oomph, a neat figure, big blue eyes and the most wonderful curly hair which she washes half an hour before a party and gives a shake, and is ready to go...'

She was the 22-year-old daughter of a publisher, and his wife who taught French at a school near Henley-on-Thames, and since their own interests were almost entirely intellectual they had never quite understood Bridget's obsession with animals, particularly horses. After helping around the local stables in return for riding lessons she had, with difficulty, persuaded her parents to buy her a grey Anglo-Arab mare. When

Grey Owl went lame she bred a replacement and it was this handsome bay youngster who had accompanied her to Fforest Farm.

Mummy always allowed the girls who worked for her to bring their horses or dogs, and I think this relaxed attitude to animals en masse attracted Bridget as much as her parents' relaxed attitude to guests who spent all day with their noses in a book attracted me when I visited her home near Nettlebed.

For the moment, though, she was very busy imposing proper standards of agricultural efficiency on our few remaining milking cows, weighing their rations according to their yields instead of carelessly dumping a couple of scoops of nuts into each manger as had been my habit, maintaining meticulous hygiene in the dairy, and keeping scrupulously exact records of the amount of milk produced each day instead of topping up the churn with water to bring it to a round figure as I often used to when in charge of the cow-shed.

She was quick and clever and efficient, loved riding about the hill and giving a hand with the shepherding, and she and Mummy got on like a house on fire. Her downbeat, laconic turn of phrase often made us laugh.

'What have we got for dinner?' I remember Mummy asking her.

'Well, there's this rotting stew,' drawled Bridget, taking the remains of a rather good Sunday roast from the larder, and instantly *rotting stew* was adopted into our own family-speak.

Her brother Duff was the same age as Gerry and David and had been in the same house as them at Eton. Along with the rest of their year, all three were now doing their National Service, and having survived their Basic Training were serving in the British Forces in Germany, Gerry with the Royal Horse Artillery at Osnabruck, and Duff and David with the Coldstream Guards at Krefeld.

One day I found Bridget chuckling over a letter which she passed to me to read. Duff, who had never shared her interest in horses, had been persuaded by a brother officer to come for a ride on one of the Saddle Club's hacks, and all went well until his mount, who had been schooled for dressage, reacted to some aid Duff didn't know he'd given it, by performing a high-stepping passage across a field of cabbages. The more he tried to make it go forward, the more it danced sideways, and he tried desperately to keep his seat while making apologetic placatory gestures to the owner of the cabbage patch who was yelling abuse and waving his hoe.

The inevitable happened. He lost his balance, the horse deposited him in the mud and galloped for home, leaving him to creep back to barracks past the grinning sentries...

I laughed and handed back the letter, and Bridget said thoughtfully, 'You know, you ought to meet my brother. I'd sure you'd get on well.'

I gave a non-committal grunt because as it happened I had already met him two years earlier at Eton's Fourth of June celebrations and, in my censorious teenage way had formed a low opinion of his manners. After a lavish picnic lunch with strawberries and cream on Agar's, we had been strolling round the cricket field, when my parents stopped to speak to his. In front of their canvas chairs a boy with wildly curling fair hair was sitting cross-legged, wholly absorbed in the game. When called by his mother to come and say hello, he did exactly that, smiled, shook hands, and instantly returned to watching the cricket without giving a second glance at my fashionable finery: a head-hugging hat made entirely of blue and pink petals, white gloves, a cornflower-blue starched shirt-waister whose full skirt was puffed out with net petticoats in the latest style, stockings with clocks round the heel, agonisingly tight shoes, the lot.

I felt obscurely rebuffed and had no particular wish to renew our acquaintance. Besides, during this glorious whirl of parties, my address-book, which had up to now been a man-free zone, had suddenly filled with the names and telephone numbers of chaps in their twenties, with jobs in the City and membership of London nightclubs, all looking – even if in a somewhat desultory fashion – for a soul-mate, helpmeet or wife. Beside them my brother's friends, too cash-strapped to take a girl out to dine and dance, had begun to seem mere boys, and most of them were in Germany anyway.

From time to time they reappeared on leave, with very short haircuts and lots of new jargon. Gerry, that pillar of rectitude, winner of the Sword of Honour at his passing-out parade, brought a party of friends down to Fforest Farm and produced from his kitbag a thunderflash 'left over'

— ahem — after a training exercise. On market day, when Mummy had taken a trailer of pigs in to Hereford, we went on to the hill above the farm to try it out. The boys took it gingerly from the rucksack, and spent some time deciding where to dig the hole with the dear little collapsible spade Gerry had brought in his pack.

'Stay here and don't move,' he ordered, leaving us in a patch of bracken. He and Richard walked off and disappeared over the brow.

We waited for what seemed a very long time. They weren't far away, because we could hear them arguing and giving one another instructions. It sounded as if they were having trouble with the fuse.

At last we heard Gerry say: 'That's it! Now, light it — quick!'

We watchers had been creeping stealthily forward on hands and knees like disobedient gundogs. We saw Gerry and Richard bending down staring at the ground, then they straightened suddenly, chorused, 'Retire briskly. Do not run!' and sprinted back towards us. Panting, they flung themselves down in the bracken.

All the girls clapped their hands over their ears and again there was a long, breathless wait. Nothing happened. Gerry and Richard looked at each other questioningly.

'Must be a dud,' said Richard, shrugging.

Gerry nodded. 'Or perhaps the fuse went out.'

He stood up. 'I'll go and — '

Before he could move there was a dazzling flash of white light, followed by an ear-splitting ker-umph!

Clods of turf erupted like a black fountain, some of them landing very close to us. Curlews and gulls took off in a cloud from a nearby pond and, startled from their afternoon doze, sheep and ponies bounced out of the bracken and galloped away to the horizon.

'Definitely not a dud,' said Richard with satisfaction.

As the Season advanced and the days lengthened into early summer, cocktail parties gave way to Coming Out Balls, mostly in London to begin with — 6, Belgrave Square and Londonderry House in Park Lane were favourite venues — and then, more memorably, up and down the country. I say more memorably because there is only so much a hostess can do to make a dance in a rented house unique and splendid, whereas every country ball was different and usually involved staying with generous neighbours of the hostess, who went to great trouble and expense to entertain the parties of four, six, possibly even eight young strangers parked with them for the weekend.

Since in those pre-disco days most country bands refused to break the Sabbath by playing after midnight on Saturday, these dances were held on Friday night, starting round about 10pm and preceded by a lavish dinner with your house-party. Drinking and driving were rarely frowned on, and in any case there was much less traffic about on country roads, so I never felt the least qualm about being driven to the dance by a young man who would in today's terms be way over the limit. The only terror was that he would take some other girl home and leave me stranded.

Getting out of the warm cocoon of the car and braving the lights, music and bustling throng of strangers was rather like diving into a swimming pool – all right as soon as you got your shoulders under and there was no going back. I would look desperately for someone I recognised in a sea of strange faces and feel completely rudderless, but at the beginning of the evening you could rely on being asked to dance by the male members of your house-party, which gave you a breathing space in which to identify other people you knew already.

Supper, and judicious visits to the loo could be used to fill in wallflower moments, and round about two o'clock I would begin to look around anxiously for the man who had driven me to the dance. If he had vanished, the outlook was dire. Either I would have to ask for a lift from another couple, thus kyboshing any romantic plans they might have in mind, or seek out one of the weary chaperones charged with seeing that we all got home safely, and hang about endlessly while she checked and rechecked the scattered members of her house-party, then bundled all the stragglers into her car. Both options left one feeling a social failure.

On Saturday it was almost a point of honour not to get up until noon, which did at least give your toiling hostess a bit of time for essential admin. Only the grandest houses had enough servants to cope with the needs of half a dozen guests, and often you would find your hosts polishing shoes or bringing in logs while the idle visitors sat about reading the newspapers.

After a leisurely lunch, there might be a tennis or swimming party with other neighbours, plus a small informal hop with gramophone records and rolled-back carpets, at which romantic liaisons begun at the dance would firm up.

It quickly became apparent to me that the young Englishmen I met at such parties were very very different from their French counterparts – truly another breed. It was useless to expect compliments or chivalrous gestures from them; but a house-party where most of the young men had been at school together would often turn into a non-stop running cabaret of jokes, fantasy, teasing and catch-phrases which made me laugh until I could hardly breathe.

The year I came out, there was a particularly strong clique from Ampleforth, who had gone on to Cambridge, written sketches for the Footlights, and were very bright sparks indeed. They were asked every-where, and their repartee at breakfast could be cripplingly funny. It was the same with Etonians or Wykehamists or men who had done their National Service in the same regiment: the better they knew each other, the faster and racier their wit, and since every hostess likes her party to go with a swing, they were often invited en bloc, and knew very well they would be expected to sing for their supper by keeping the table in a roar of laughter.

House-parties and dances, race-meetings and cricket matches were jammed so close together that it was like bingeing on meringues, delicious at first but ultimately nauseating. As the summer advanced through Ascot, Wimbledon, Henley Regatta and Glorious Goodwood, I became increas-ingly glad of the chance to return for a few days of our normal bread-and-butter regime at Fforest Farm.

For some reason, I never felt very well in London and if ever I had to stay there alone for the weekend, a paralysing gloom and inertia would settle on me, so I hardly had the energy to leave the flat. It was a kind of agoraphobia. Nothing seemed worth the effort of getting dressed and going out into the street.

This may have been due, in part at least, to the extreme discomfort of the clothes considered suitable for town life. No question of slopping about in jeans and trainers: London meant tidy clothes – skirt, stockings, high heels, and very often hat and gloves as well – and that was only the outer layer. Underclothes were far worse. Even at this distance I shudder to think of cramming myself into the rubberised instrument of torture known as a 'roll-on' which had replaced my simple school suspender-belts. Tube-shaped and constructed from particularly resilient elasticated mesh, it was worn next to the skin, under your pants, and kept in place by the four suspenders that connected with the tops of your stockings. All day long it squeezed you into a smaller size than Nature had designed, and every time you sat down it doubled over at the top in an agonisingly tight belt that had to be unrolled surreptitiously as you stood up again.

Then there was the question of how to spend a weekend in London. Far from there being too little to do, there was such a bewildering choice that I would find it impossible to decide whether to go to a film or a museum or exhibition or concert or play, whether to ring up a friend or go shopping. I would fiddle around in the flat, reading old Georgette Heyer paperbacks and eating yoghurt and potted shrimps, which Daddy always ate for breakfast in the touching belief that they were not only slimming but would make you live for ever. Morning would turn into afternoon, afternoon into evening, and finally it would be time to go to bed having wasted the entire day.

As the hours ticked by I would become ever more zombified, until I settled for the same solution as A.A. Milne's shipwrecked sailor. *And so in the end he did nothing at all/ But sat on the shingle wrapped up in a shawl/ And I think it disgraceful the way he behaved/ He did nothing but sit there until HE WAS SAVED!*

The sound of Daddy's key in the door would galvanise me into normal life again, and I would feel so ashamed of having wasted the whole weekend that I would invent a completely fictitious account of what I had done in the last two days.

Back at the Fforest, new horses more suited to carrying grown-ups were gradually taking over from the few old favourites such as Taffy and Sally who had survived Mummy's economy drives.

Daddy weighed fifteen stone and had a dodgy hip, so it had taken much expenditure in trial and error to find a horse on which he would enjoy pottering about the farm at weekends. Time and again Mummy would acquire an allegedly well-mannered, surefooted weight-carrier, only to discover that it was too keen, or joggled his hip, or refused to stand still while he got on and off, and back it would go to Hereford market. When at last she bought Peter, a big bay horse with white socks and a dash of Clydesdale blood, who had none of these defects, it was something of an Eureka moment, and for about six months everyone was happy.

Then Daddy woke one morning with his eyes full of tears, having dreamed – as he told Mummy – 'That you sold Peter and bought some rotten little thoroughbred for Phyllida.'

Of course she indignantly denied planning to do any such thing, but as it turned out, Daddy's dream was as prophetic as Joseph's. While checking the sheep one day, Harold the tractor-driver caught sight of Peter chasing a bunch of calves about the field on the other side of the road, and before he could intervene, the horse cornered one and deliberately smashed its skull with a pawing stroke of his ironshod hoof.

That was a very black mark. The calves were removed out of harm's way, and everyone watched anxiously to see if the act of violence was a one-off. Alas, no. Peter was next seen chasing sheep, who shouldn't have been in his field but had filtered through a glat in the hedge. A week or two later he turned his attention to the other ponies in with him, harassing them, biting and striking out with his forelegs like a stallion, and the sad truth became apparent that some kind of mental – or possibly sexual – kink meant he simply wasn't safe with other livestock.

Scanning the 'Horses for Sale' and 'Wanted' column in the *Hereford Times* Mummy spotted a farmer offering to exchange a five-year-old thoroughbred mare for a strong cob, and the opportunity seemed too good to miss. While Daddy was away in London, Peter went off in the trailer to his new home, and Mummy returned triumphant with a beautiful gentle chestnut called Pendant, by a high-class sprinter named Golden Cloud, out of a middle-distance mare, Mary's First. The story was that she had been left with the farmer in settlement of a debt, but wasn't up to his weight.

'He said Peter was just what he was looking for,' said Mummy, and no-one quite cared to ask whether she had made Peter's new owner aware of his failings.

Unfortunately, it soon turned out that Pendant had failings of her own. She was the first thoroughbred I had ever ridden and her smooth surge of speed was an eye-opener. As we zoomed round the paddock wild fantasies entered my head. We would win the flapping races at Erwood, the Hereford All-Comers, the Newmarket Town Plate, but the moment I pulled her up to open the gate these hopes collapsed. Her sides heaved in and out, then she seized the gate's top bar with her teeth, braced her neck and gulped in air as if in the throes of hiccups.

'Wind-sucker,' said Mummy regretfully when I reported this odd behaviour. 'So that was why he tied her up so tight in the trailer. Pity... it did seem a bit too good to be true. Well, we're stuck with her now. We'll have to see what we can do and keep her away from the other horses or they'll all copy her.'

This was much easier said than done. We tried putting a special collar on her that tightened on her windpipe when she sucked air, but it made no difference. She would latch on to any horizontal that she could get her mouth round – the stable door, the bars of the bull-pen, even a branch would serve the purpose – and rock back and forth in apparent ecstasy as she gulped, but it blew out her belly and did her wind no good at all, and it proved impossible to get her fit. She reminded me very much of Cally – so beautiful, so deeply addicted, so difficult to help. Eventually Mummy decided to put her out to grass with the pensioners who weren't likely to catch her bad habits, and there her career stagnated until Bridget came to the Fforest.

'Why not get her in foal?' she said. 'Of course, you'd have to wean it early, before it started to copy her.'

What then? wiser heads might have asked, but I leapt at the suggestion. Pendant was too young and beautiful to be put down simply because she was a *bouche inutile*, but reading the runes I guessed Mummy's thoughts were going that way. We found out that a stallion called Iena II, who had won several races, was working that season for the Hunter Improvement Society and doing a round near Ledbury, serving mares for a fraction of his usual fee, so I made an appointment to meet him at the farm where he stopped to bait – lunch – when Pendant came in season.

Looking back, I can see we were incredibly lucky that the whole operation went so smoothly. Iena's handler was a tall, taciturn weather-beaten man of sixty-odd named Ted. Six days a week he would leave his permanent base at Ludgershall, where mares had been brought overnight to be served, and lead the stallion by tracks and minor roads to the Howe, some eight miles away. There they would feed and rest, after which Iena would serve any mares waiting there for him, and set off again on a circular route to another collecting point, repeat the process, and return to Ludgershall for the night. Both horse and man looked lean and extremely fit on this routine.

We had about an hour to wait before they turned up at the Howe, Ted swinging up the lane leading a dashing, long-legged dapple-grey with black points, who danced along beside him as if on steel springs. As soon as Pendant scented the stallion she began to neigh, tossing her mane and stamping restlessly.

'Aye, she's ready,' grunted Ted, peering into her loosebox.

He fitted felt shoes on to her hind feet as a precaution, but there was really no need. Far from kicking her suitor, she received his overtures with every sign of pleasure, giving little playful squeals and grunts as he nipped and nuzzled her, and standing like a rock when he mounted, his long, well-muscled neck stretched in an arc over her as he gently gripped her crest with his teeth.

There were no other mares waiting, and Ted gave the lovers ten minutes' grace before quietly leading Iena away, while Bridget and I sighed at the romance of it all and put Pendant back in the trailer.

The whole episode seemed so like a dream that we could hardly believe anything tangible would come of this brief encounter, but eleven months later almost to the day, Pendant foaled a neat little filly, almost black at birth but later dapple-grey like her sire, whom I named after another of Napoleon's great battles, Borodino.

I'm afraid the fact that I can't remember what happened to Pendant thereafter suggests she was indeed put down soon after her foal was weaned. All that was far in the future, however, as the Season began to peter out after glorious Goodwood. Debs and their Delights ebbed away from London as sun-and-sea based holidays beckoned. Suddenly, unnervingly, the date of my own dance at Chapel House was upon us.

We had chosen the Friday before August Bank Holiday, (then at the beginning rather than the end of the month) which was traditionally a time of parties and jollification in the Wye Valley, its central event and principal *raison d'être* being the two-day needle match between Builth Cricket Club and a scratch XI raised by David Gibson-Watt, the local MP who was also Secretary of State for Wales. Up and down the Valley, friends and neighbours had responded nobly to Mummy's dance invitations, offering to entertain house parties throughout the long weekend, and an immense amount of correspondence both written and telephoned had gone into distributing equal numbers of girls and boys among the houses, briefing guests on where they were staying, train times and so on, and their hosts on whom to expect.

A marquee was hired and sited on the terrace and lawn between the house and chapel, with the corner where the venerable Mr Pilbeam's band would sit perilously poised over the Whee-air Jump. Daddy persuaded five of the staff from the Garrick Club to take charge of the wine, both flowers and catering were provided by local firms, and all crockery and cutlery was firmly stamped Shufflebotham. (Years later coffee spoons with this logo would still be turning up in the flowerbeds.)

The weather looked promising. Everyone was pitching in to help in a thousand ways, and I felt confident that this dance, at least, was going to be fun from start to finish. No question of facing a roomful of strangers and wondering what to say. Here we were at home, secure among friends. Everyone knew everyone else in the Wye Valley, and no-one would dream of making snarky remarks if the drink ran out or the band played the wrong tunes.

Another cause of pleasure was my dress. Granny had given me a dream of a ballgown, made to measure by her own London milliner, Leila Read, who had translated my vague instruction that it should look like a cascade of water flowing over the Claerwen Dam into a most glorious creation. Descending tiers of gold-edged, gold embroidered white muslin flounces swirled out from a strapless bodice, perfectly fitted, with a dark blue ribbon under the bust and the cleavage defined by a pink rose. As soon as I tried it on, morale soared. It was the most beautiful dress I had seen all through the Season.

Mummy and Daddy checked lists and ticked off their *Jobs to Do* memoranda. 'Have a think about what we might have forgotten,' Mummy said, and we all racked our brains and shook our heads. As far as we could tell, every angle was covered, nothing left to chance. Nevertheless one large fly lurked in the ointment.

Immersed in preparations for the dance and shamefully uninterested in politics anyway, I had been only peripherally aware of rumblings of trouble over the Suez Canal. I knew that Egypt resented British suzerainty there, and that we were determined to hang on to it. But all the same it came as a surprise when President Nasser, who looked like a dark, lean-jawed wolf, announced on July 26th that he had nationalised the Suez Canal Company.

The British press was outraged and went into full jingo mode. All the following week the Suez Crisis dominated the headlines, the general opinion being that the Egyptians wouldn't be able to run the Canal Company for toffee nuts and would soon have to hand it back.

None of this seemed to affect us directly but on August 2nd, the very day before my dance, the picture changed abruptly. The Government announced the recall of reservists, and all leave for the Armed Services was cancelled as preparations were made to take the Canal back by force.

This threw our carefully planned house-parties into chaos. The sudden absence of soldiers and sailors (I didn't seem to know any airmen) opened up great gaps in the guest list, since we had been relying on Gerry and David and many of their handsome, uniformed friends to balance the hordes of debs I had invited from London.

Prospects for the dance looked black, but Mummy wasn't beaten yet. Like the feastgiver in the parable whose guests refused his invitation, she began to comb the highways and byways for replacements. Up and down the Wye valley, any man with a dinner jacket in his wardrobe, from sprightly eighty-year-old generals to boys still at school, was hastily telephoned and invited, and bless their hearts they rallied round with a will.

And then on the six o'clock news, when all the placements had been rearranged, we heard the invasion of Suez had been put on hold. Our military guests could have come after all – but then, of course, it was too late. Even if they left London at once, they would be stuck at Hereford around midnight. Of all the missing National Servicemen only David Caccia actually made it, arriving by taxi from Hereford just as the dance was running out of steam at 2 am. It was an heroic effort and he said it was worth it, even though he was dead tired and the fare cost him £12 – in those days an enormous sum.

I suppose in the end it all went pretty well, though when we came to compare notes afterwards, each of us had such diverse memories that we might have been at different dances. I remembered with horrible clarity the thin plume of smoke rising from a glowing cigarette stub that had fallen on the drawing-room hearth rug, and the scramble to stamp it out. Mummy recalled the frightful crash as a waitress misjudged the length of the scullery draining-board, and put down a whole tray of glasses just off the end of it, and also her tussle to get the band to play an extra hour after the agreed time. Daddy's worst moment had been finding one of the waiters stretched out on Granny's chaise longue among the ladies' coats, totally blotto. With the help of a neighbour, he had manhandled him downstairs and into the old servants' hall, and wedged the door shut until the last of our guests had departed.

So ended my Season, for although the parties continued sporadically for the rest of the summer the shades of the prison-house had begun to loom. It was time, high time, I began to earn my living.

Ever since, at the age of nine, I had won a competition in *Collins Magazine*, which required you to match close-ups of animals' eyes to the proper owners, I had wanted to be a journalist.

In the intervening years I had never wavered from this somewhat arbitrary choice, and that was why my parents, who admired consistency, had given me a portable Olivetti typewriter on whose strangely spongey keys I learned to touch-type at fair speed while I was still at school. Short-hand – also essential to a journalist – was not so easily acquired, but I jibbed so hard at the suggestion of going to secretarial college that Daddy persuaded his partners in Trower, Still, & Keeling to find me a job in their typing pool where I would, he hoped, pick up this useful skill.

A vain hope, alas. Like maths, shorthand simply refused to stick in my mind. I couldn't get the hang of listening to the sounds of words without bothering about their sense, and though I could produce a fairly accurate draft of what had been dictated by relying on my memory, it wouldn't actually be what had been said, and this drove the two young articled clerks for whom I worked to tooth-gnashing distraction. They hadn't the clout to fire a partner's daughter, but I know they would have liked to, and they encouraged me to take time off to go for interviews with magazine editors, hoping no doubt to get rid of me as soon as possible.

Aunt Nancy, then Ambassadress in Washington, had powerful friends in the world of fashion, and kindly pulled strings to secure me an introduction to Beatrix Miller, then editor of *Vogue*. I found her frankly terrifying, with her glossy hair and quick, sharp questions, very *grande dame* in her enormous, pale-carpeted, minimally furnished office, and I was relieved when she said she didn't think I was suited to work on *Vogue*.

Much more to my taste was the interview which Michael Gilbert, one of Daddy's partners who also wrote detective stories, arranged for me with Miss Sutherland (Peggy to her friends and DMS to everyone else in the office), who not only edited the monthly magazines *Woman's Journal* and *Argosy*, but was also the only female director of the Amalgamated Press. She was far more approachable than Miss Miller, seemed pleased when I admitted that reading was my favourite pastime, but taken aback when, offered the choice of a job on one of her magazines, I unhesitatingly plumped for *Argosy*.

This was regarded as something of a backwater by the fashionistas of Amalgamated Press, but it suited me just fine. From Monday to Friday, from 9.30 to 5.30 with just an hour off for lunch, I devoured short stories submitted by literary agents or aspiring authors, wrote reports on them, and either sent them back whence they came or supervised their inclusion in the next month's magazine. For what hardly seemed like work at all, I was paid £8. 17s per week, a splendid advance on the fiver from Daddy's office, and though I sometimes left the office feeling quite woozy from spending so much time in fictional worlds, the half-hour bus journey from Farringdon Street to Marble Arch – it cost 3d. – had the effect of bringing real life back into focus.

It was a leisurely, civilised introduction to journalism. The staff was small, friendly, and entirely female, consisting of the editor and her secretary plus a features editor, chief sub-editor, and two sub-editors – me and another girl my age – but considering that the format of the magazine never varied apart from the colour of the cover, and its content was entirely written by outsiders, we could and should have done twice the work in half the time.

Down the corridor the offices of *Woman's Journal* were an entirely different environment, full of drama, hustle and bustle, with photographers dashing in and out, people telephoning with their spare hand blocking the spare ear to shut out the din, doors slamming, the Chief Sub throwing tantrums, heaps of dresses draped on chairs and desks, an air of urgency and expectancy whenever the door of the Editor's office was flung open. A tremendous fuss was made over things that I couldn't see mattered: whether the figures referred to in a caption were numbered from the left or right, or whether the Cookery Pages were before or after the Fashion Pages in the front of the book. It was a relief to retreat to the three rooms occupied by *Argosy* where only the rustle of turning pages and an occasional telephone call broke the silence.

Though I enjoyed the work and realised I had been lucky, untrained as I was, to land a job so much to my taste, I greatly resented the restrictions it imposed on my liberty. The Editor was a charming, earnest, scholarly spinster, tall and frail with a chronic back problem that made her stoop, and I was not alone in thinking she would have been better suited to nitpicking her way through a new translation of the Bible than editing a commercial magazine, but for her *Argosy* really was the be-all and end-all.

She made a good job of it, too. Every short-story writer of note was eager to be published in it and in terms of sales, *Argosy* more than washed its face. Editorially speaking, each month's edition had to be as perfect as we could make it, each page scrutinised a dozen times, and our Editor had a completely blind spot about the social lives of her junior staff. We had to be there on the dot of 9.30, take our lunch hour between 1pm and 2pm precisely and never leave the office before 5.30.

I found this absolutely infuriating, since there were no department stores near Farringdon Street and there was never time to dash back to the West End, do one's shopping, and get back to the office by 2 o'clock. By the time I reached Oxford Street on the journey home, all the shops would be closing.

Peggy, the secretary and Pat, my co-sub-editor, accepted these restrictions quite calmly, though each had a far longer journey home than me. Peggy's father worked for the *Times of India* and in retrospect I suppose she was Anglo-Indian herself, though the subject never came up between us. She was small and tubby, with thick black hair cut *en brosse*, big, dark eyes and strongly-marked eyebrows which she would sleek into shape with a comb before putting on her coat to leave. Her telephone manner was a marvel to me. Nothing ever ruffled her calm, efficient politeness, and her filing was a model of neatness.

Pat was Irish, with deep-blue eyes and straggling wavy hair, and rather played up the wildness of her ancestry, though she lived conventionally enough with her family in Sevenoaks. Her father voted Labour and Pat was keen on supporting the union – the NUJ – who would from time to time order us to attend meetings of the direst tedium, and demanded dues which I felt thoroughly disinclined to pay. But even I had to admit it was an agreeable surprise when I found extra money in the little brown envelope I collected from the Accounts Department in the bowels of Amalgamated Press at lunchtime on Fridays, after the union had blackmailed the management into pay-rises across the board.

Pat and Peggy each had a boyfriend, or rather a series of boyfriends, but only one at a time. They considered it disloyal, even immoral, to go out with anyone who invited them in the happy-go-lucky way I thought normal, and though they would sometimes switch allegiances with maximum drama – tears, confrontations, accusations – and then latch on to someone else, they always detached completely from the old before attaching to the new boyfriend.

Another maddening restriction was on private telephone calls. Even a message to say that someone was ill or in hospital was received with black looks, and the Features Editor, a widow with two children, had the greatest difficulty juggling their school pick-ups and visits to dentists without falling foul of office rules. Worst of all for me, though, was the taboo on leaving early which made it almost impossible to join Daddy at Paddington in time to catch the 4.45 train to Hereford on Fridays.

It took a good half-hour to get from Farringdon Street to Paddington, and having asked for and been reluctantly granted permission to leave at 4, I would stand in the Editor's office with a pile of proofs for her to sign off in thick green ink, glancing surreptitiously at my watch and feeling tension rise in me as she re-read pages that had already been initialled by me and the Chief Sub, and made miniscule alterations then re-instated the original, and vital minutes ticked past. Daddy didn't like waiting for the 6.45 since it meant we wouldn't get back to Fforest Farm before midnight, and there was no way of letting him know I was held up…

At last she would hand back the last page. 'Off you go, then,' she'd say graciously but with a subtext of, 'Some people don't know what work is,' and I would gasp my thanks and scuttle down the fire escape, run like hell all the way up Farringdon Road to the Underground station, and pray that the next train would be Paddington-bound.

The net result was that I went home less and less, and gradually grew out of touch with both family and animals at the Fforest. Nevertheless, as soon as I did arrive from London, I would be subsumed into the latest crisis. Mummy preferred to live at fever pitch, and if events looked like going off the boil she would quickly give them a stir. Actually, few of my family were around just then. Gerry had finished National Service and gone up to Oxford to read History. Olivia had left school and was spending a year in New England with the family of one of Mummy's bridesmaids. Miranda had whizzed through the local school before she was old enough to go to Lawnside, so had been sent to learn French in Switzerland, leaving George my sole sibling at the farm.

As for the animals, they were there, just as they had always been and I always expected them to be. Ponies to ride, cows to be fed, sheep to be driven from one field to another. And then there was Scot with his bright button eyes and shag-pile hearthrug of a coat, the grand old man of the farmyard, devoted as ever, bowing and waving his tail at me with never a look of reproach for coming to see him so seldom.

So it was a nasty jolt to me a few days before Christmas when Mummy said, 'Have you noticed how poor Scot's gone?'

Poor in that specific sense meant thin, emaciated.

I looked at Scot, lying as usual on his sack under the bench in the porch where people sat to put on their boots. His enquiring round eyes and sharp nose poked out of the great curly ruff of coarse black coat and his thin, foxy-looking legs, now sprinkled with silver, were stretched in front of him.

I shook my head. 'He looks just the same.'

'Look properly. Put your hand on his back.'

So instead of stroking his head as I usually did, I felt carefully along his loins and had a shock. Under the big thick coat, Scot had shrunk to a mere skeleton. Every rib, every knob of his backbone was sharp under my fingers. I could hardly believe it.

I had known that he was slowing up, less keen to jump into the Land Rover, more inclined to lie in the sun at the top of the drive monitoring people coming and going than to trot behind the ponies on long rides, but I'd had no idea how much he had declined since the summer.

'He's not eating up,' she said. 'It's not just age.'

'His teeth?'

'Idris took a look and they're all right. He says it's internal. Something's gone wrong inside him.'

I said helplessly, 'I didn't know.'

'Well, you're not here much.' There was a long pause, and then she said, almost angrily, 'You can't just let him fade away. He's your dog.'

She put only a tiny emphasis on 'your' but it was enough to send a wave of guilt over me. Scotty had given me his life, and what had I done for him? Left him for others to look after for months on end, and now I hadn't even noticed that he was suffering. This was one responsibility I couldn't duck out of. I bent down to scratch him under the chin and he pressed his silver muzzle against my hand.

Mummy watched him for a moment in silence. 'Well?' she said at last.

'All right,' I said reluctantly.

Scot had never visited the surgery in his life, but he followed me in willingly enough, then retreated to the door and whined. He knew he wasn't allowed indoors. I said to the receptionist, 'I'll wait outside,' and we went and sat in the sun on the surgery steps for what seemed a very long time.

I tried not to cry because that would give the game away, but it seemed the blackest treachery to go on chatting to Scot and stroking his head when I was about to have him killed. The vet came out, looked at us and said doubtfully, 'Are you all right?' and when I sniffed and nodded, said, 'Bring him into the car park, then.'

He shaved a patch on Scot's forearm while the boot-button eyes watched me anxiously, but he never moved as the needle went in.

'Good dog. See you soon,' I said as I always did when going back to London, and a moment later the spark faded from Scot's eyes.

How soon is soon? How long is a piece of string? Every religion has its own notion of celestial bliss, but none of the official versions come anywhere near what I would consider Heaven. Harps and nighties? No, thanks. Seventy-two virgins? A recipe for strife. The formless perfection of Nirvana? Hardly a stimulating prospect.

On the other hand, the certainty of a life after death in which I would see again everyone I had loved on earth is extremely appealing, and that would include my animals – goats, rabbits, sheep and all. If Scot and Taffy and all the rest are not waiting for me on the other side of the Pearly Gates, I shall know I've come to the wrong place, and request an immediate transfer.